For Forever I'll Be Here
THE ART OF MARCI WASHINGTON

First Published in the United States of America
January 2014

First Edition

Gingko Press, Inc.
1321 Fifth Street
Berkeley, CA 94710, USA
www.gingkopress.com

ISBN: 978-1-58423-515-6

Printed in China

Special thanks to Modern Effects and Jessica Skloven for photographing the paintings within. Thanks also to Myleen Hollero for the in-studio photographs.

LEEDS
COLLEGE OF
ART

Part of the work featured in this book is from a solo exhibition of Marci Washington's paintings at Leeds College of Art, November 2011.

COVER IMAGE: **THE SUMMONING, A RECKONING**
Watercolor and Gouache on Paper

OPPOSITE: **NO PLACE**
Watercolor and Gouache on Paper

PAGE 4: **ON THE DOOR**
18 x 24", 2010, Watercolor and Gouache on Paper

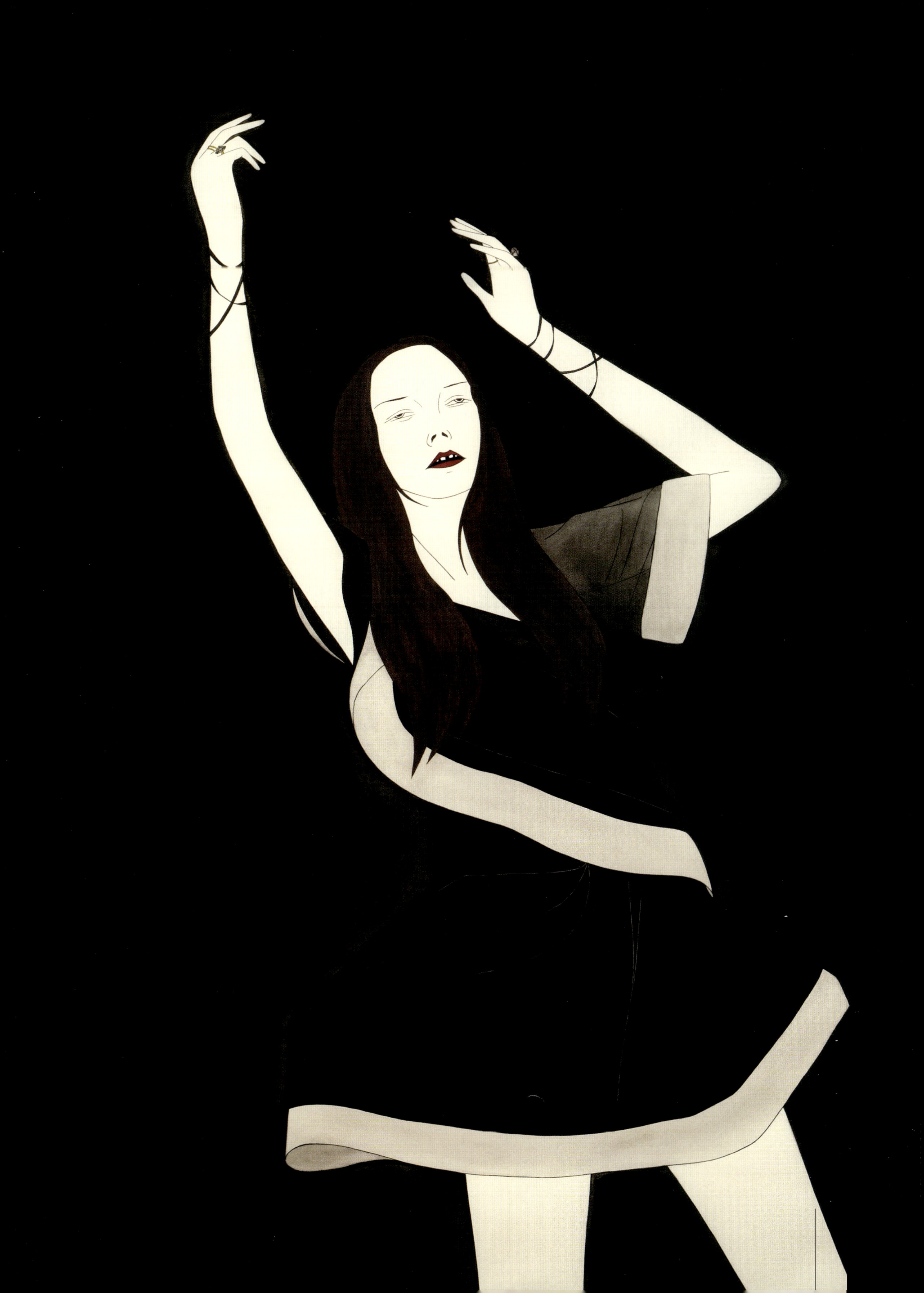

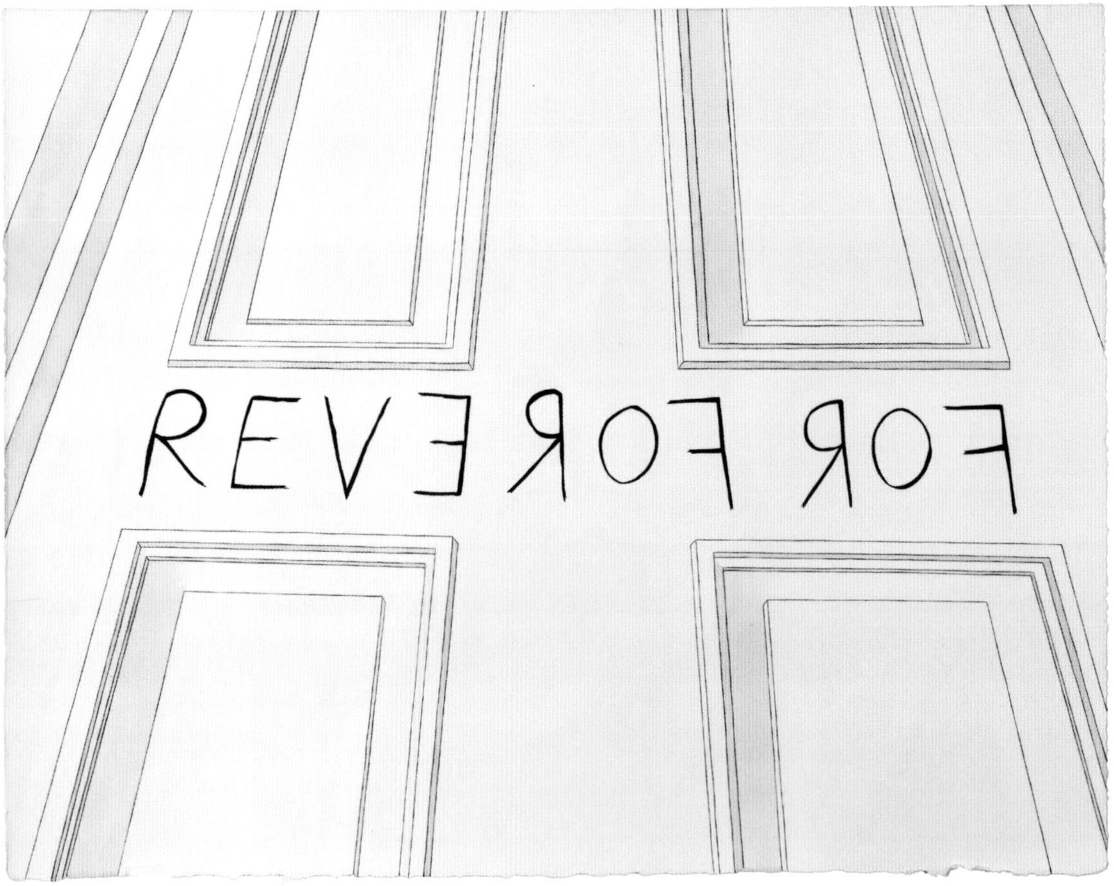
REVƎЯOF ЯOF

For Forever I'll Be Here

THE ART OF MARCI WASHINGTON

SELECTED WORKS

Gingko Press

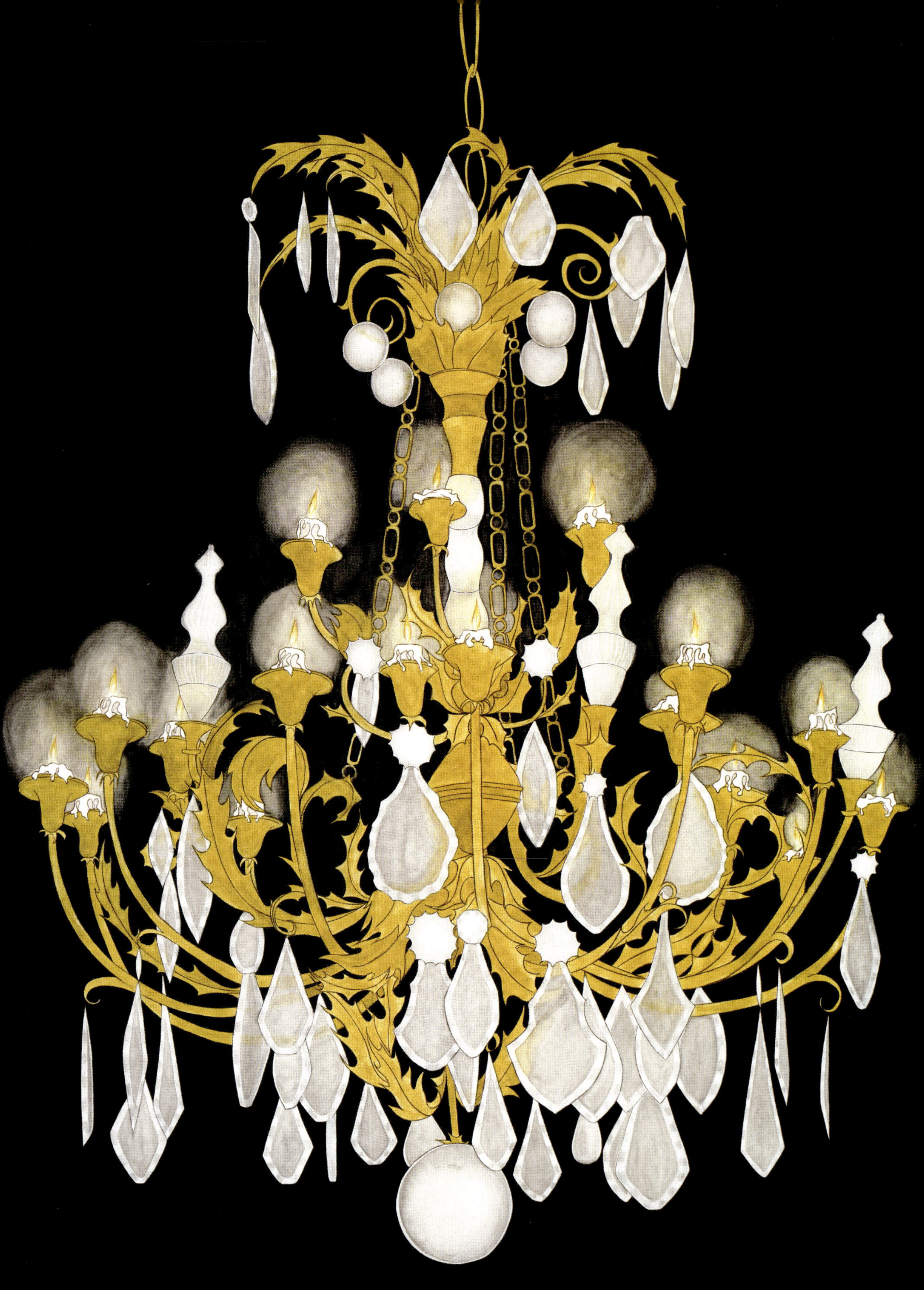

Through Marci Washington's Dark Mirror

by Nathaniel Rich

Marci Washington's work is an invitation to step inside a dream. Not her dream—yours. Her paintings disinter those aspects of human nature that we tend to crush into a ball, lock in a safe, and bury deep underground. Viewing Washington's art is, to borrow the name of one of her series, like staring into a dark mirror. You want to look away, but you can't look away. So you look deeper into the darkness. And you sense that in the darkness there is something, or someone, staring back at you.

As in any vivid dream, the paintings are filled with familiar images reconfigured in startling ways. Her figures—pale beauties with attenuated limbs and high cheekbones who wear silk crepe blouses, sheath dresses, and schoolboy blazers—seem to have been abstracted from the pages of a Calvin Klein catalogue. The features are as simple and flat—childlike, even—as those of an airbrushed model. Only there's something wrong with their eyes. Their eyes are dead.

There also tends to be something wrong with their arms, legs, or heads. Often these appendages have been severed from the rest of their bodies, or are bleeding profusely, or both. "Like a Fucked Up Face" is an understatement of a title: a woman appears to be hemorrhaging blood from her nostrils and eyes. "The Heart" is plated on a porcelain dish, beside a knife and fork. And in "After the Dinner Party," a woman in a white cocktail dress sits cross-legged on her rug after a party, an empty bottle of Cristal champagne and a pair of Christian Louboutin heels scattered by

THE COMING DARKNESS
Watercolor and Gouache on Paper

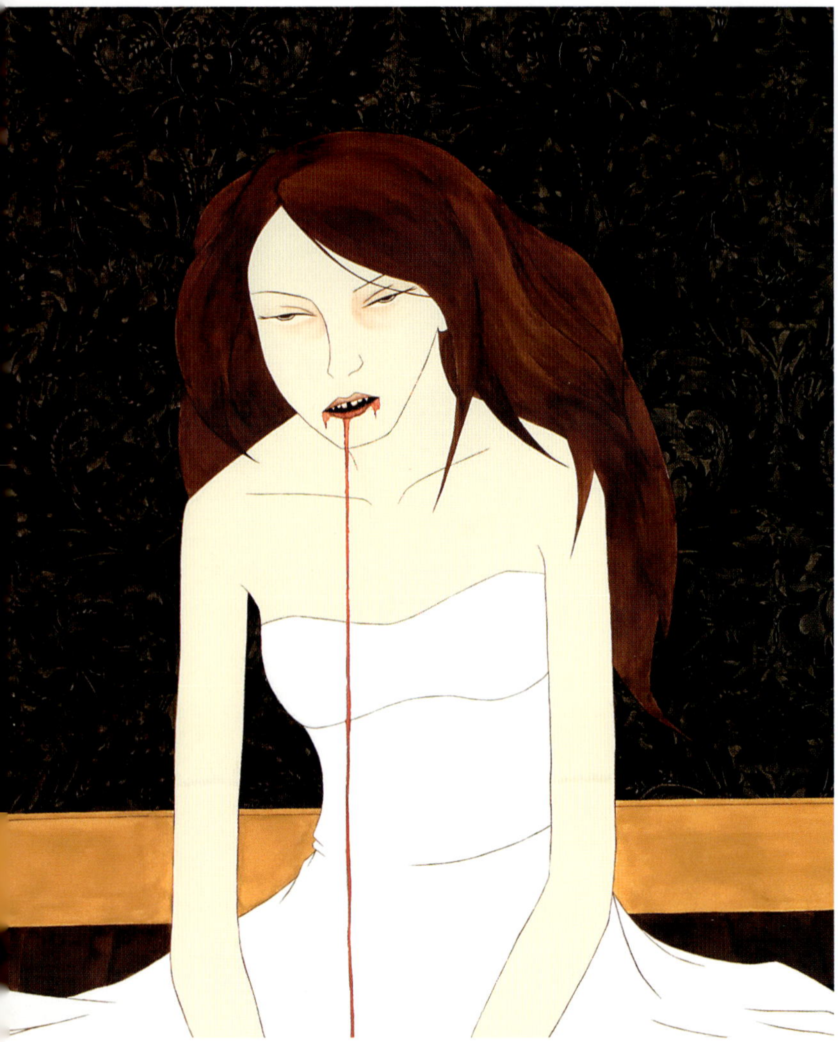

AFTER THE DINNER PARTY (DETAIL)

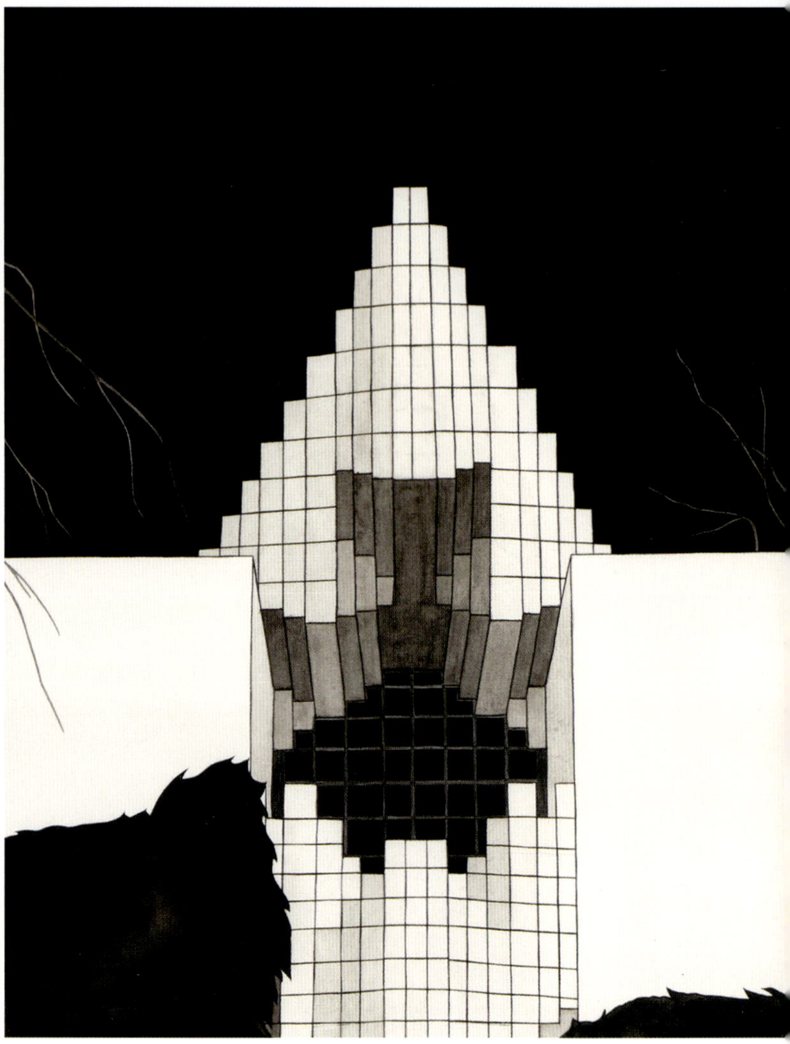

THE DOCTOR'S HOUSE (DETAIL)

her feet, while a saliva trail of blood falls from her mouth and pools on the rug. The decapitated heads that appear in paintings like "From Within" and "From Without" might be those of Lars Burmeister or Kate Moss.

But what killed them? The Cristal and the Louboutins are clues. In other paintings you can glimpse a Dolce and Gabbana belt, a Cartier bracelet, and a Chanel slipper. The haunted houses in which the models find themselves are just as opulent. They tend to be either baronial manors, plush with damask wallpaper and velvet carpeting (in the "Dark Mirror" series), or art deco mansions (in "For Forever I'll Be Here") with shiny reflective surfaces that render them haunted houses of mirrors. Most chilling of these is "The Doctor's House," modeled after the John Sowden house in Los Angeles, where it is suspected that Elizabeth Short, the Black Dahlia, was tortured, murdered, and dissected by the physician George Hodel.

Washington specializes in Black Dahlia figures—carefree young people who have fallen into a gory nightmare. Not all of them are dead, at least not outwardly. But all appear under a spell. They wear catatonic expressions that might pass for either extreme dread or sexual satiation. Are "The Count," "The Widow," and "Boy" lobotomized zombies, or sex fiends? What about the slightly disheveled woman who is "Lost in the Crags"? With her distant, sleepy eyes, parted lips, and splayed arms, she might be running away from a ghostly pursuer, or lost in a blissful

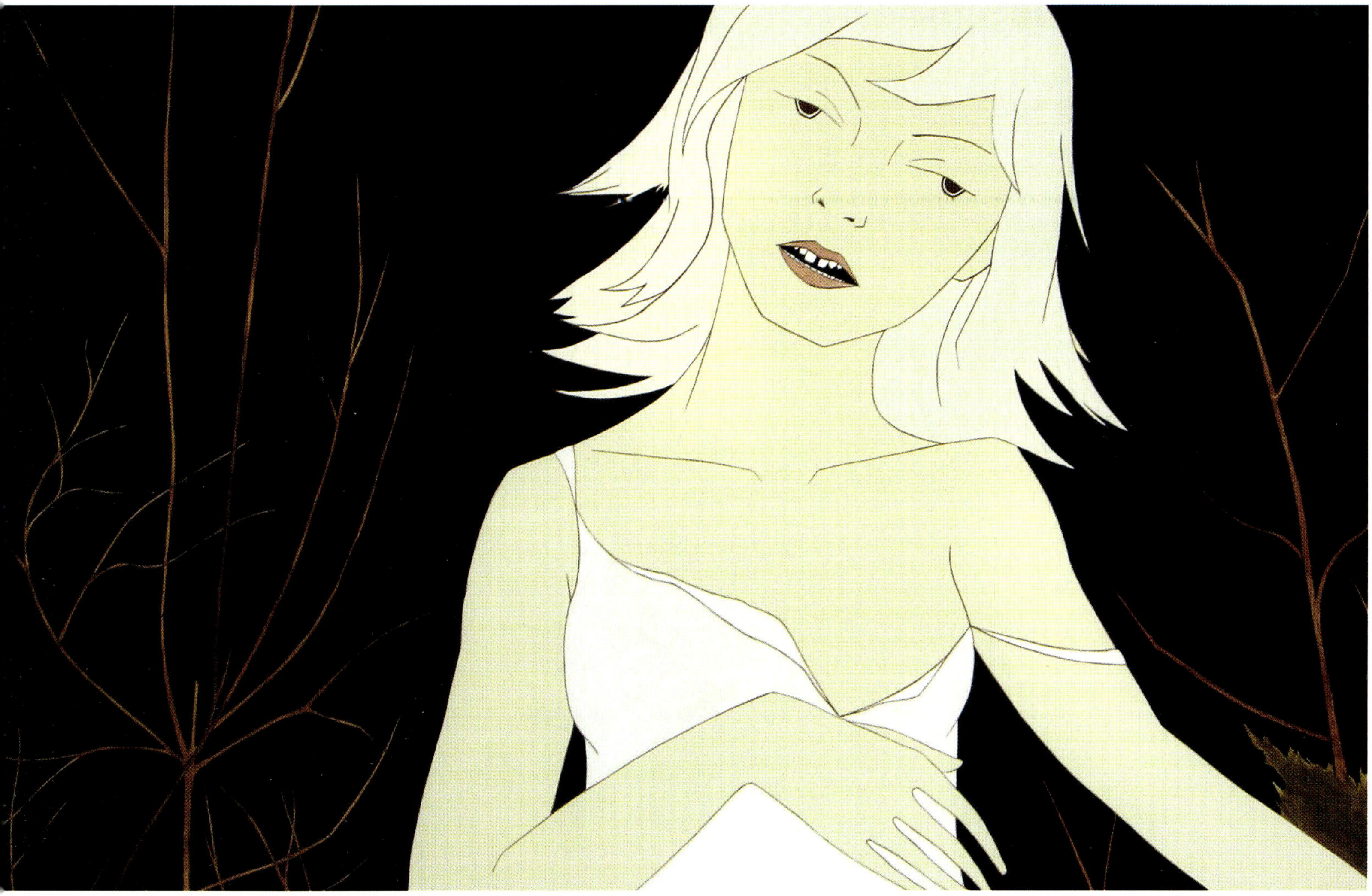

LOST IN THE CRAGS (DETAIL)

post-coital reverie. Is the slumped-over woman who is bleeding out of her mouth in "After the Dinner Party" a recent murder victim or a sated cannibal, drooling blood in gluttonous ecstasy? In Washington's dark mirror, both seem plausible.

The paintings resist obvious characterization. They are not merely a critique of the vapidity of popular culture. They are not, in fact, at all polemical. In their mingling of death and eroticism, they are far more unsettling than that. They tell a story. Washington has described her paintings as "illustrations from a novel that hasn't been written, film stills from a movie that hasn't been made." But many of the images are borrowed from films and books that do exist. The woman in the trench coat in "Like a Fucked Up Face" is borrowed from Georges Franju's *Eyes Without a Face*; the owl "BOB" has swooped in from *Twin Peaks*. "The Architect's House" and the clock of "In Between Time" are from Edgar G. Ulmer's *The Black Cat*; "The Hospital" appears in the cult horror film *Dead Girl*; "The Boathouse (For Agatha)" is Agatha Christie's own boathouse, which she used in her novel *Dead Man's Folly* (in which a dead girl is found inside the boathouse, strangled with a cord). The "Dark Mirror" series evokes Nathaniel Hawthorne's *House of the Seven Gables* and Henry James' "The Turn of the Screw," both visually (as in "Just Such an Old House," a title taken from James' ghost story) and in the paintings' uncanny representation of a past that refuses to die. The blankness we see in

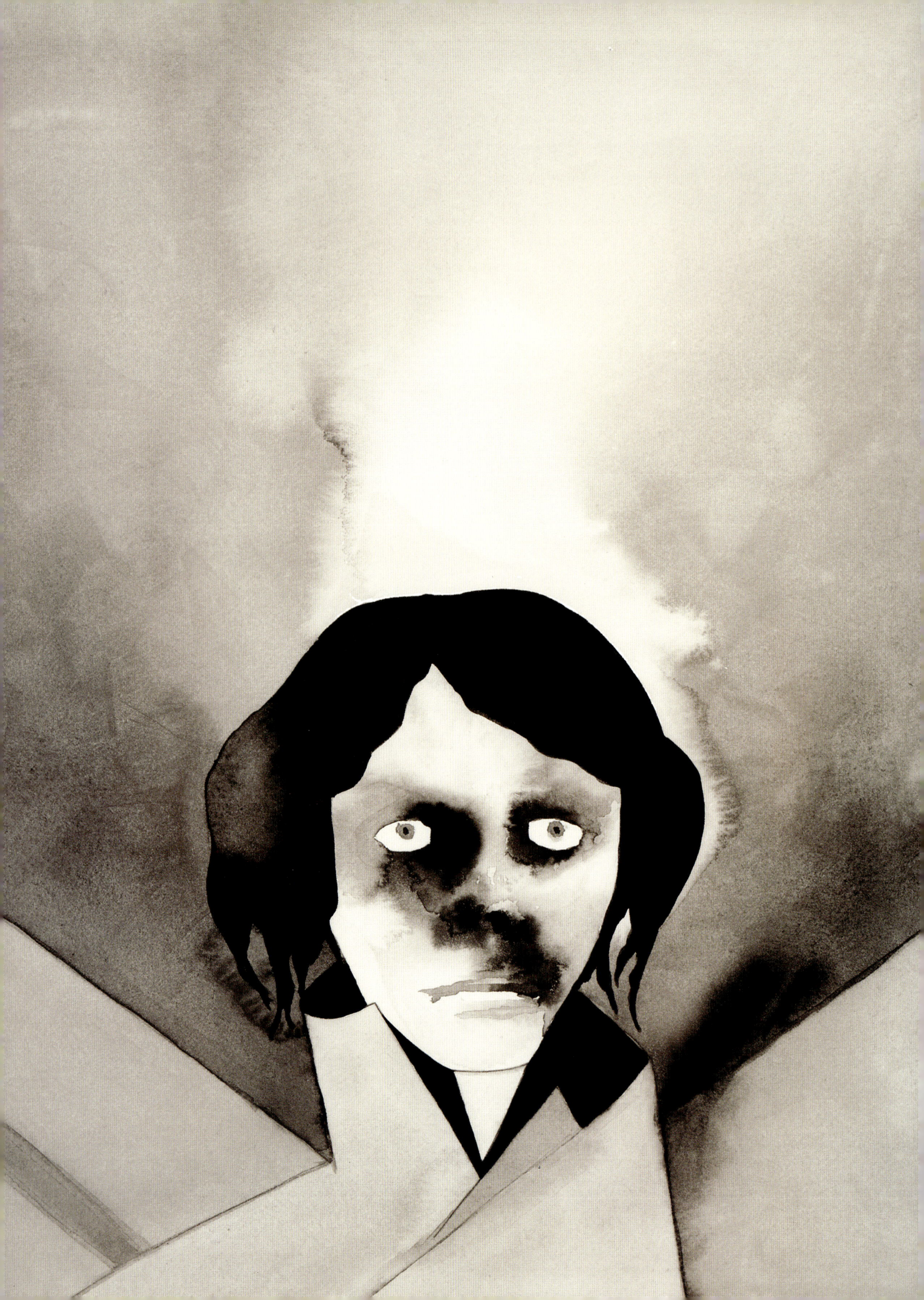

the eyes of Washington's characters recall Hawthorne at his bleakest:

> With a mysterious and terrible Past, which had annihilated his memory, and a blank Future before him, he had only this visionary and impalpable Now, which, if you once look closely at it, is nothing.

Washington has also drawn considerably from Dark Romanticism, which was recently the subject of a major exhibition at the Musée d'Orsay. Washington's gloomy, twisted trees, gesticulating like mangled fingers, her forsaken moors, and her looming, immense boulders, recall Caspar David Friedrich's tortured landscapes. The pale victim of "Drowned," half-submerged in a black lake, her head inclined toward the viewer, bears more than a passing resemblance to Paul Delaroche's *La Jeune Martyre*. And Washington's disembodied heads seem to be nodding to the decapitations of Odilon Redon.

The visual language of the Dark Romantics was adopted by Hollywood filmmakers in the early 1930s, with films like Tod Browning's *Dracula* and James Whale's *Frankenstein*, and its power on the public imagination remains, as the success of the recent *Twilight* films attests. But Washington's work, which predates that series, reclaims the language of the uncanny—resisting clichés and finding new ways to unnerve. There is nothing reassuring in her paintings. There is only dread. One of the ways she accomplishes this is by reconfiguring the familiar iconography of celebrity culture in unsettling ways. Though Robert Pattinson seems to have stepped out of one of Washington's paintings—he bears a strong resemblance to "The Count" and also to the man gushing black disease in "Escape into the Woods—Overcome"—it is hard to imagine him appearing in a film in which his body parts are severed one at a time and hung from tree branches.

Washington's paintings call out to each other, mournfully, like separated twins. They demand to be seen in tandem. In isolation, a Washington painting is like a trailer to a film, or the first chapter of a novel. It presents clues and elicits questions. What kind of maniac is hiding inside the Grey Lodge, we want to know. What kind of diabolical experiments are being conducted in the Architect's House, or the Hospital? When confronted with paintings like "Falling Teeth" or "The Rotten Arm," we want to know to whom the floating molars and incisors and bloody limbs were attached. Each painting is a cliffhanger. We want more.

Now we have it. Though Washington has previously collected her series in the form of zines, the publication of *For Forever I'll Be Here* is the richest articulation yet of her work. The three series, when placed side by side, tell a ghost horror story in three acts. "At Night" serves as an atlas of Washington's landscape—the manor on the moors, the dark lake, the sinister forest—and portraits of the lost souls who inhabit it. "In a Dark Mirror" takes us inside the manor. Washington's characters have just completed a terrible dinner party, in which they were both guests and meal. The survivors have contracted something dreadful called "the black infection," which makes them bleed blackness from their mouths. Some of them have fled for the woods, which frankly does not seem like a very good idea.

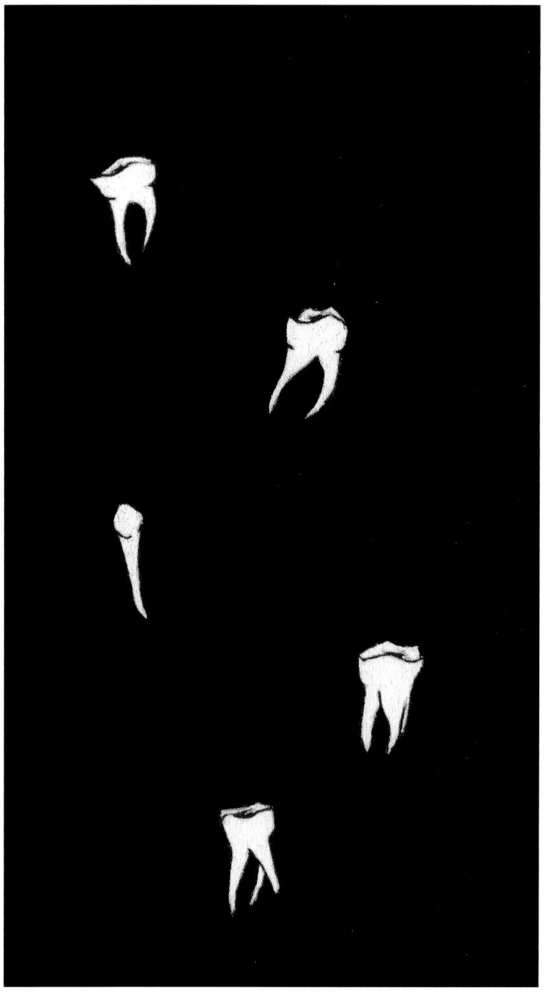

LIKE A FUCKED UP FACE (DETAIL)

FALLING TEETH NO.2

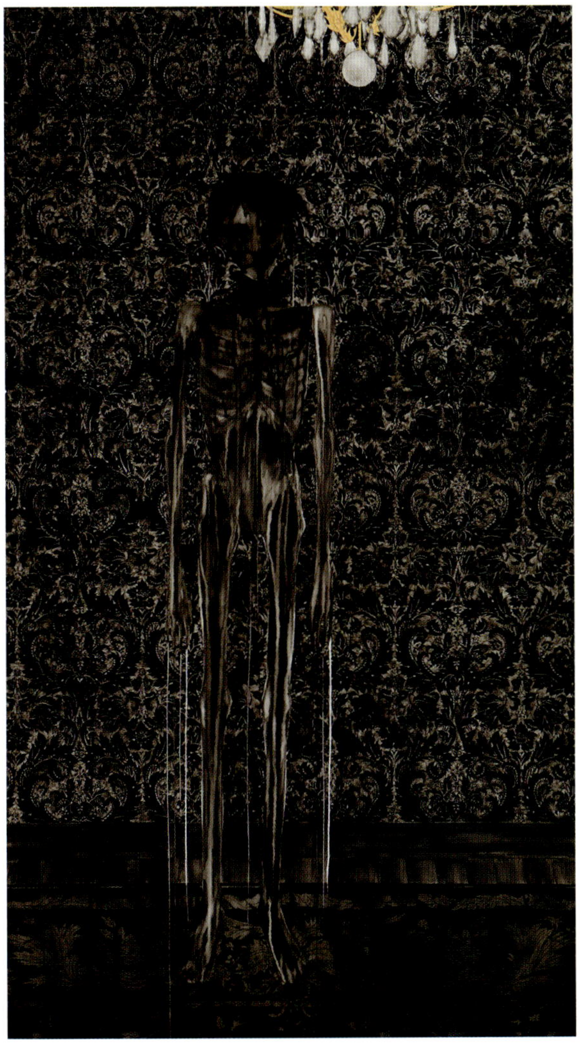

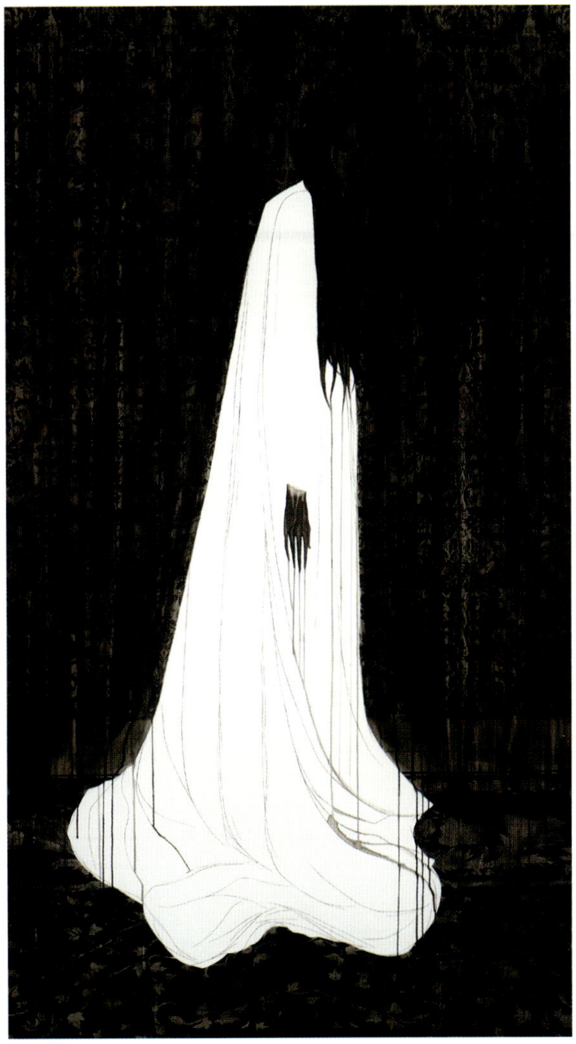

At the center of this section lie three uncanny masterpieces—"And the Blood Will Rise to Meet the Shadows," "To Walk These Halls—Unnamed and Unmourned," and "Through the Thinnest of Veils"—in which figures are seen in the midst of a transfiguration between life and death. The blurry figures merge into, or out of, her ubiquitous acanthus-print wallpaper, in a kind of gothic camouflage. The figures evoke, as powerfully as any of Washington's paintings, the shapelessness of our greatest fears. And they dramatize the way we summon our unconscious terrors into existence. They are Washington's scariest creations.

In the final act, "For Forever I'll Be Here," we find ourselves at another party. It's not late, exactly, but it's not early. We're "in between time," a realm filled with spotless modern homes where everything, and everyone, is clean and shiny and dead.

But the story isn't complete. Like all great narrative art, Washington's paintings create a world—or a manor house—that the viewer must populate with his own demons. Live with these paintings and they enter your dreams. And, before you know it, you enter them. You wake up in the middle of the night and find yourself lying on an operating table in the Doctor's House. Something is stepping out of the wallpaper. You are running through a dark forest, pursued by an elegant man who is bleeding from the corners of his mouth.

A beautiful woman in a white bikini invites you to a night swim. The sky is black. The water is very cold. Her eyes are empty. Won't you join her?

AND THE BLOOD WILL RISE TO MEET THE SHADOWS (DETAIL)

TO WALK THESE HALLS—UNNAMED AND UNMOURNED

THROUGH THE THINNEST OF VEILS

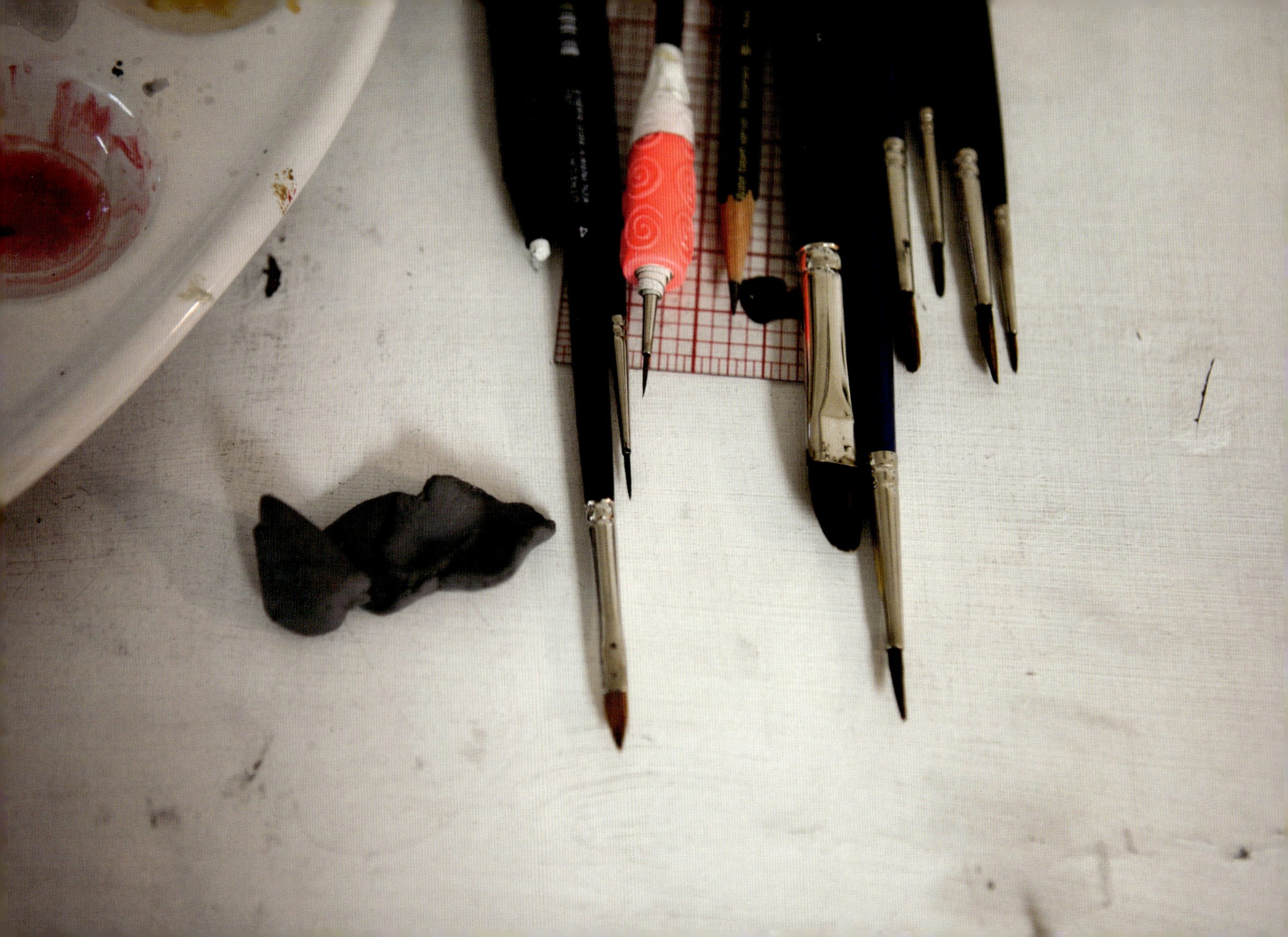

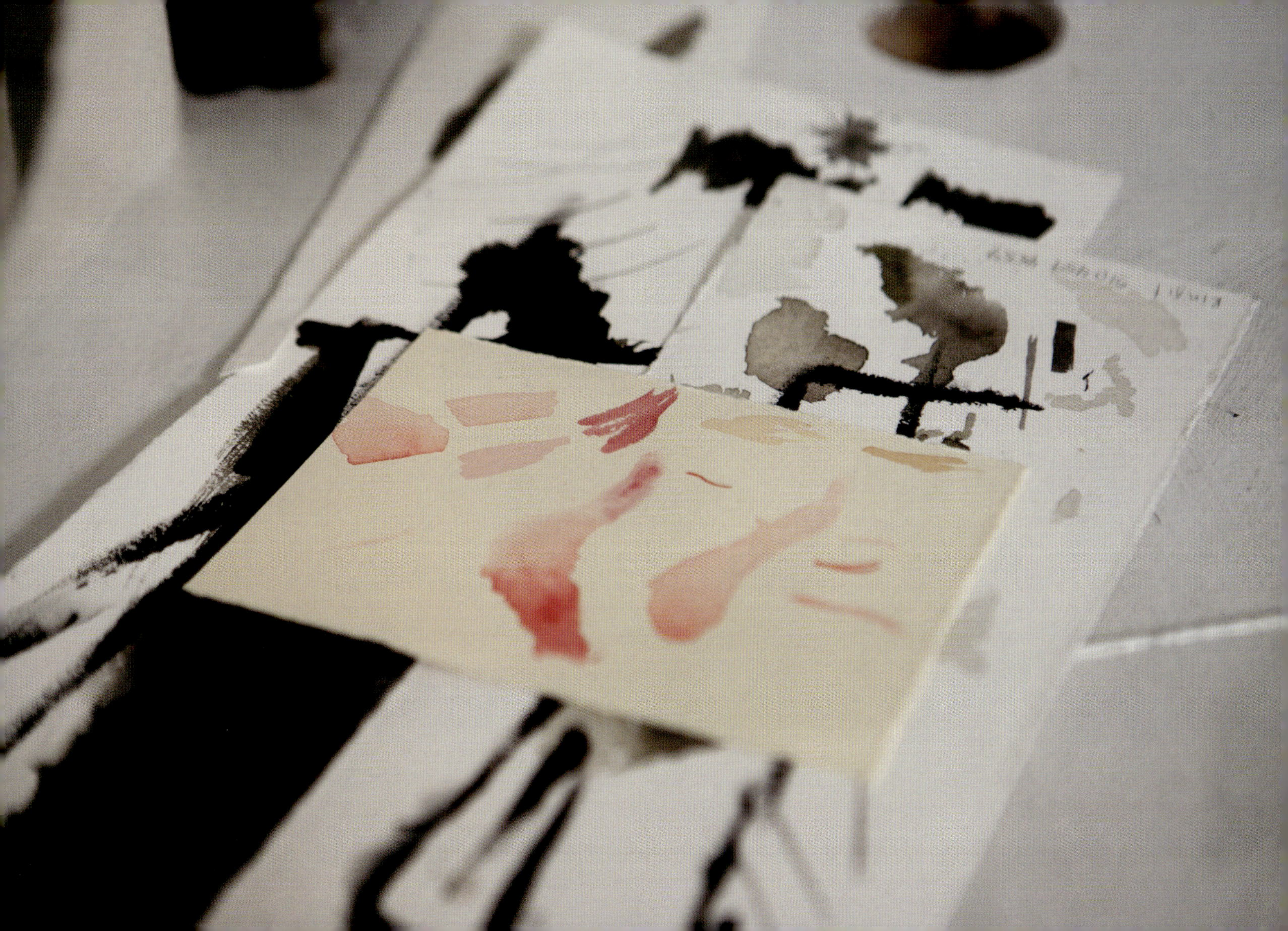

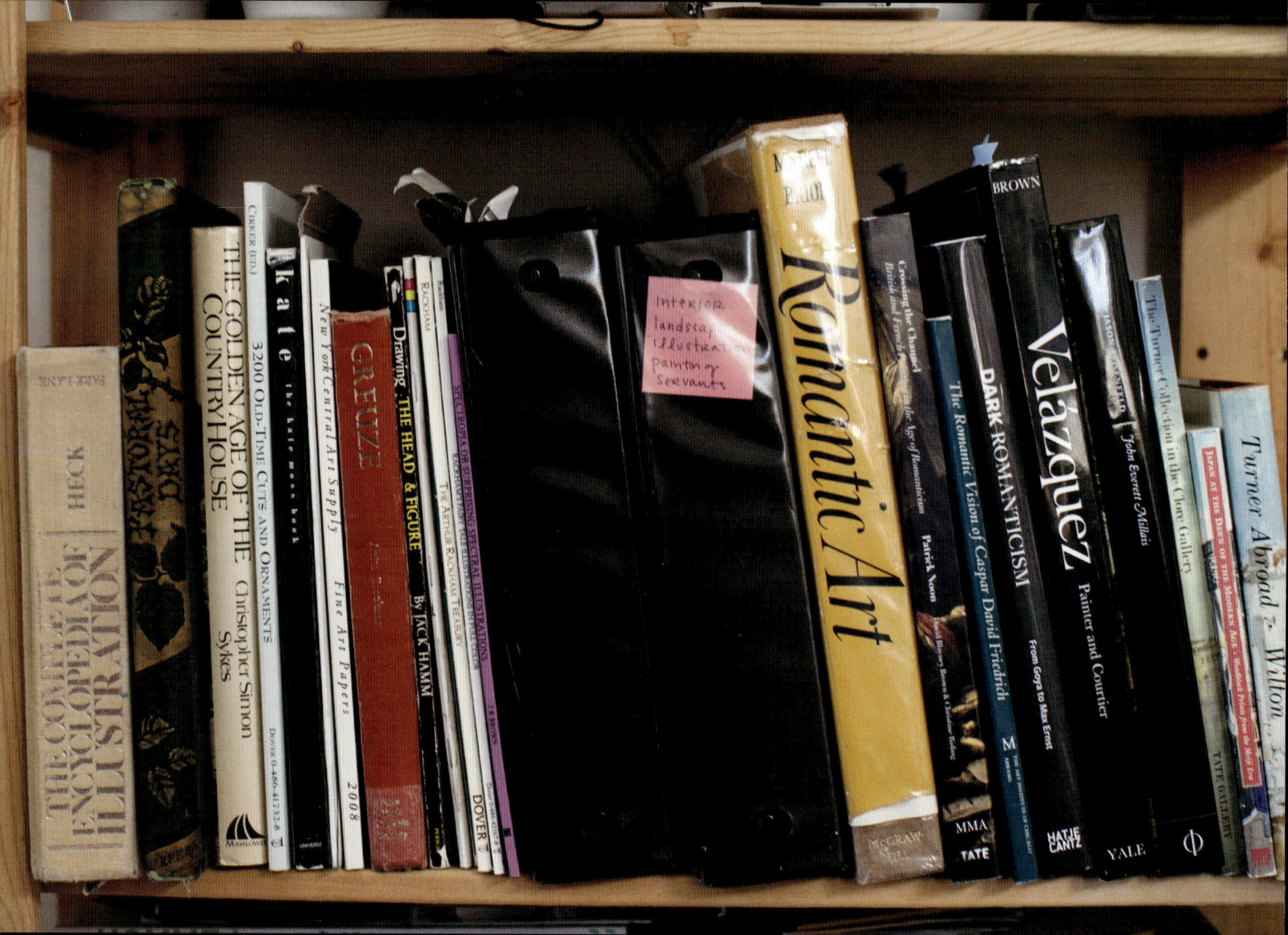
HECK
THE COMPLETE ENCYCLOPEDIA OF ILLUSTRATION
PARK LANE
PASTORAL DAYS
THE GOLDEN AGE OF THE COUNTRY HOUSE
Christopher Simon Sykes
MAYFLOWER
CIRKER (ED.)
3200 OLD-TIME CUTS AND ORNAMENTS
DOVER 0-486-41232-8
kate
New York Central Art Supply
Fine Art Papers
2008
GREUZE
Drawing THE HEAD & FIGURE
By JACK HAMM
RACKHAM
THE ARTHUR RACKHAM TREASURY
DOVER
SPECTROPIA OR SURPRISING SPECTRAL ILLUSTRATIONS
J.H. BROWN
Interior
landscap
painting
servants
Romantic Art
Crossing the Channel
Patrick Noon
MMA
TATE
The Romantic Vision of Caspar David Friedrich
BROWN
DARK ROMANTICISM
From Goya to Max Ernst
HATJE CANTZ
Velázquez
Painter and Courtier
YALE
John Everett Millais
The Turner Collection in the Clore Gallery
TATE GALLERY
Turner Abroad
Wilton

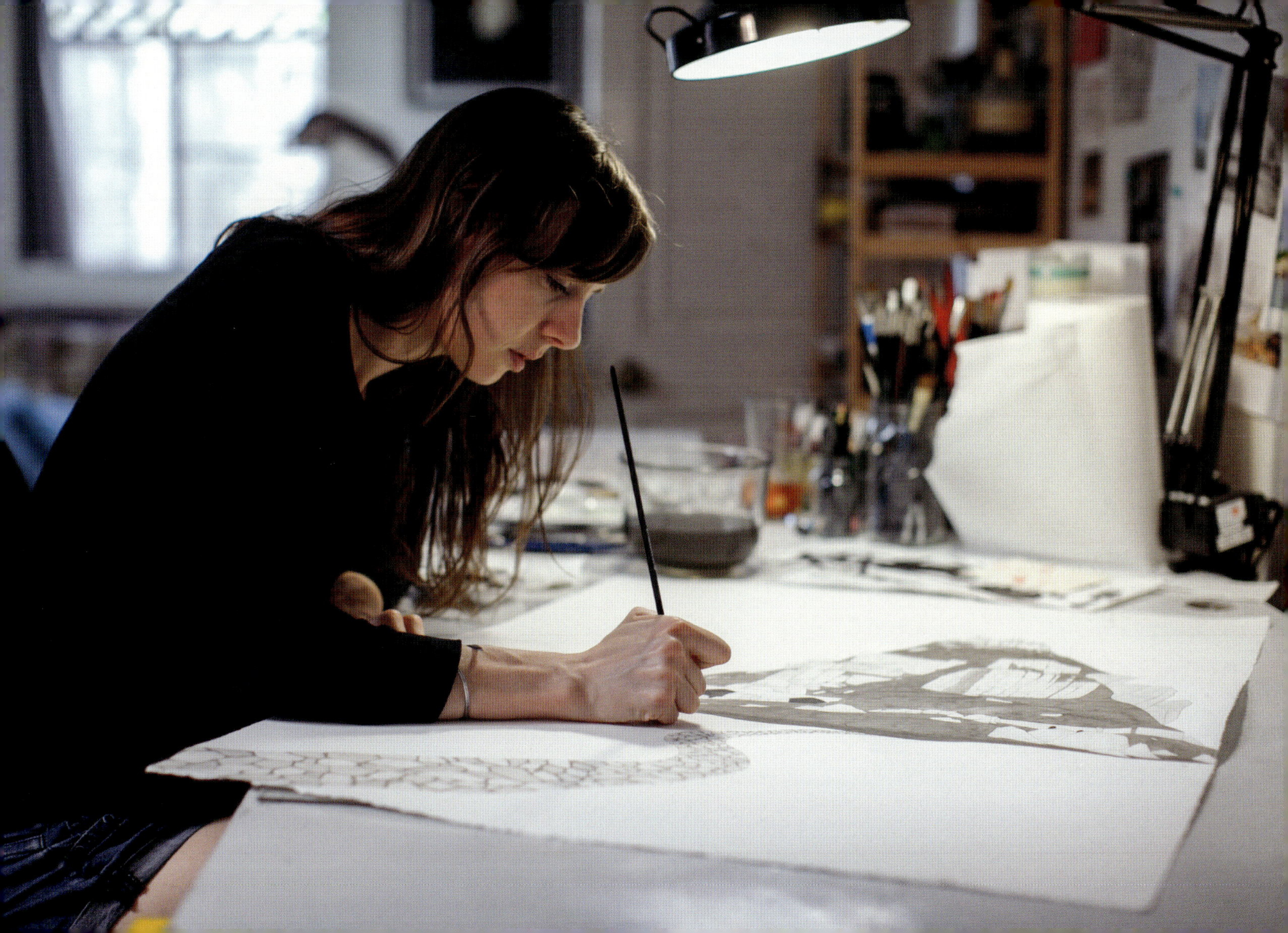

CHAPTER ONE

At Night

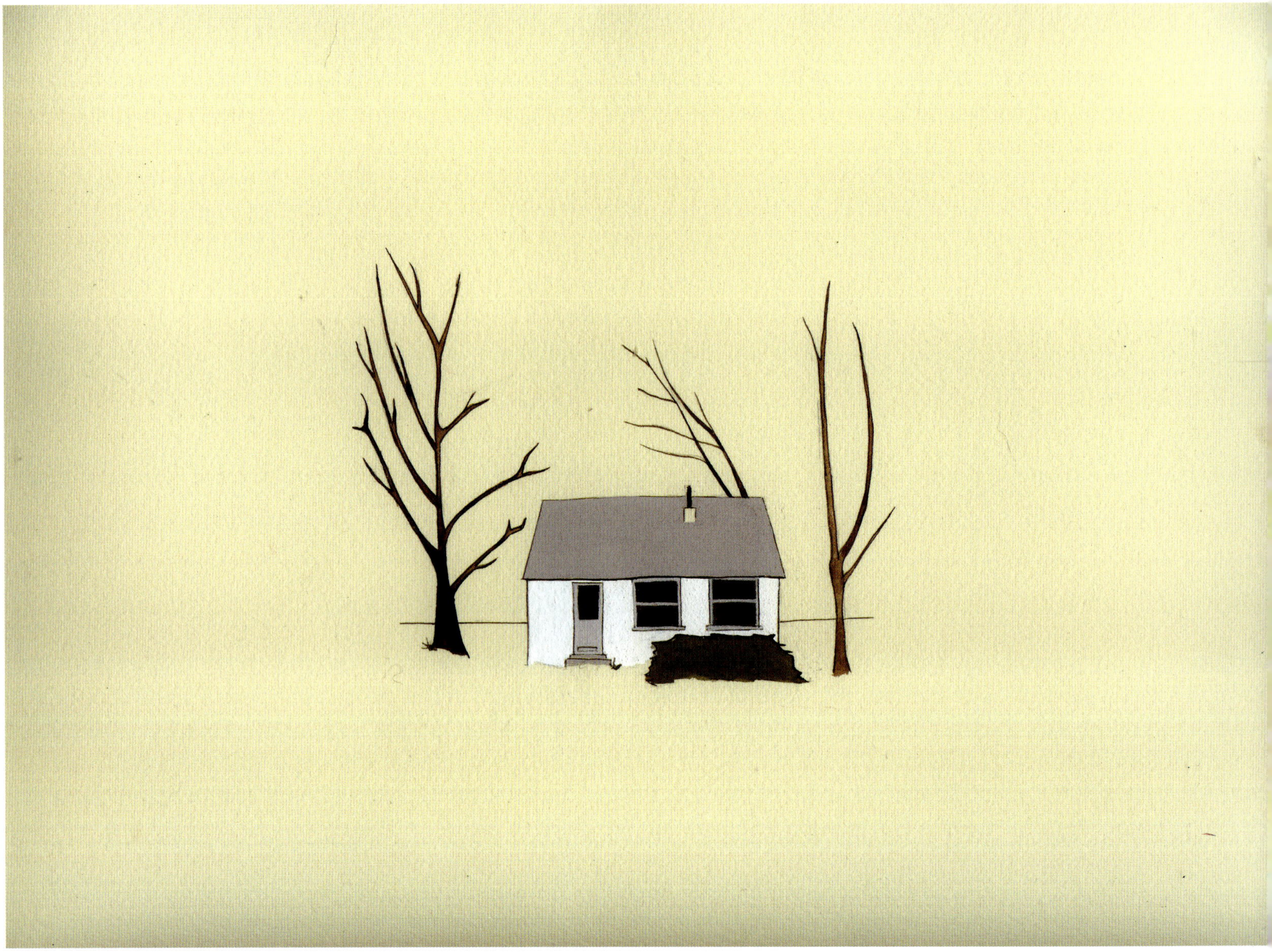

HOUSE
16 x 20", 2005, Watercolor and Gouache on Paper

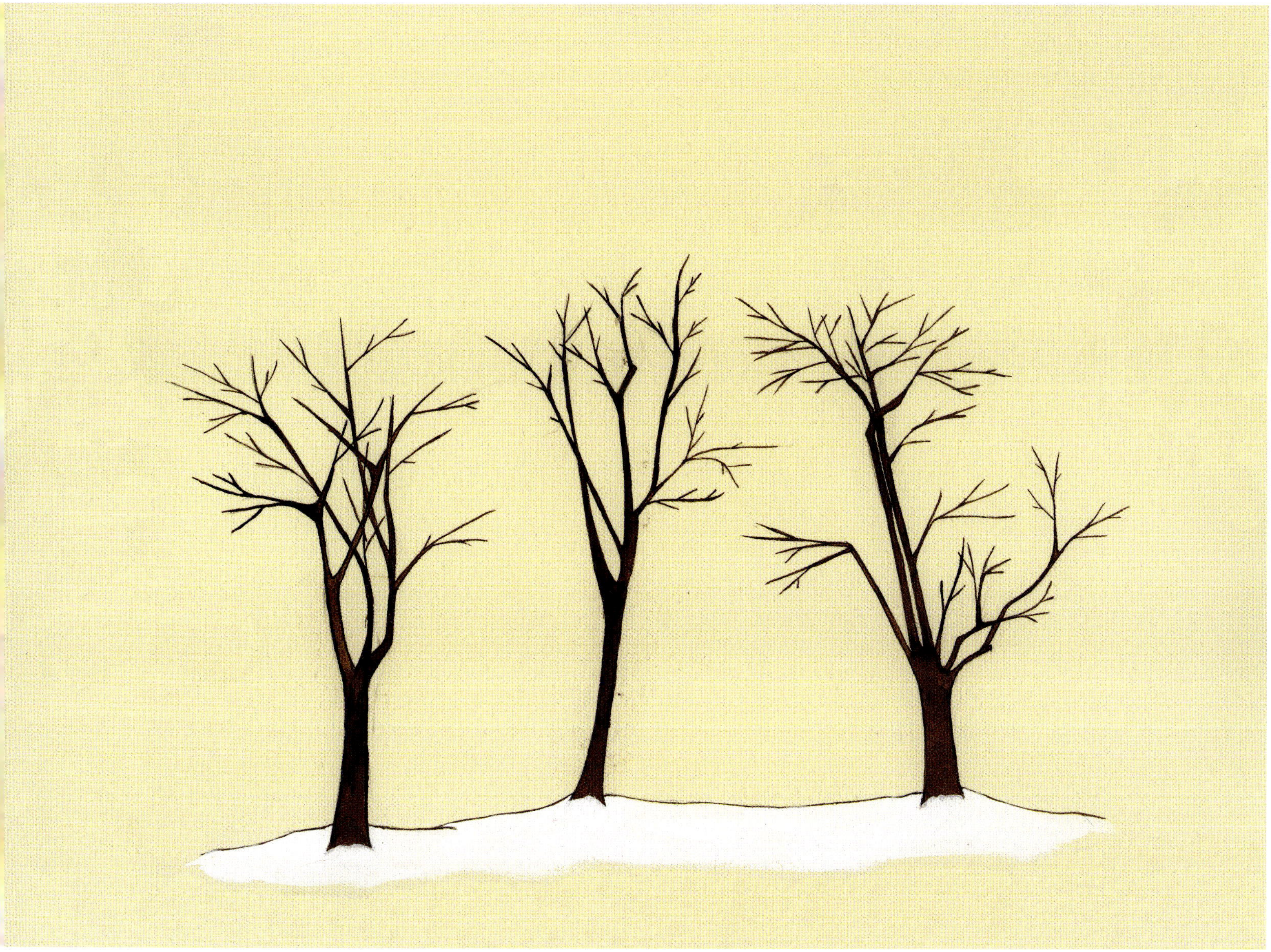

THREE TREES
11 x 14″, 2005, Watercolor and Gouache on Paper

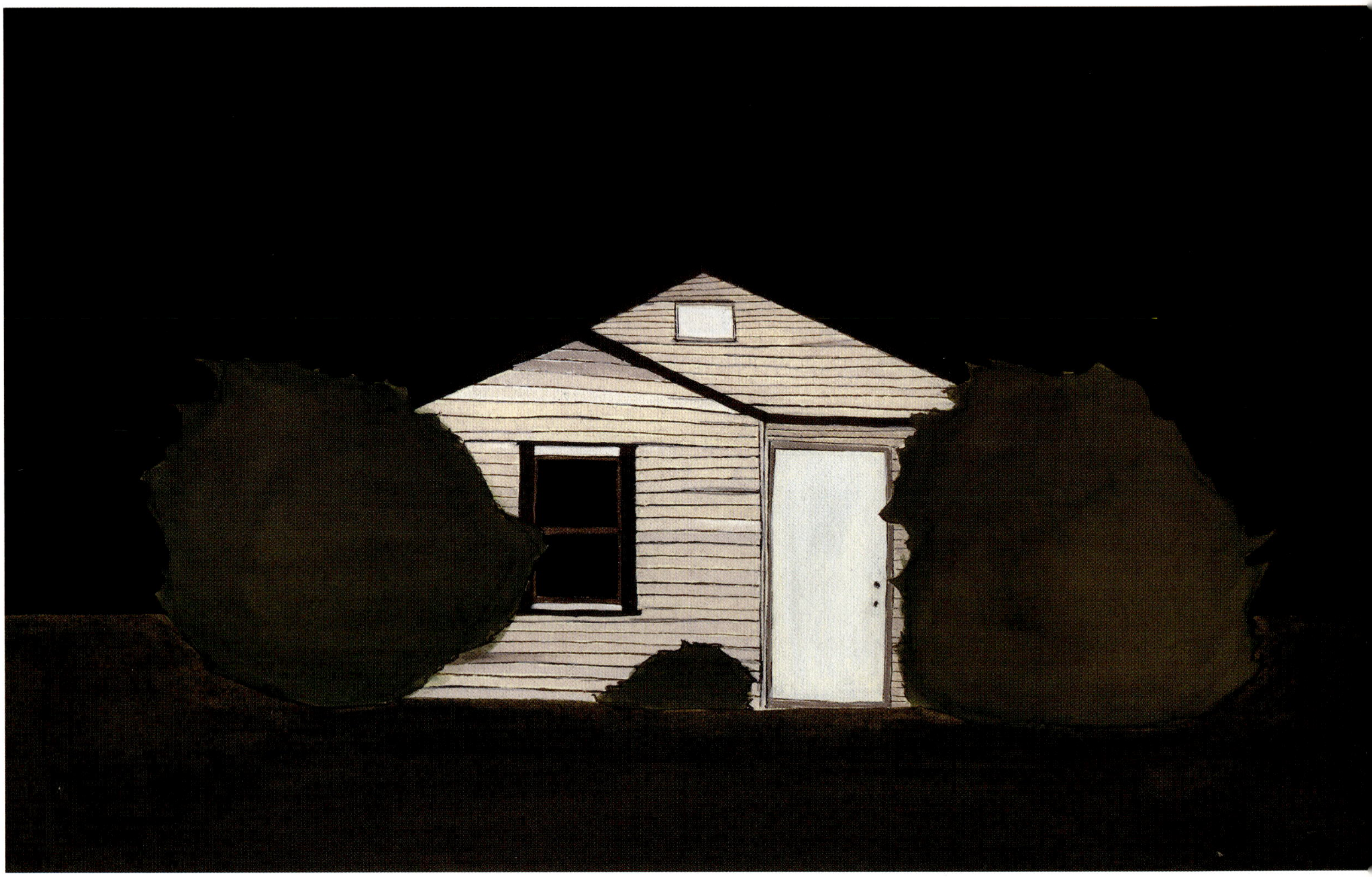

FONTANA HOUSE
16 x 20″, 2005, Watercolor and Gouache on Paper

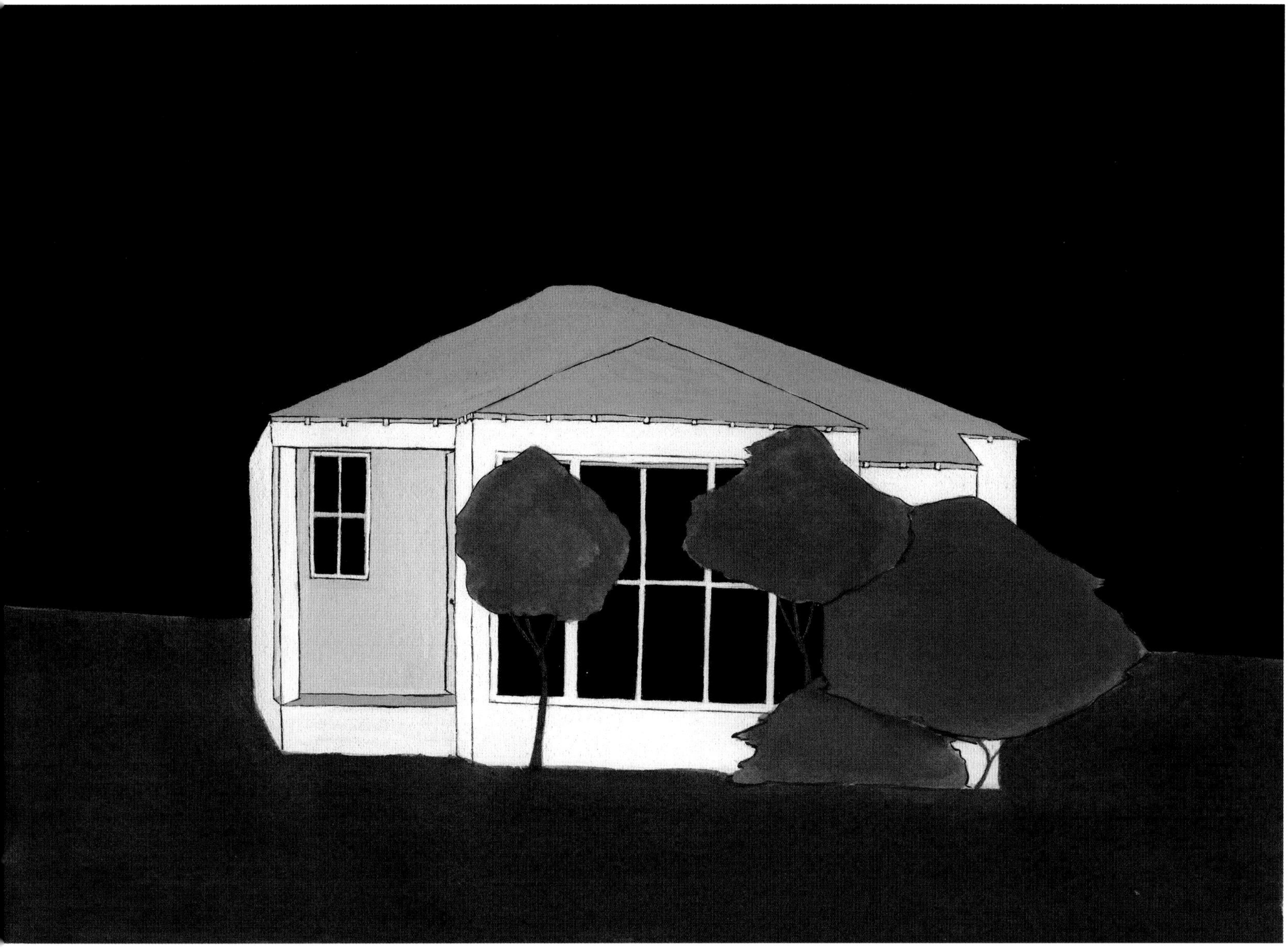

TILDEN HOUSE
16 x 20″, 2005, Watercolor and Gouache on Paper

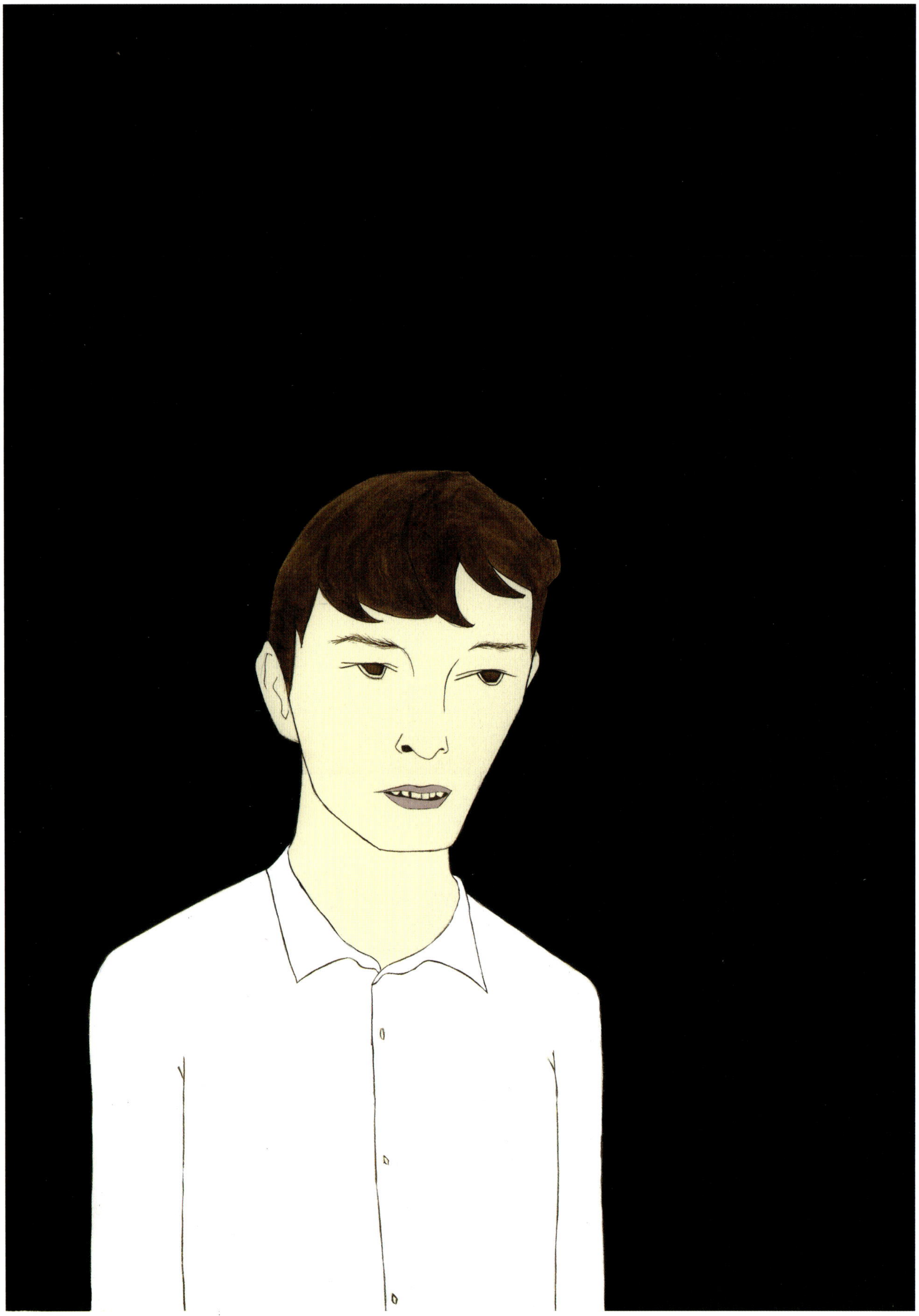

BOY
24 x 18″, 2005, Watercolor and Gouache on Paper

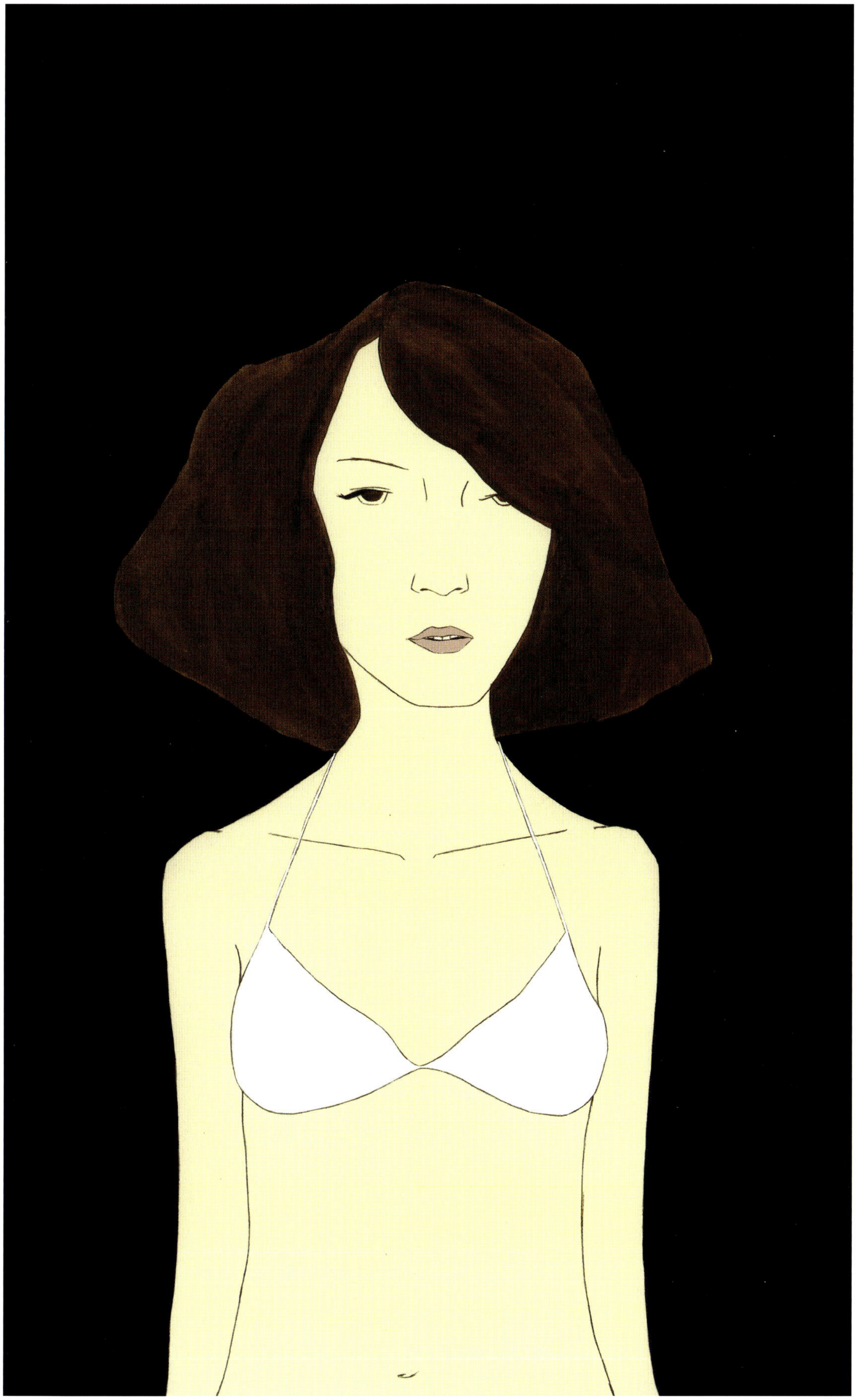

NIGHTSWIM
24 x 18″, 2005, Watercolor and Gouache on Paper

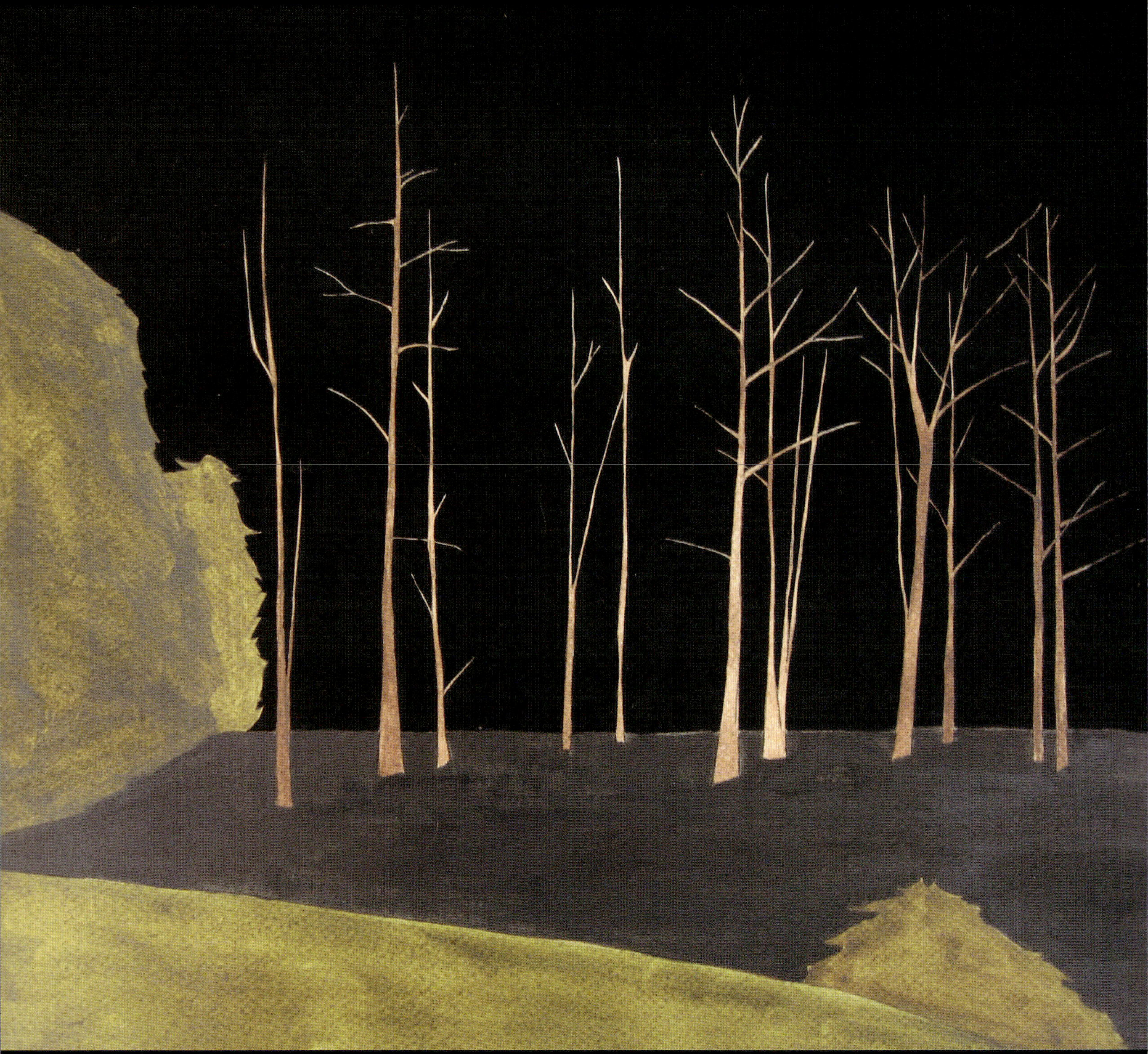

AT THE EDGE OF THE LAKE
15 x 17½″, 2006, Watercolor and Gouache on Paper

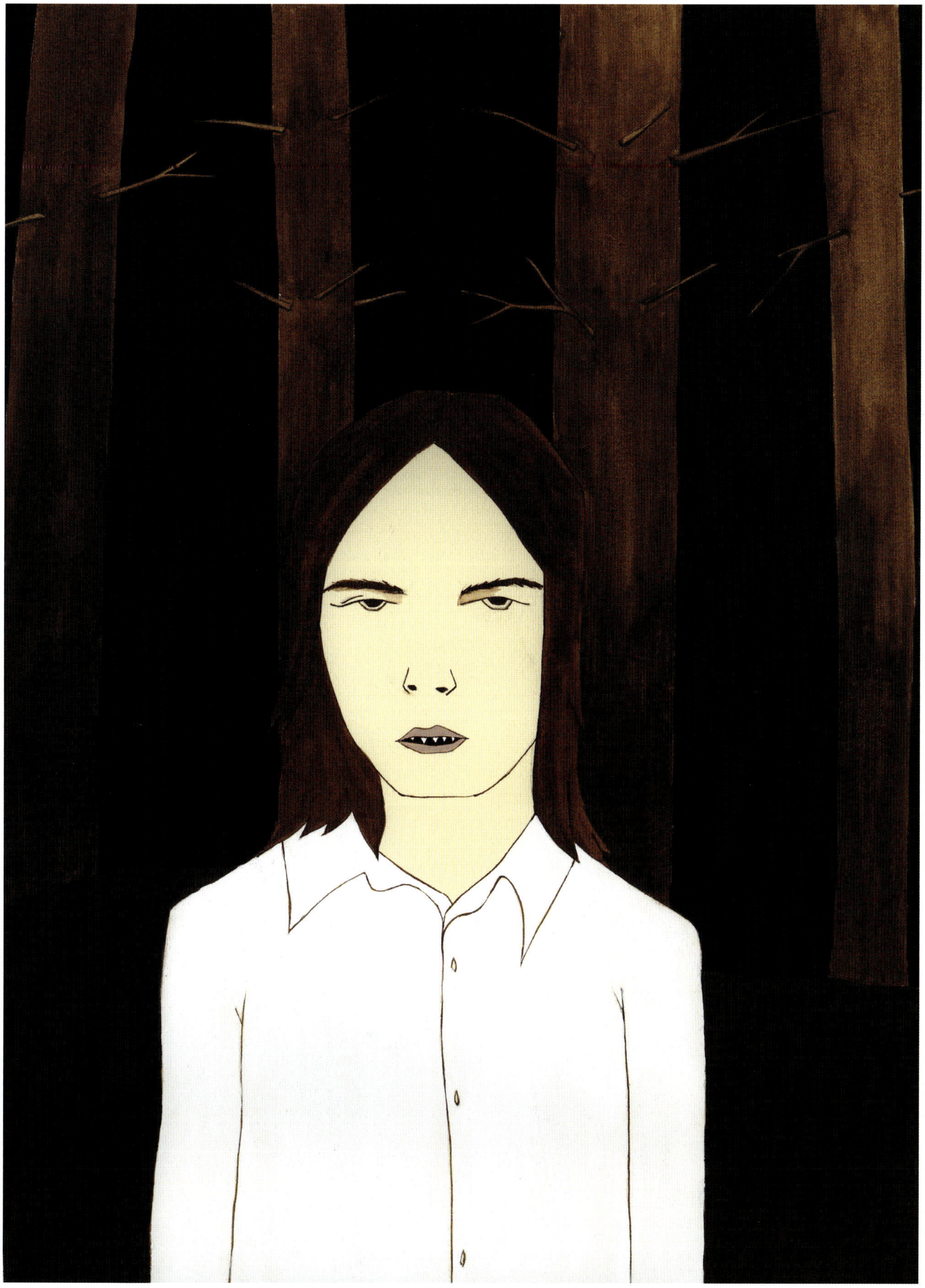

IN THE FOREST
24 x 18″, 2005, Watercolor and Gouache on Paper

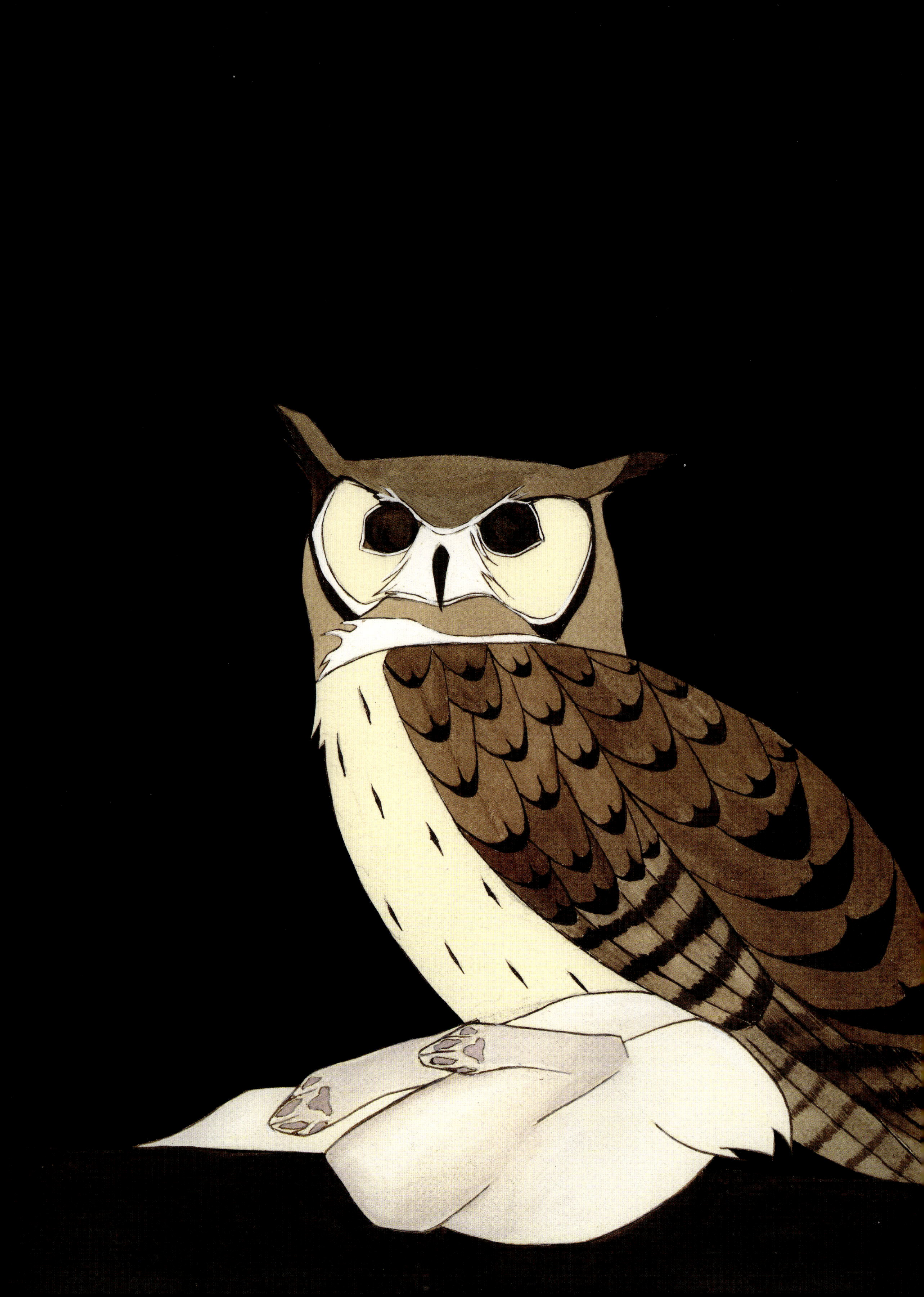

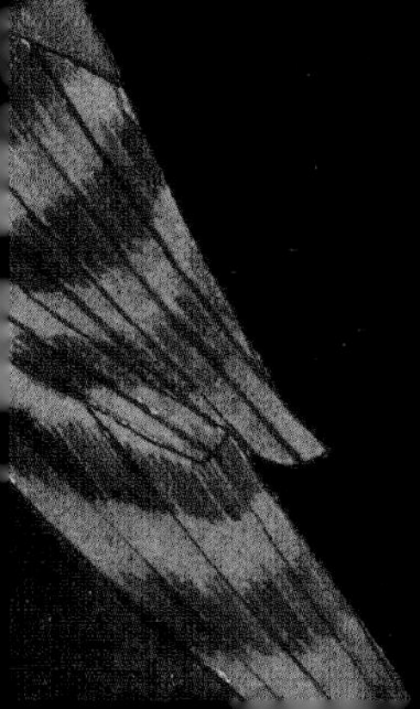

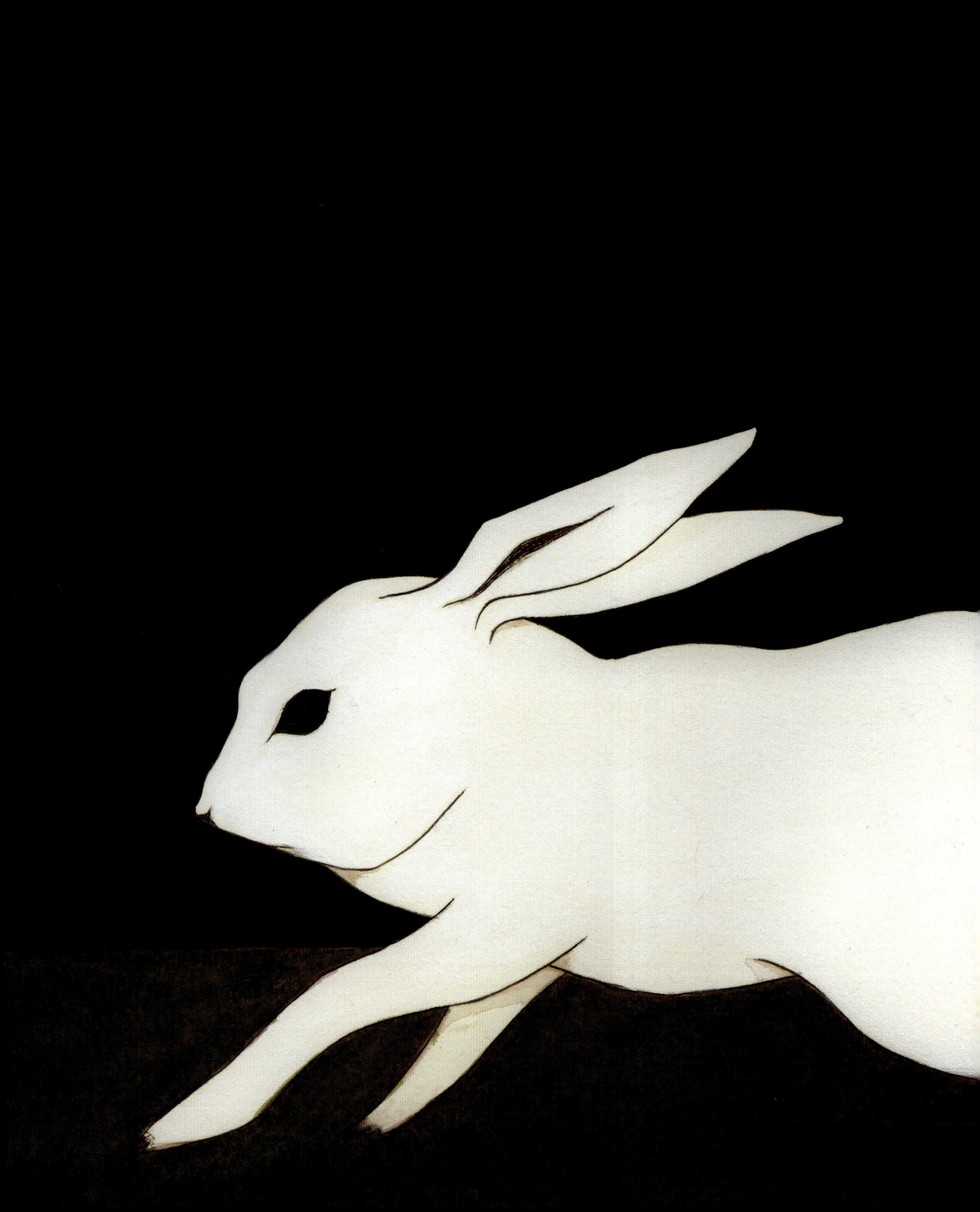

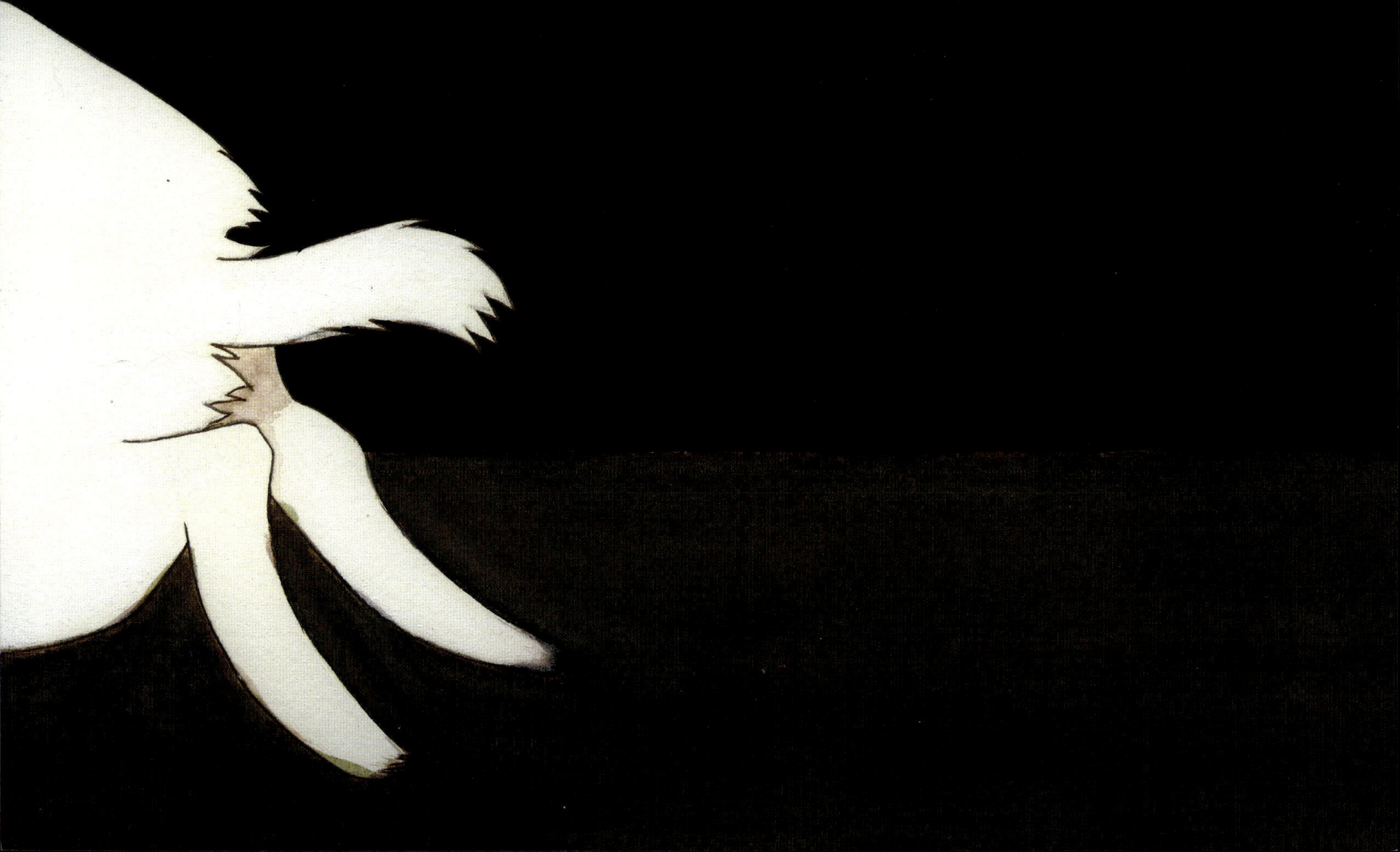

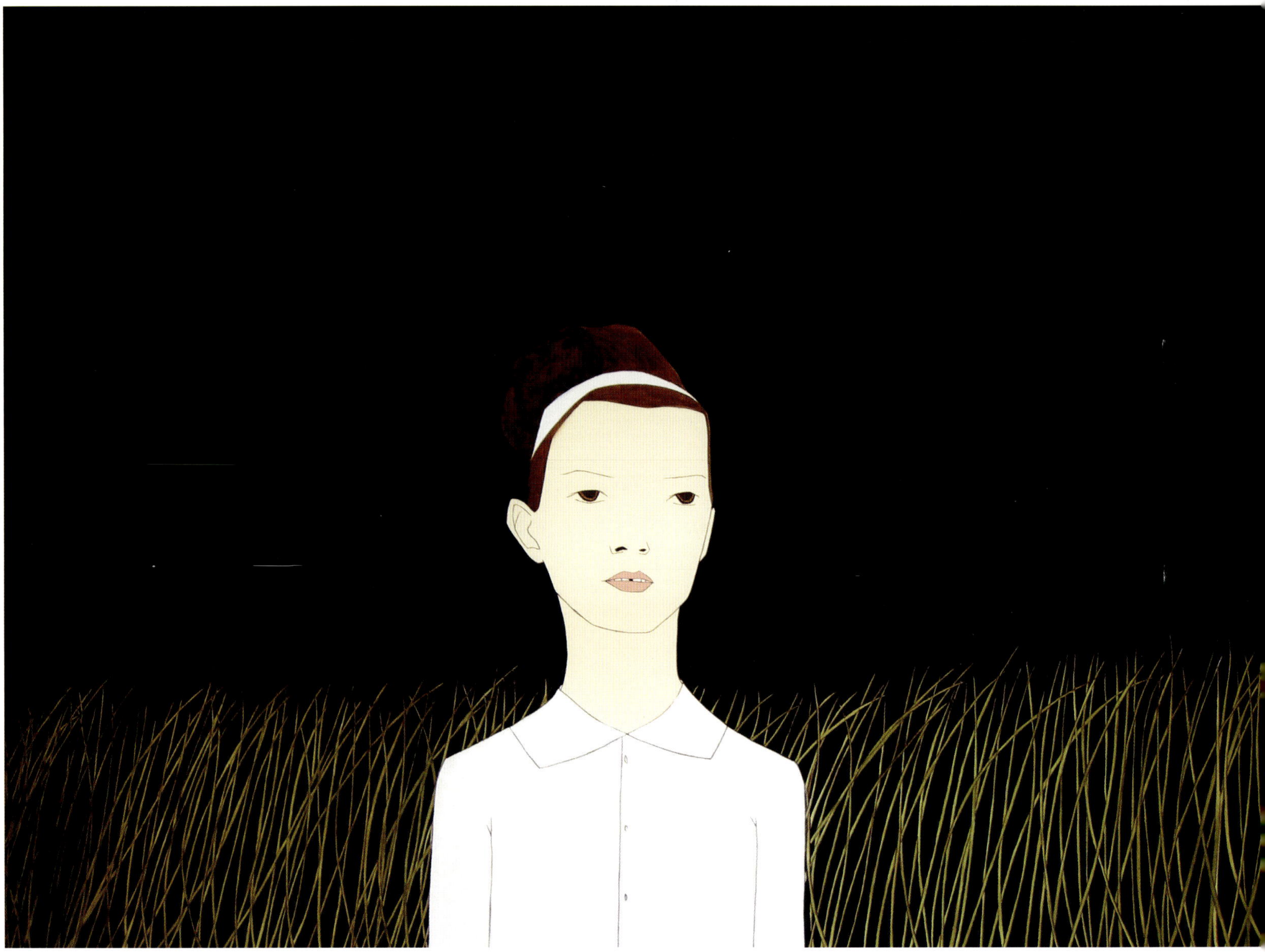

AWAY FROM THE BIG HOUSE
26 x 34″, 2005, Watercolor and Gouache on Paper

PAGE 30-31: **OWL**
18 x 24″, Watercolor and Gouache on Paper

PAGE 32-33: **RABBIT**
18 x 24″, Watercolor and Gouache on Paper

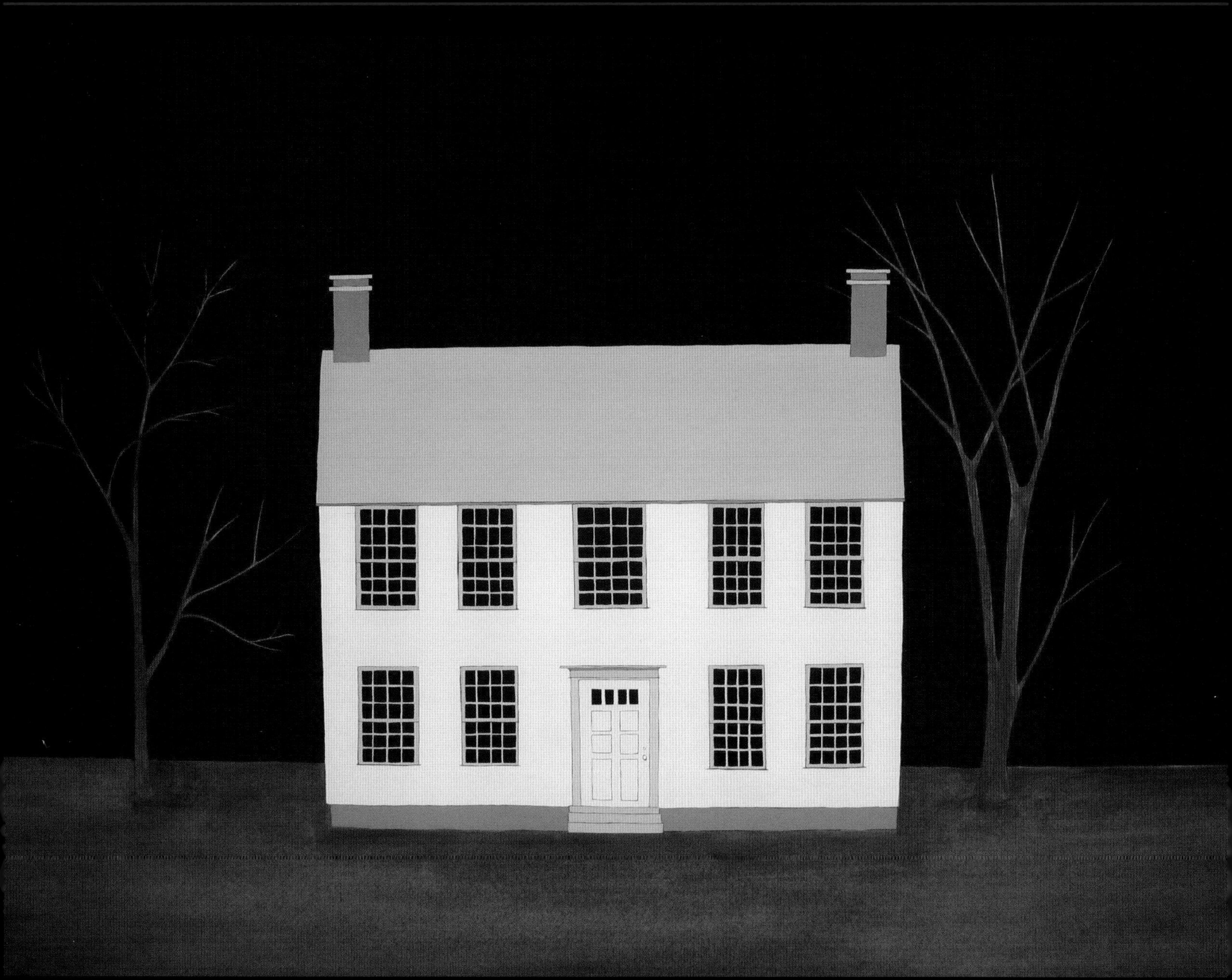

THE MANOR ON THE MOORS
26 x 34″, 2005, Watercolor and Gouache on Paper

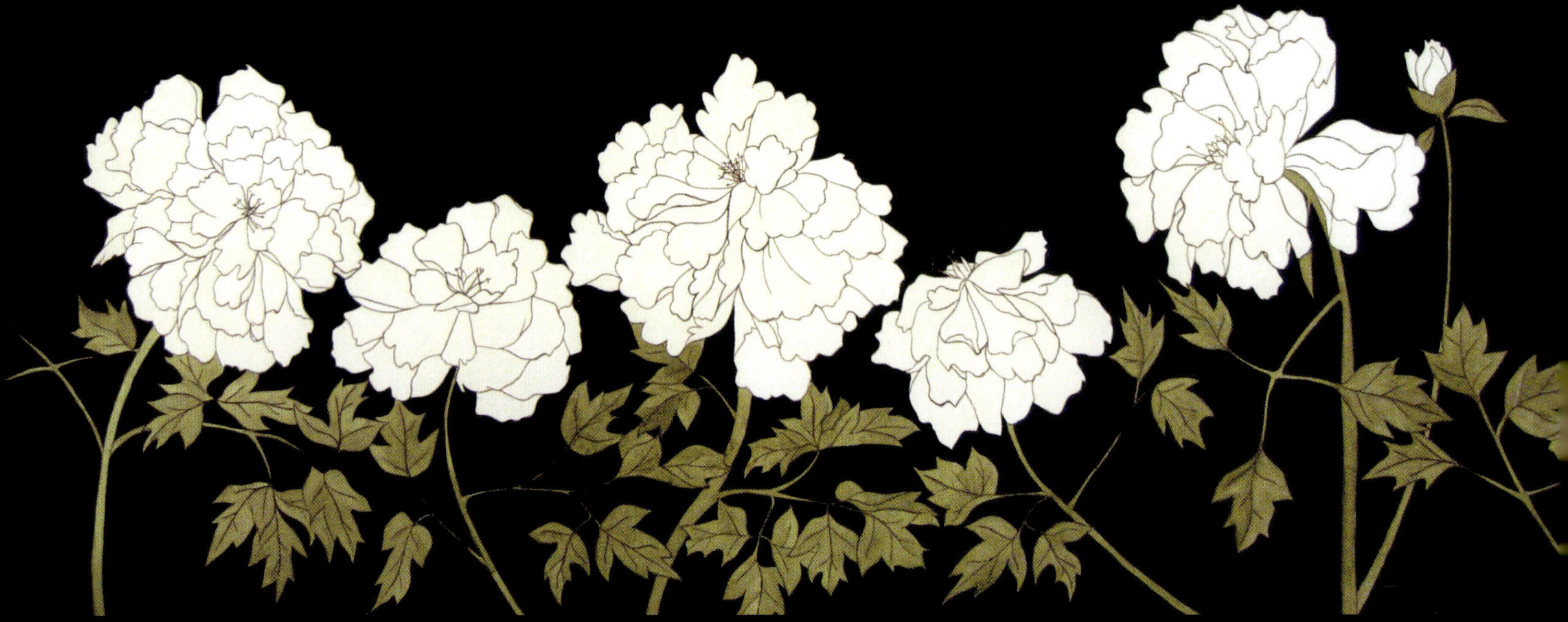

PEONIES

18 x 24″, 2005, Watercolor and Gouache on Paper

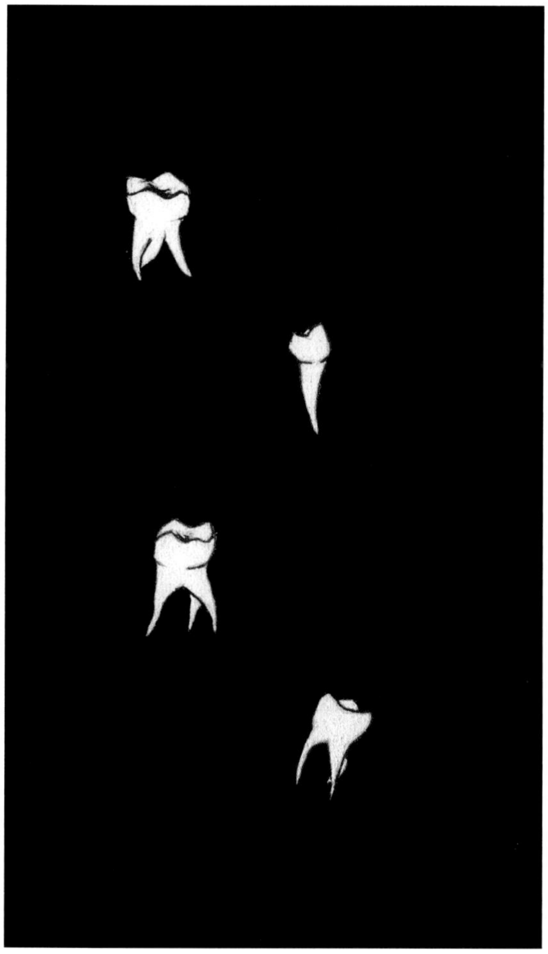

FALLING TEETH NO.1
8 x 6″, 2006, Watercolor and Gouache on Paper

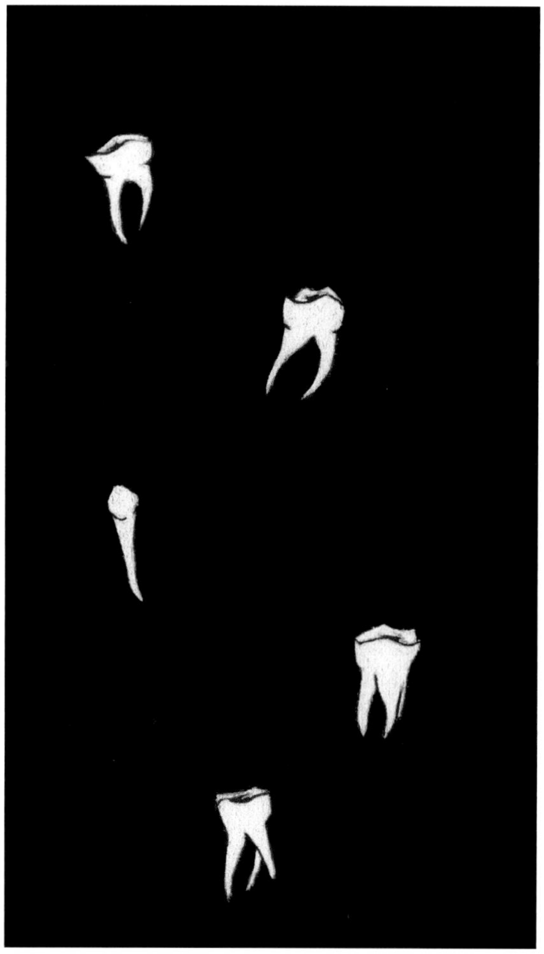

FALLING TEETH NO.2
8 x 6″, 2005, Watercolor and Gouache on Paper

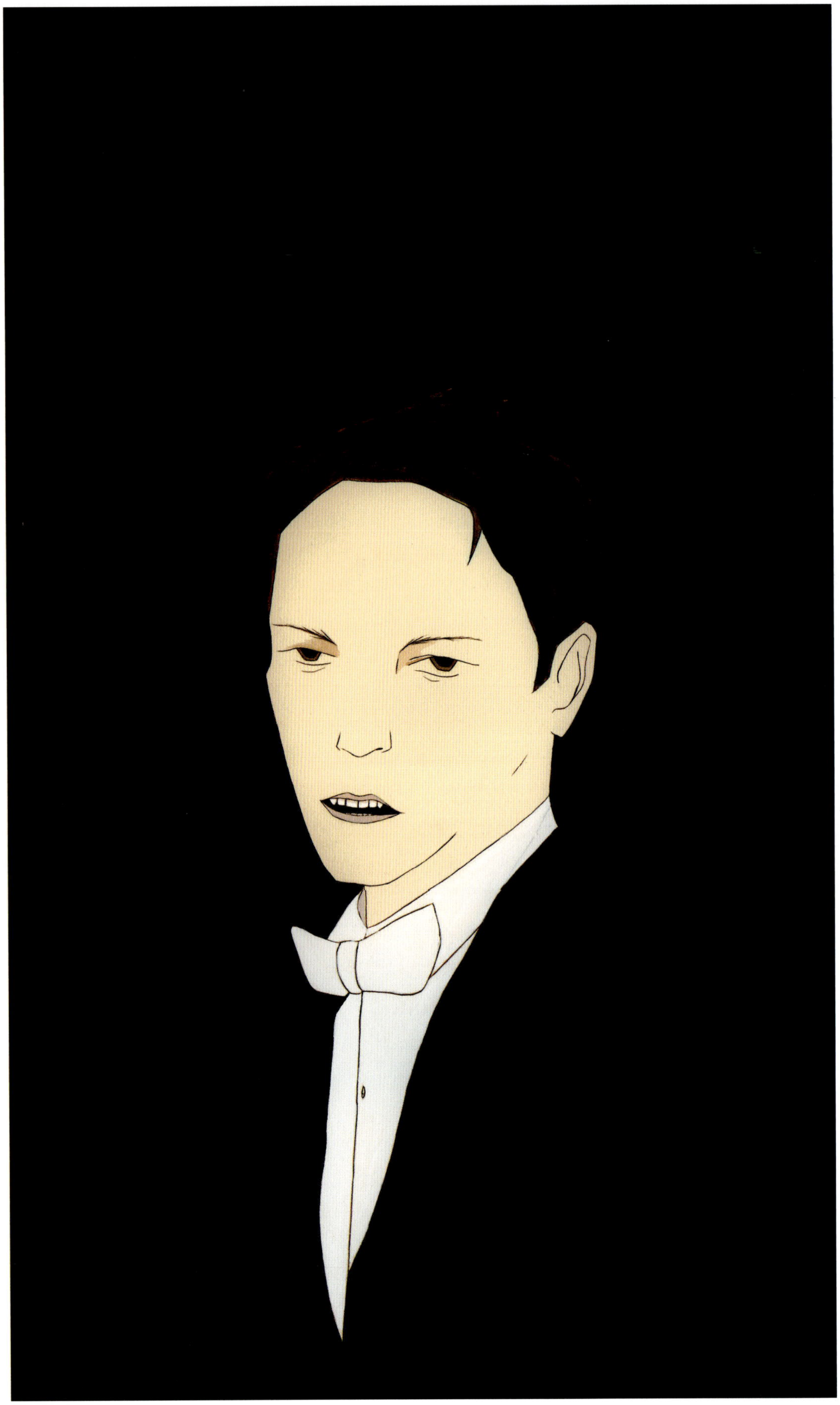

THE COUNT
24 x 18″, 2005, Watercolor and Gouache on Paper

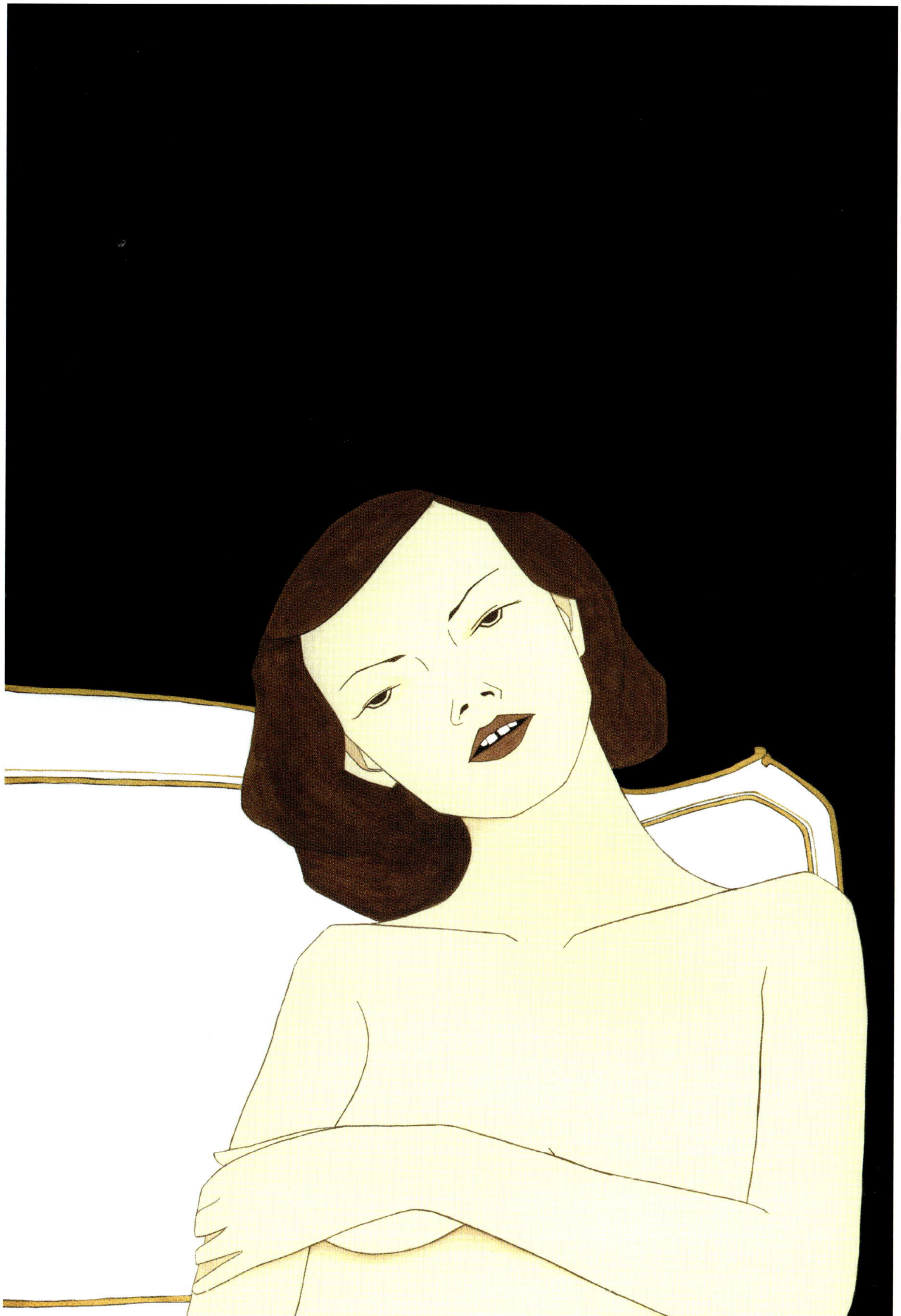

ON THE LOUNGE
24 x 18″, 2005, Watercolor and Gouache on Paper

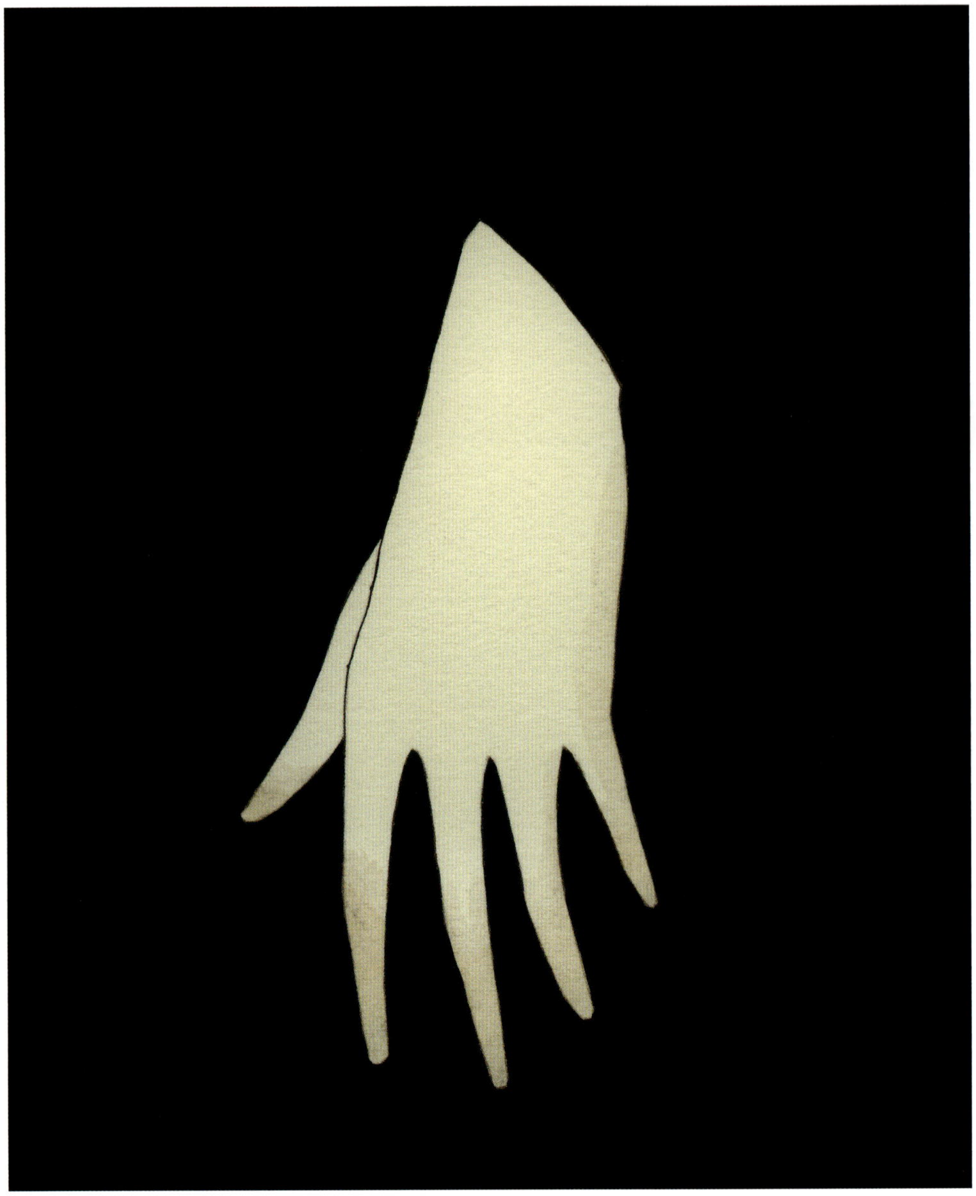

THE GLOVE
10 x 10″, 2005, Watercolor and Gouache on Paper

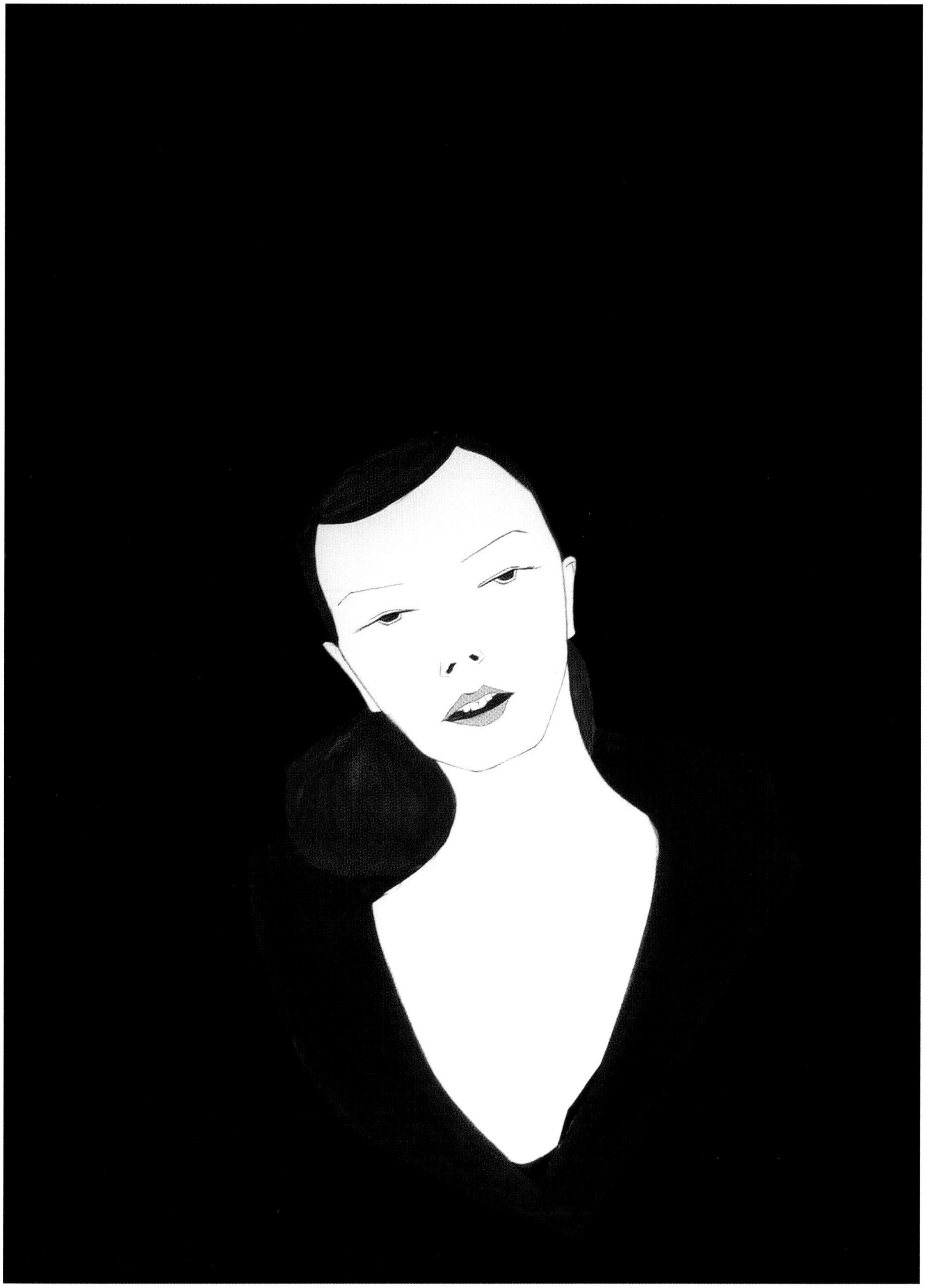

THE WIDOW
24 x 18″, 2005, Watercolor and Gouache on Paper

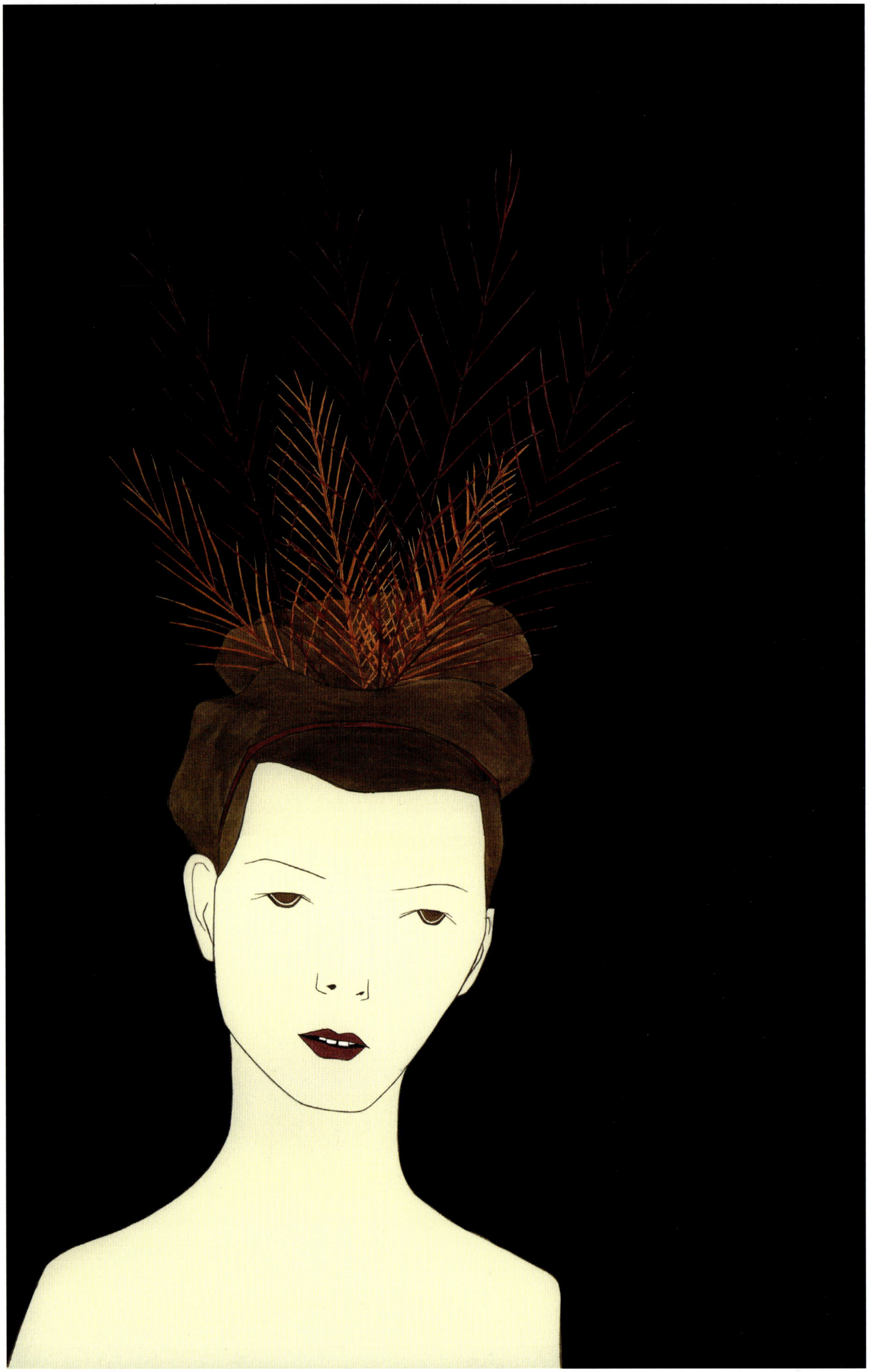

THE FEATHERED HEADDRESS
27 x 20″, 2005, Watercolor and Gouache on Paper

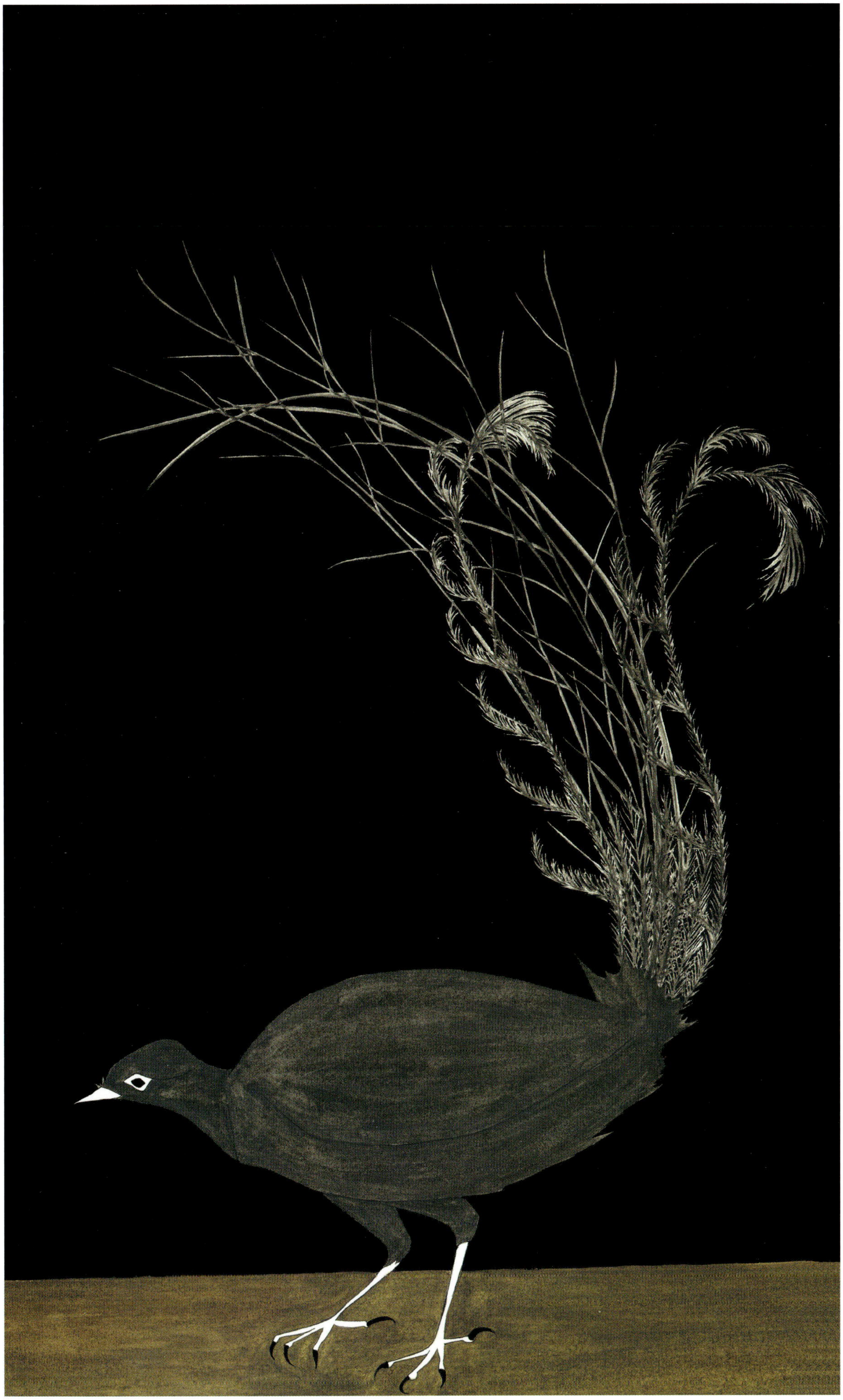

NIGHT BIRD
27 x 20″, 2005, Watercolor and Gouache on Paper

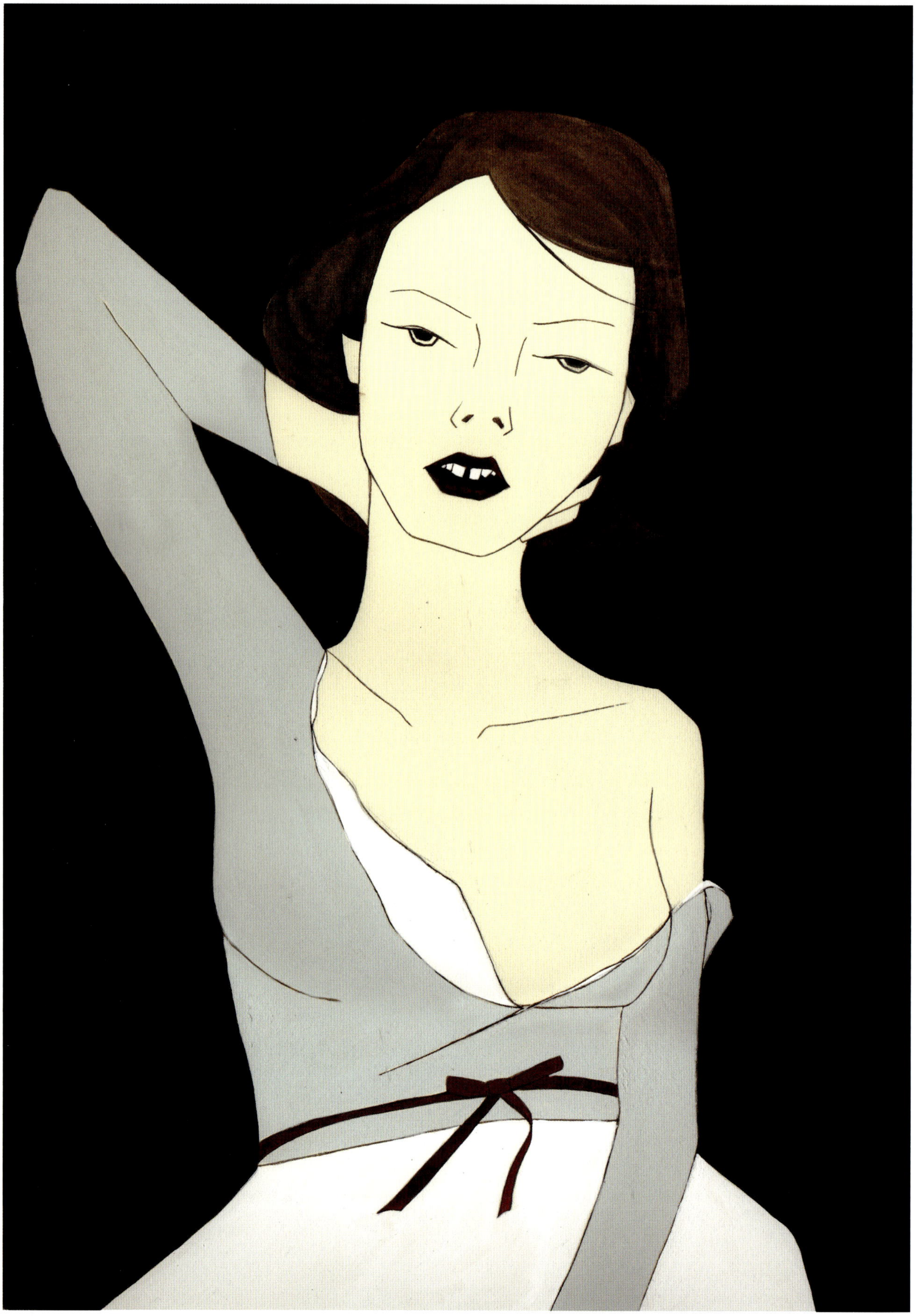

RED RIBBON
24 x 18″, 2005, Watercolor and Gouache on Paper

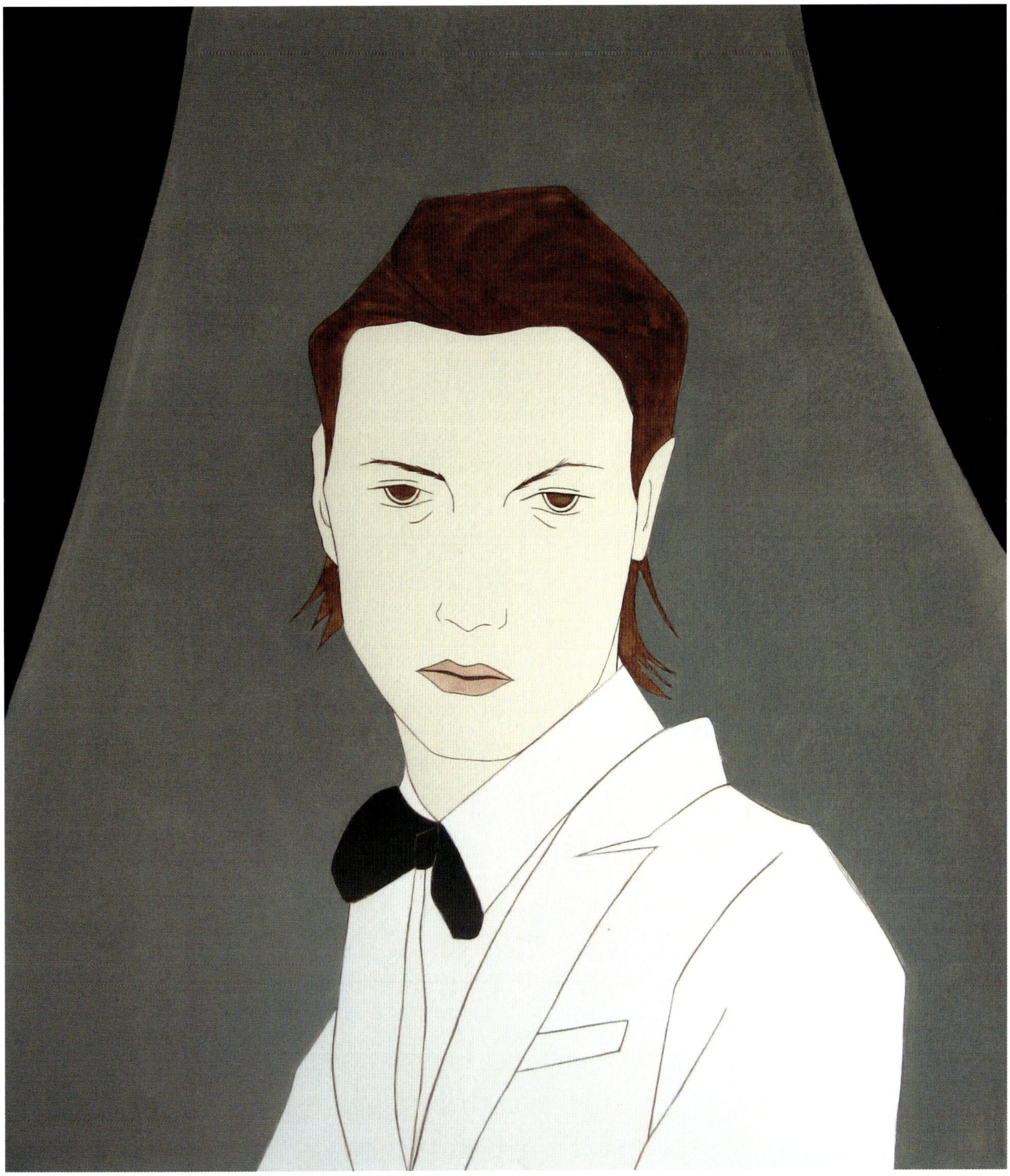

AT THE THEATER
18½ x 15″, 2006, Watercolor and Gouache on Paper

CHAPTER TWO

Dark Mirror

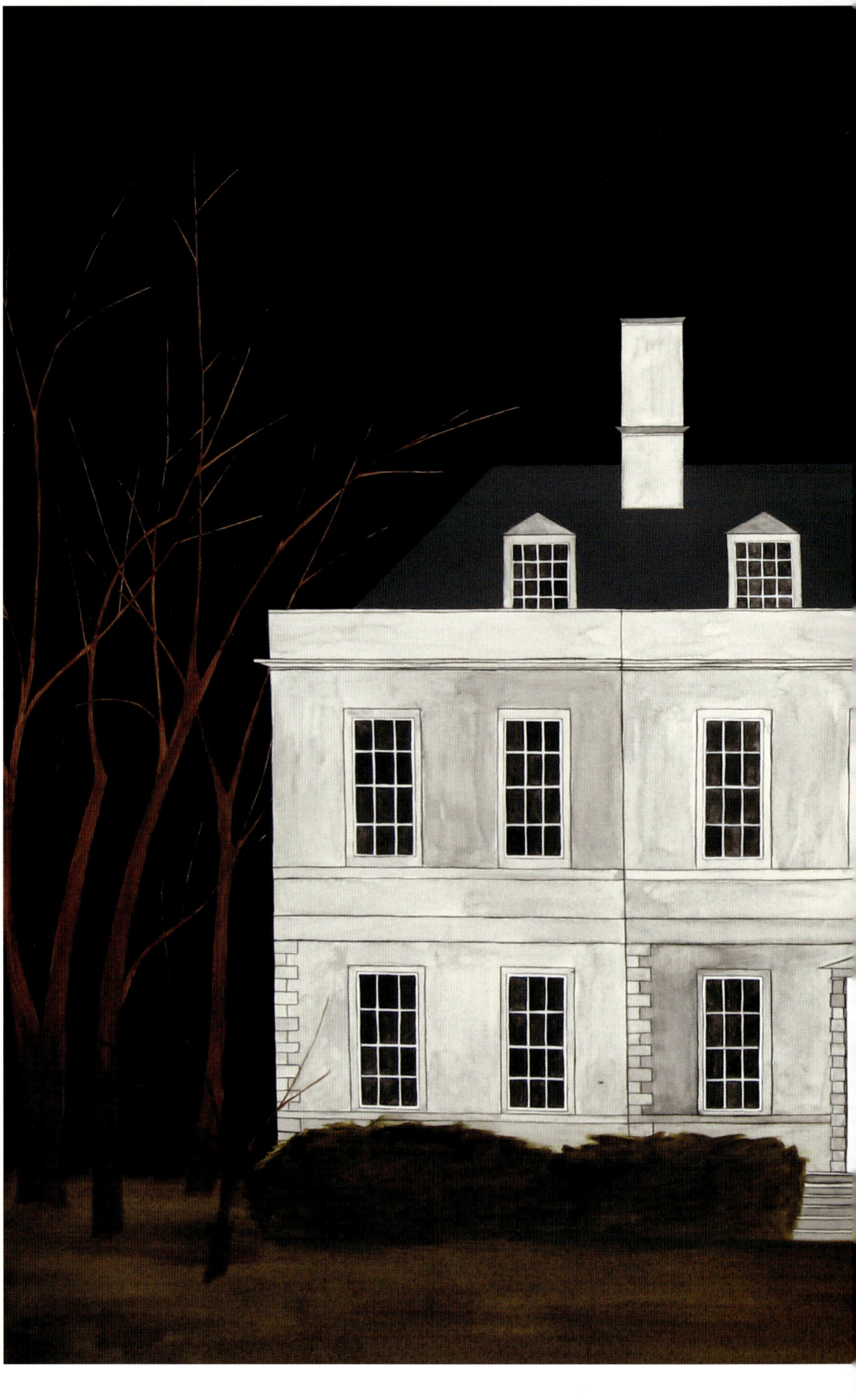

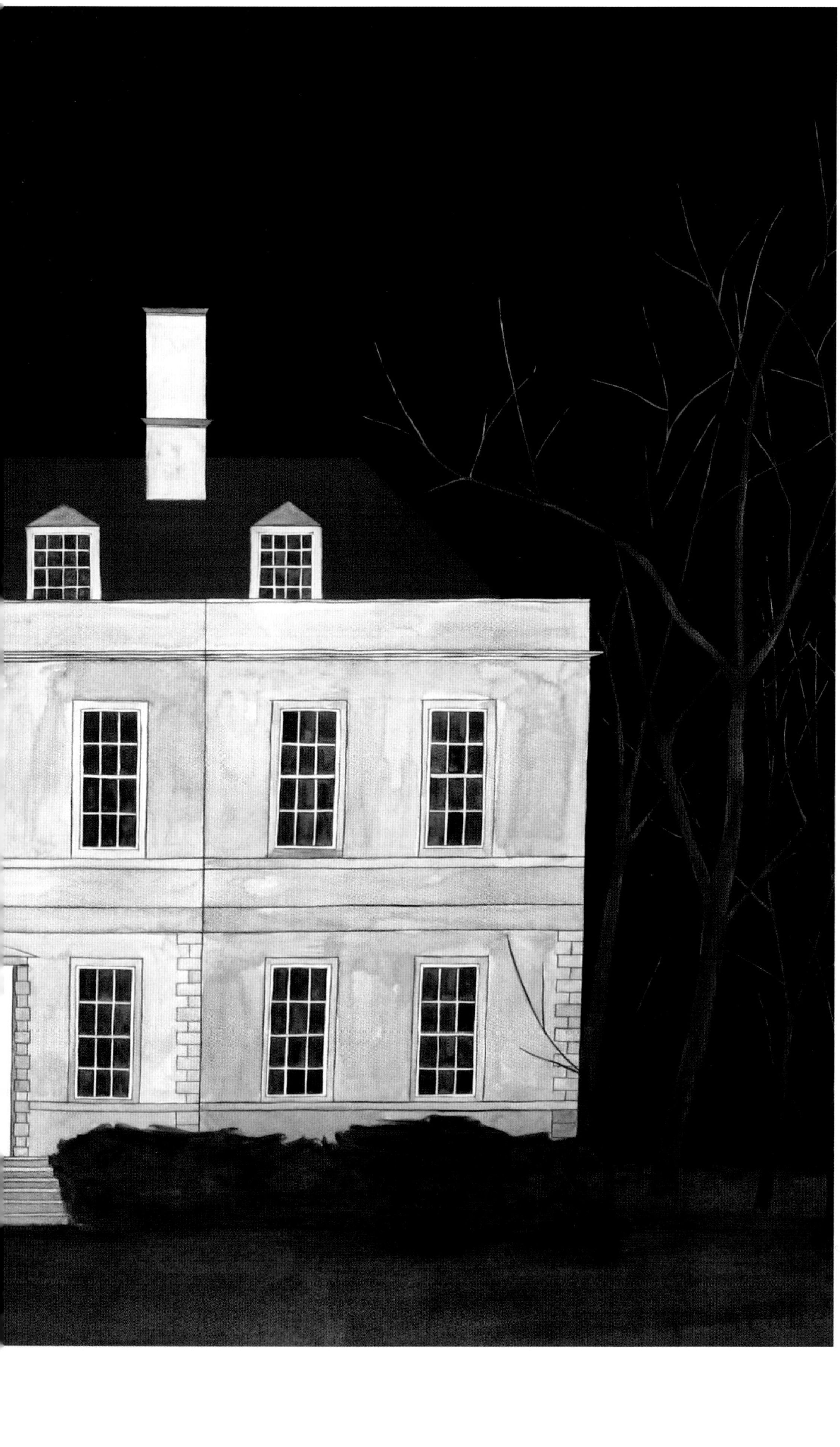

IN JUST SUCH AN OLD HOUSE
22 x 30", 2007, Watercolor and Gouache on Paper

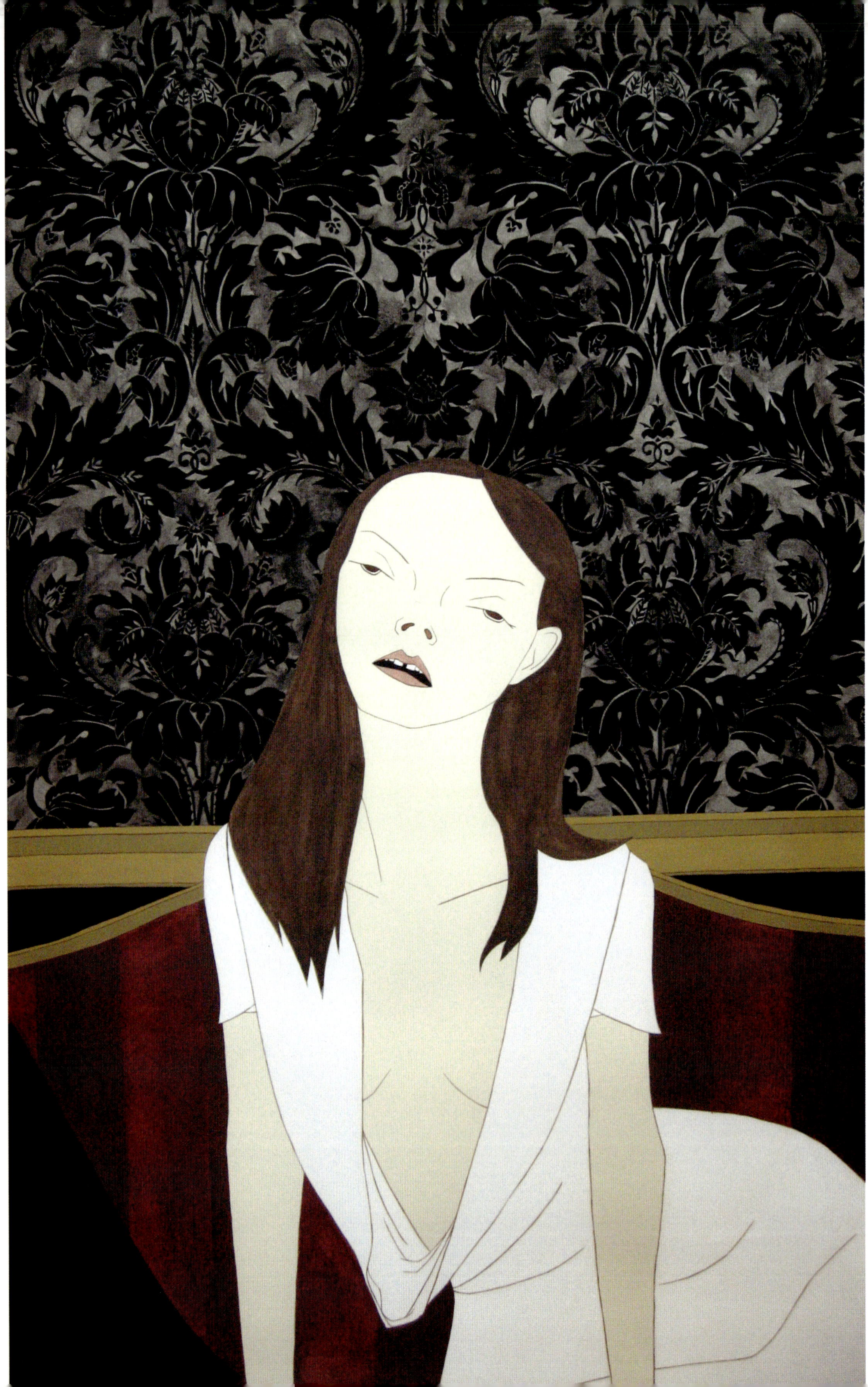

THE MISTRESS
30 x 22", 2006, Watercolor and Gouache on Paper

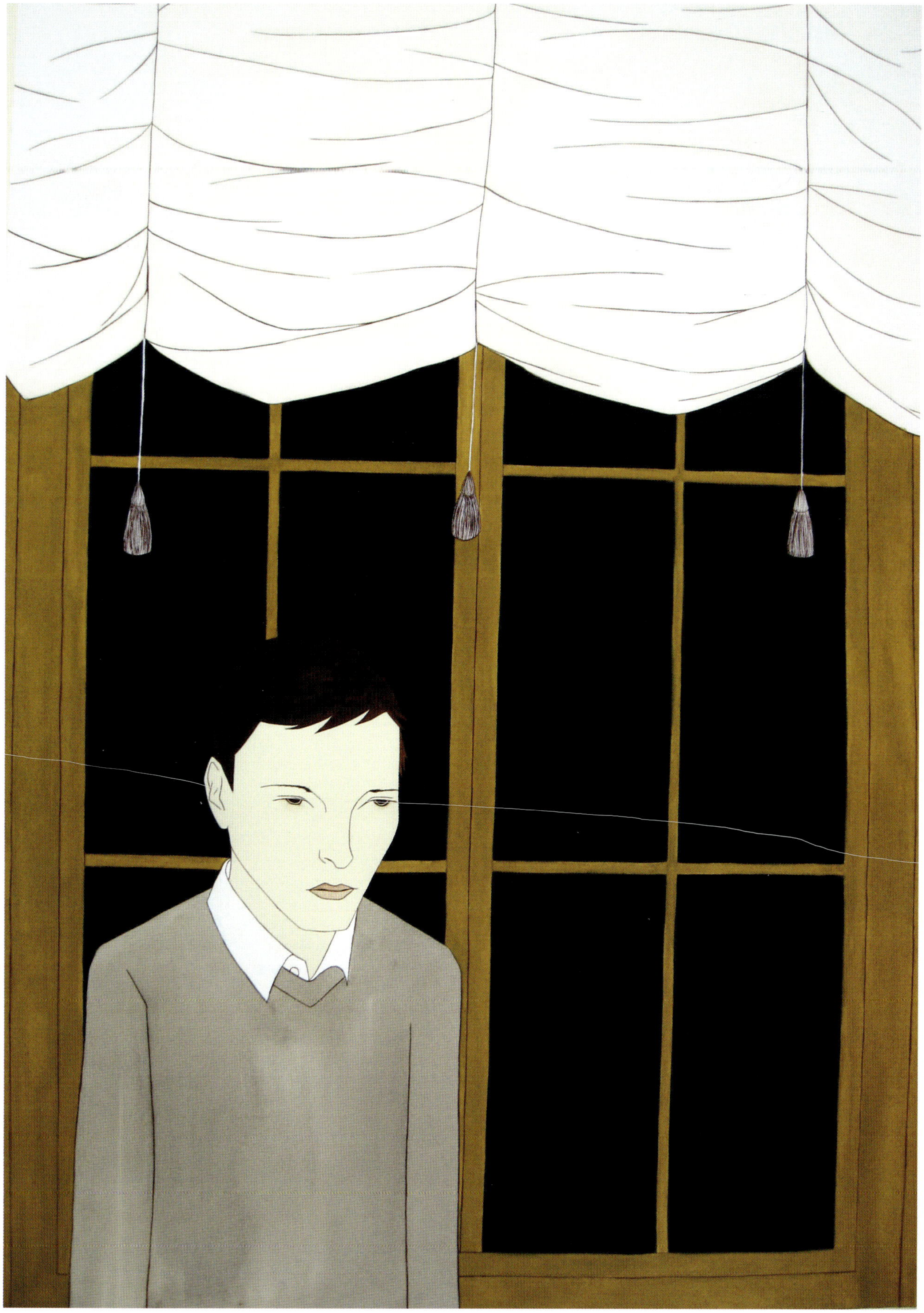

IN THE DRAWING ROOM
30 x 22″, 2006, Watercolor and Gouache on Paper

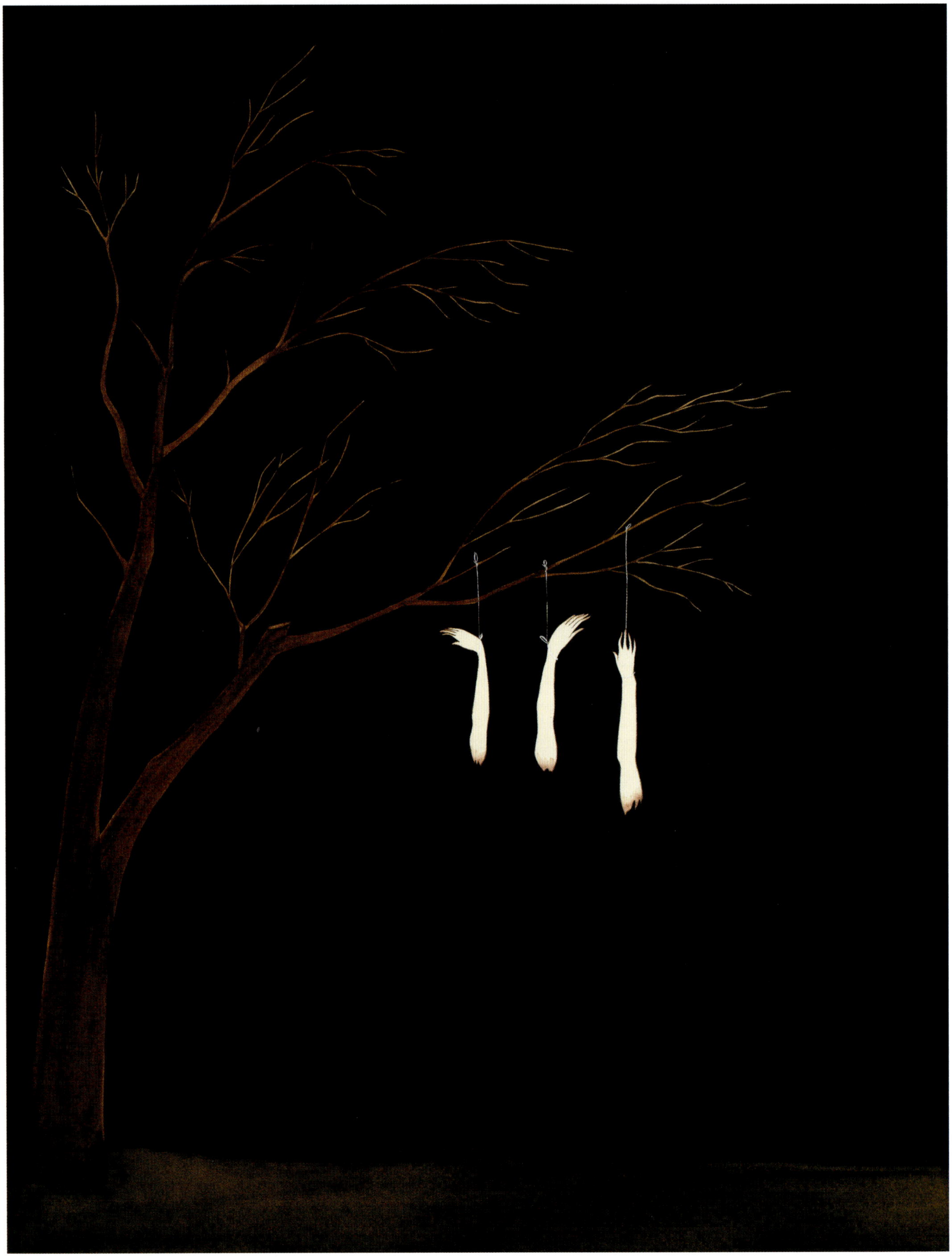

IN THE GARDEN
18 x 15″, 2007, Watercolor and Gouache on Paper

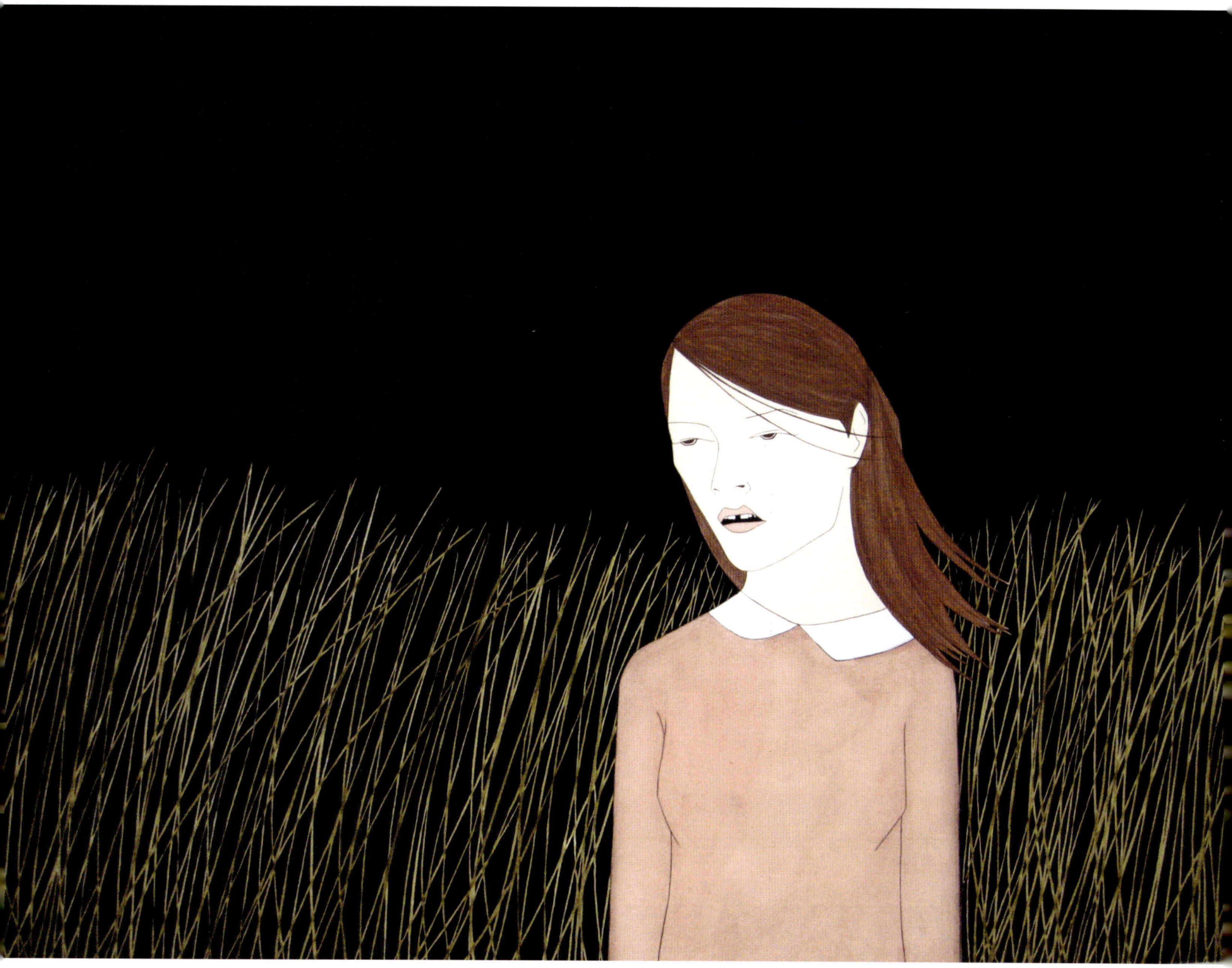

IN THE GRASS
30 x 22″, 2006, Watercolor and Gouache on Paper

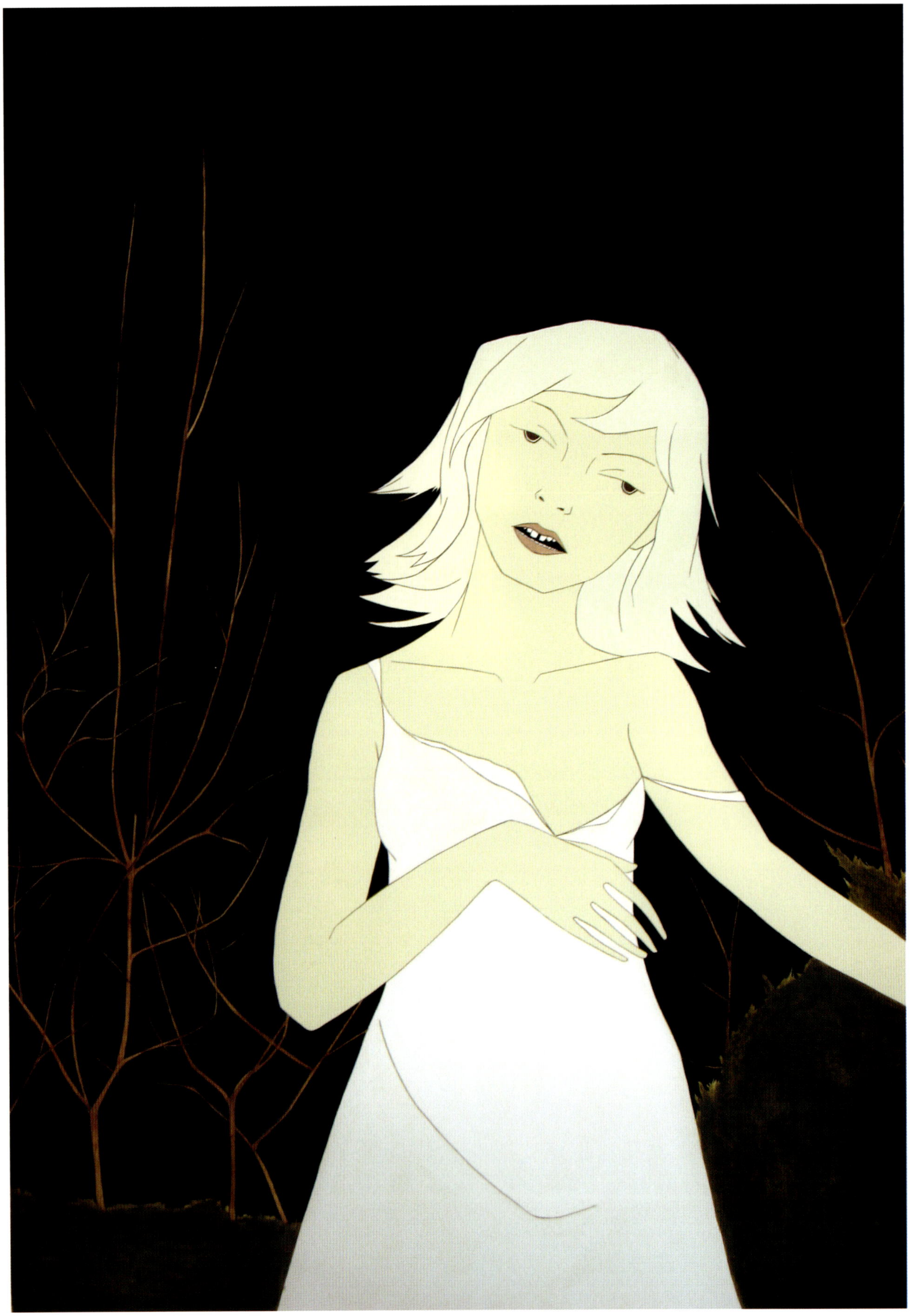

LOST IN THE CRAGS
30 x 22″, 2006, Watercolor and Gouache on Paper

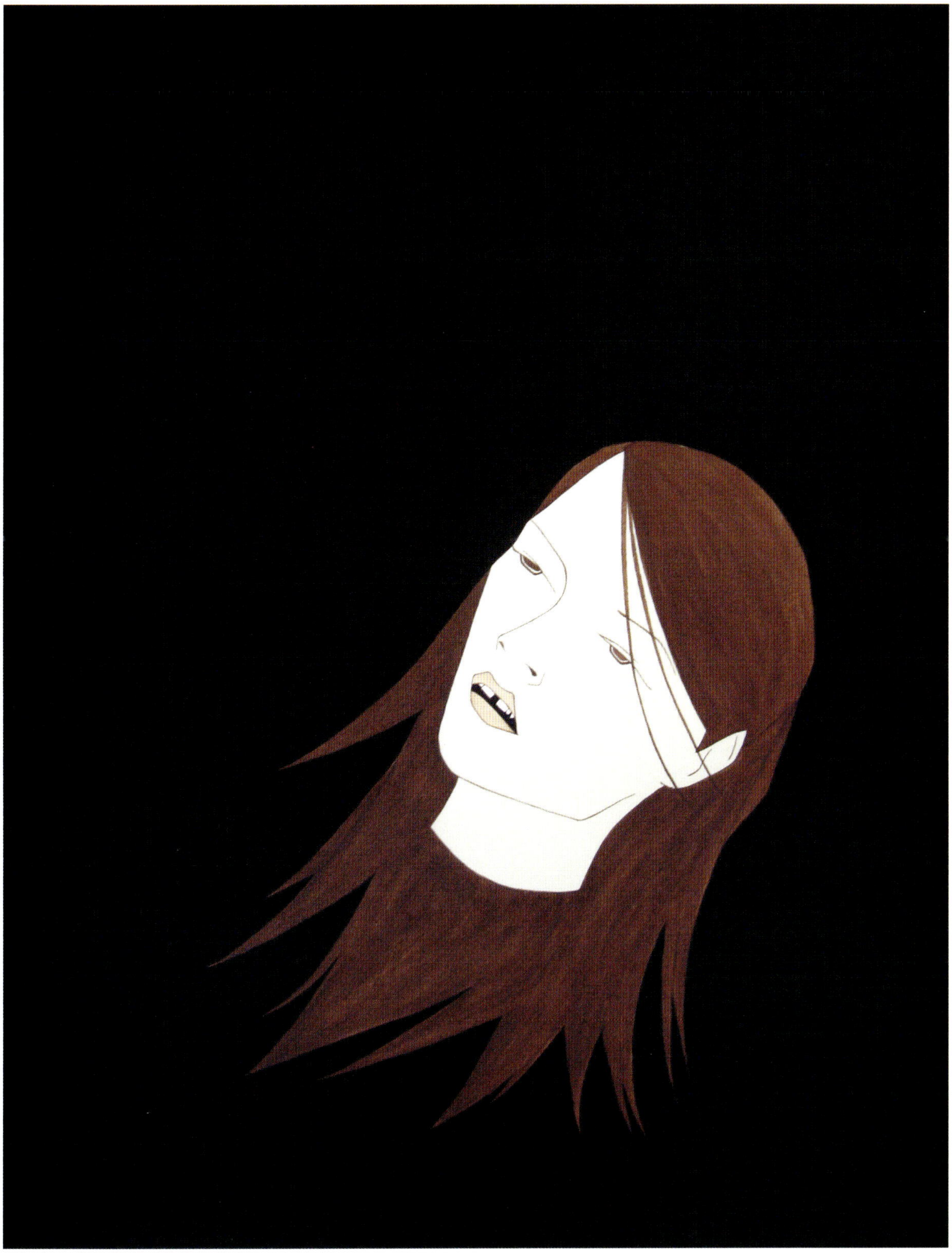

THE GIRL'S HEAD
18 x 15″, 2006, Watercolor and Gouache on Paper

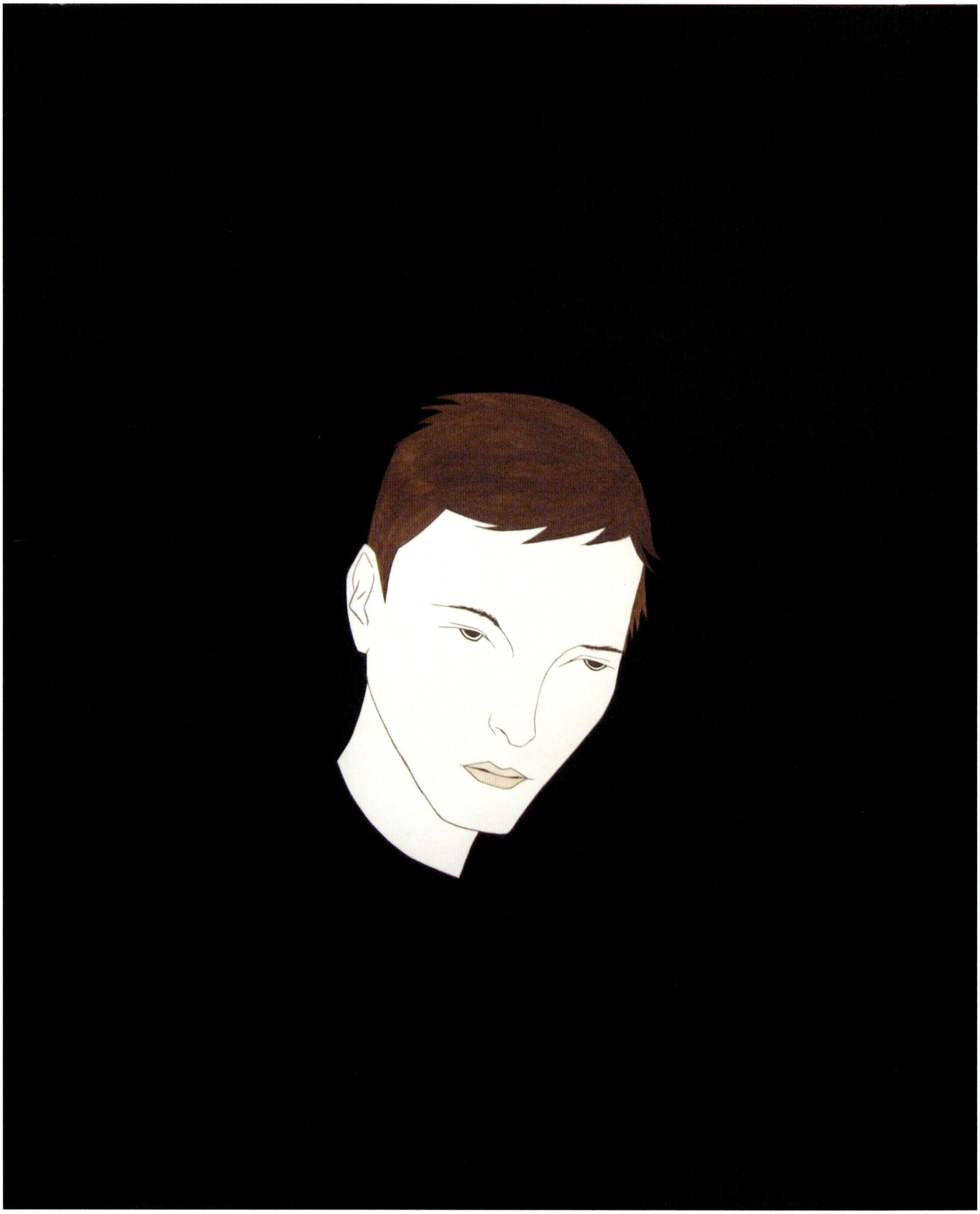

THE BOY'S HEAD
18 x 15″, 2006, Watercolor and Gouache on Paper

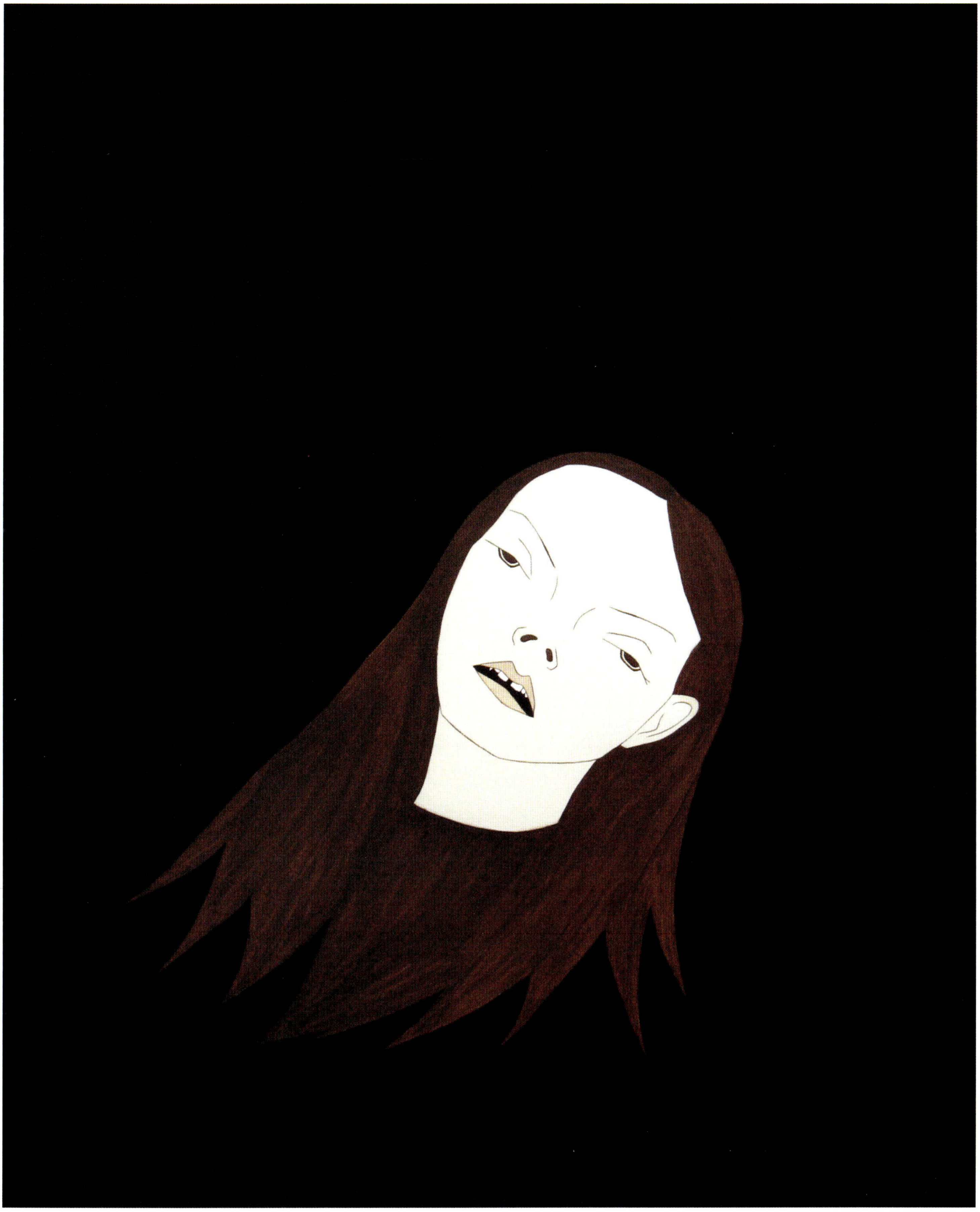

THE MISTRESS' HEAD
18 x 15″, 2006, Watercolor and Gouache on Paper

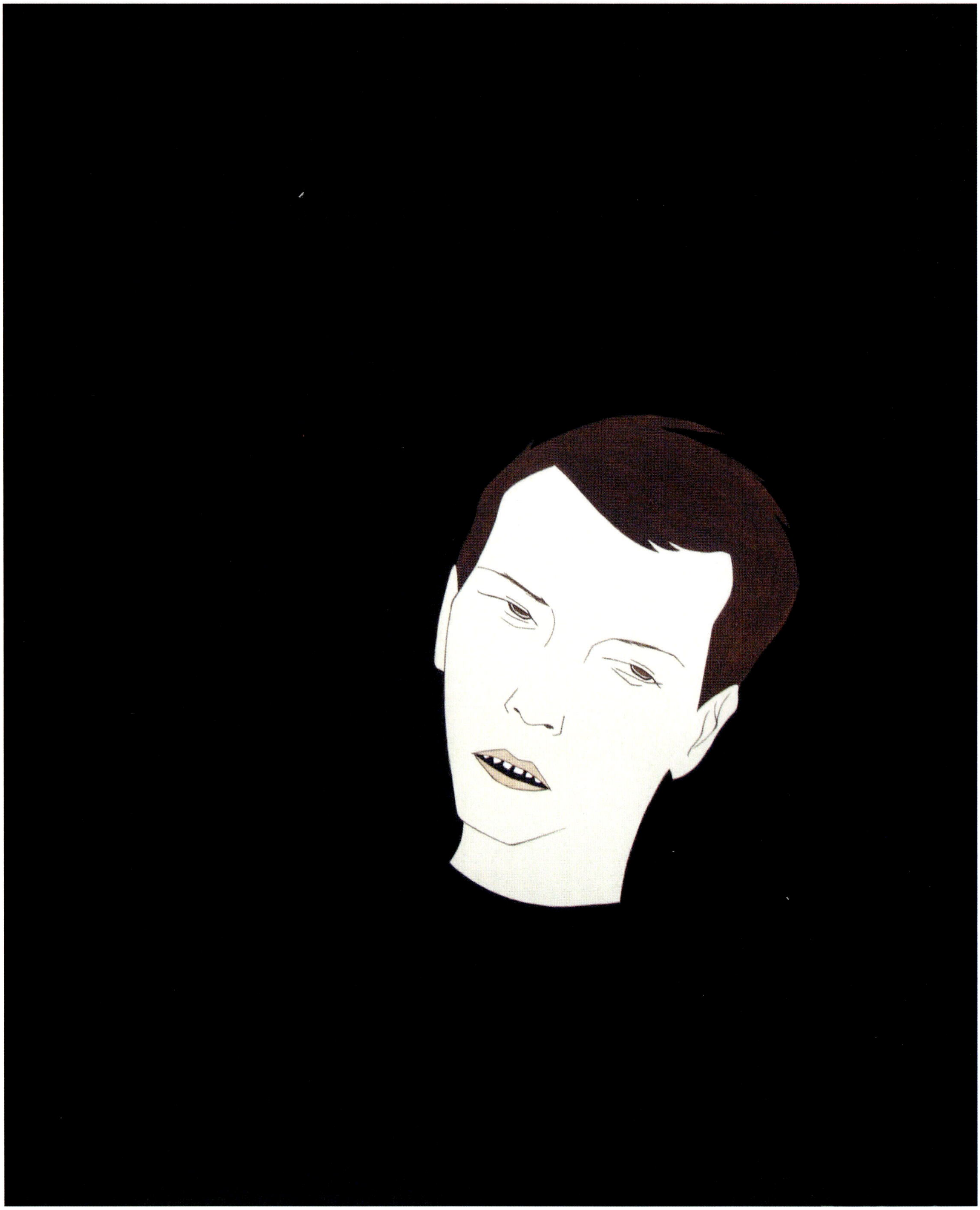

THE MAN'S HEAD
18 x 15″, 2006, Watercolor and Gouache on Paper

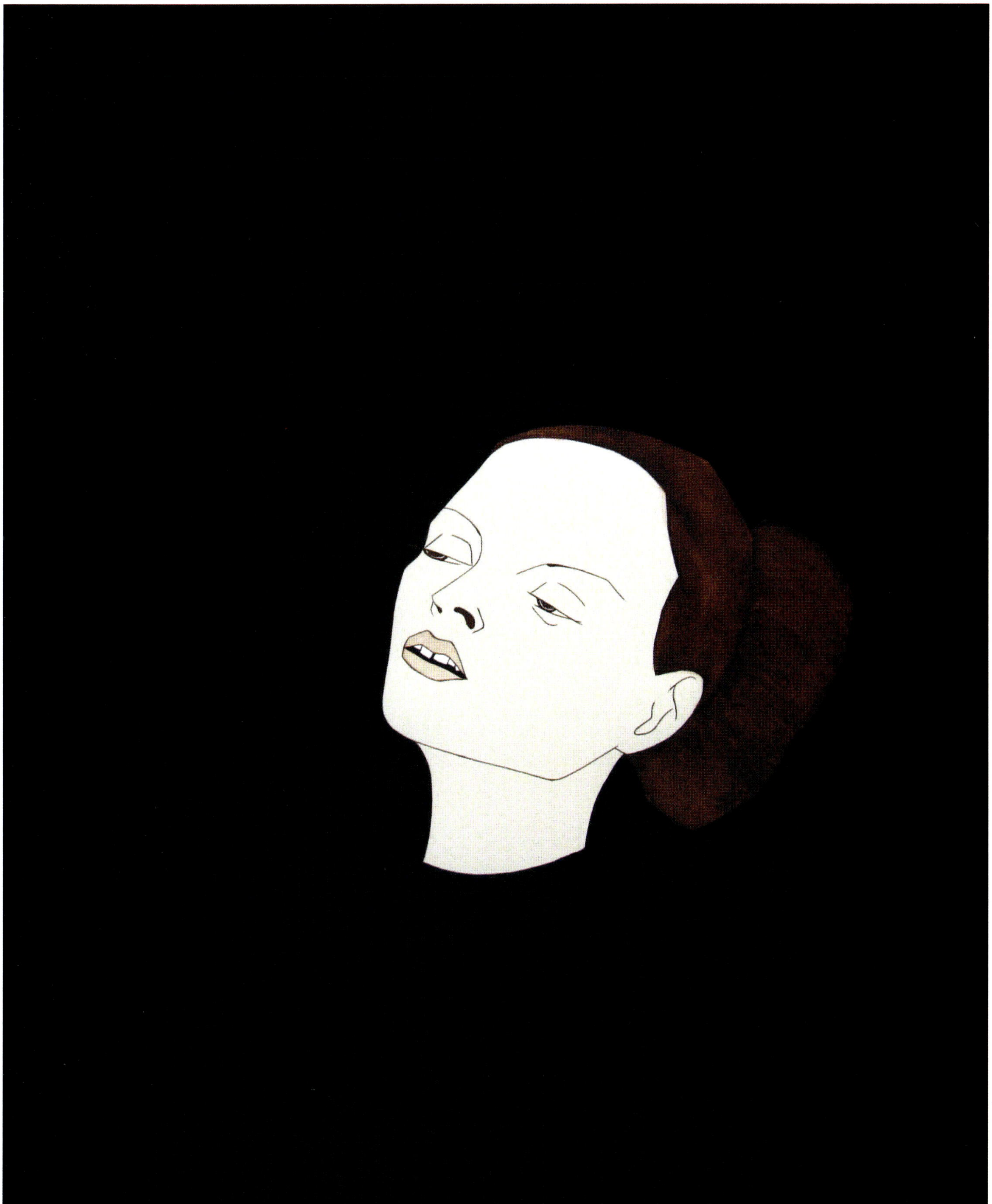

THE LADY'S HEAD
18 x 15", 2006, Watercolor and Gouache on Paper

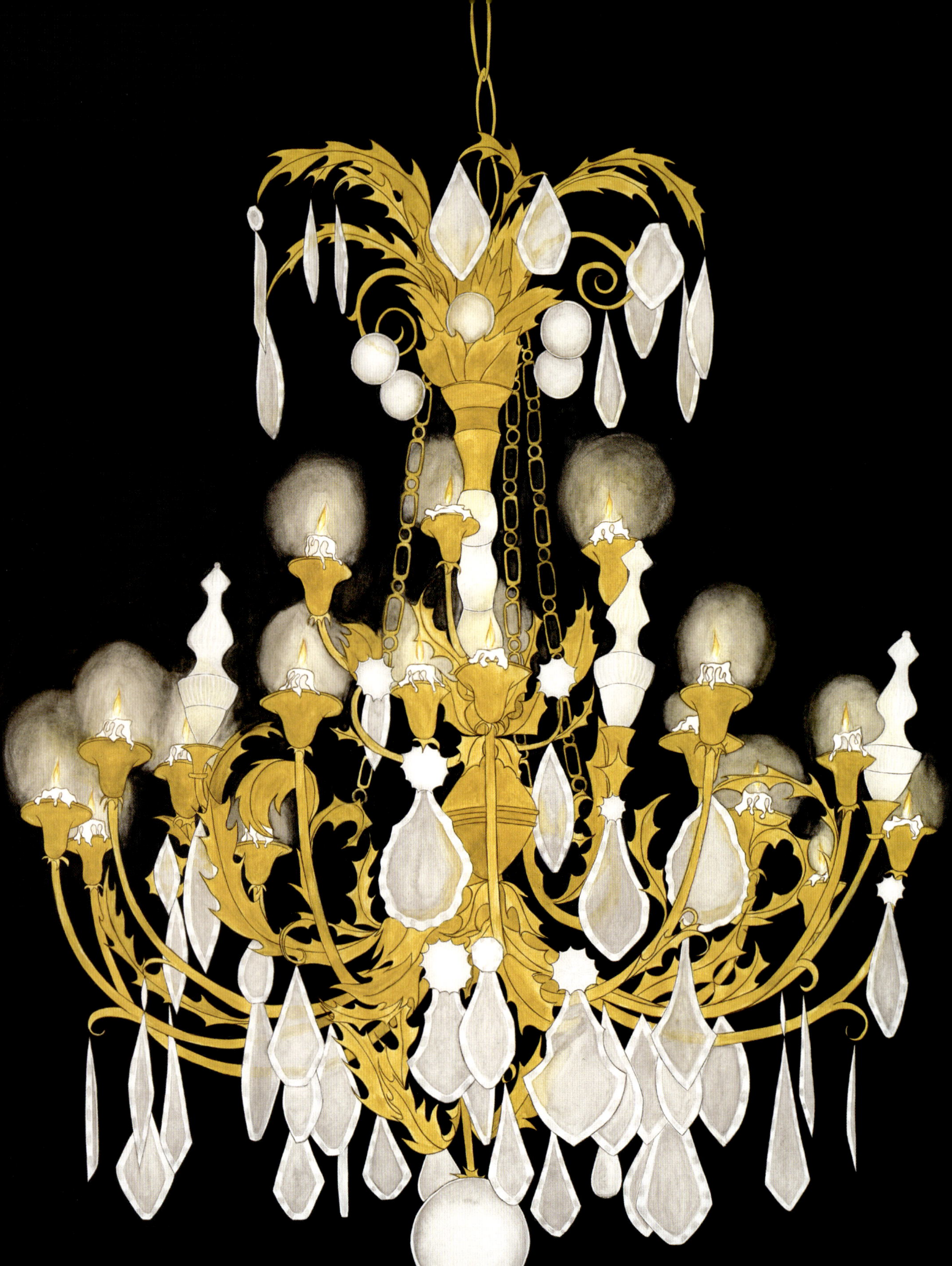

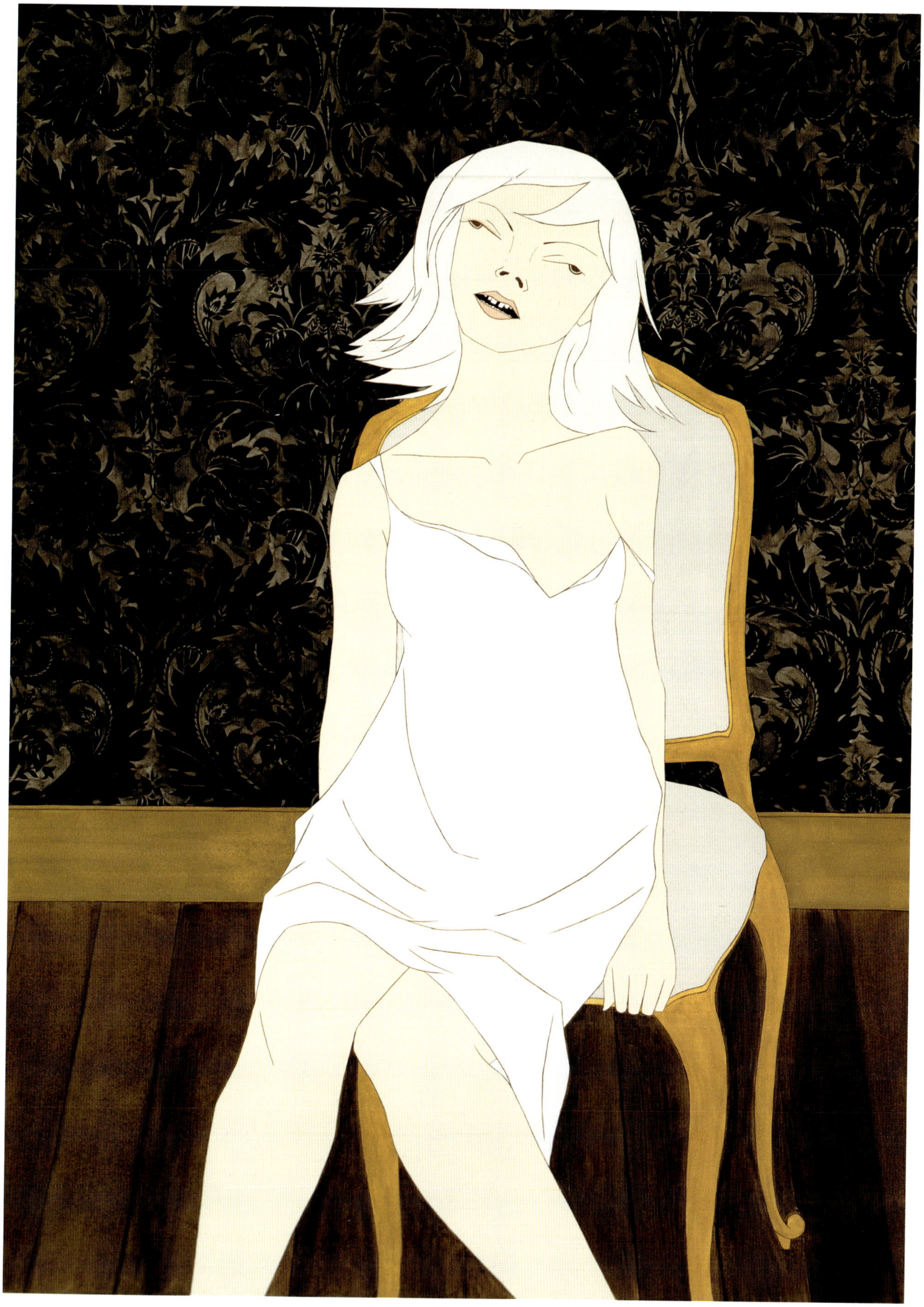

LOCKED AWAY
36 x 25", 2007, Watercolor and Gouache on Paper

OPPOSITE PAGE: **THE COMING DARKNESS**
30 x 22", 2008, Watercolor and Gouache on Paper

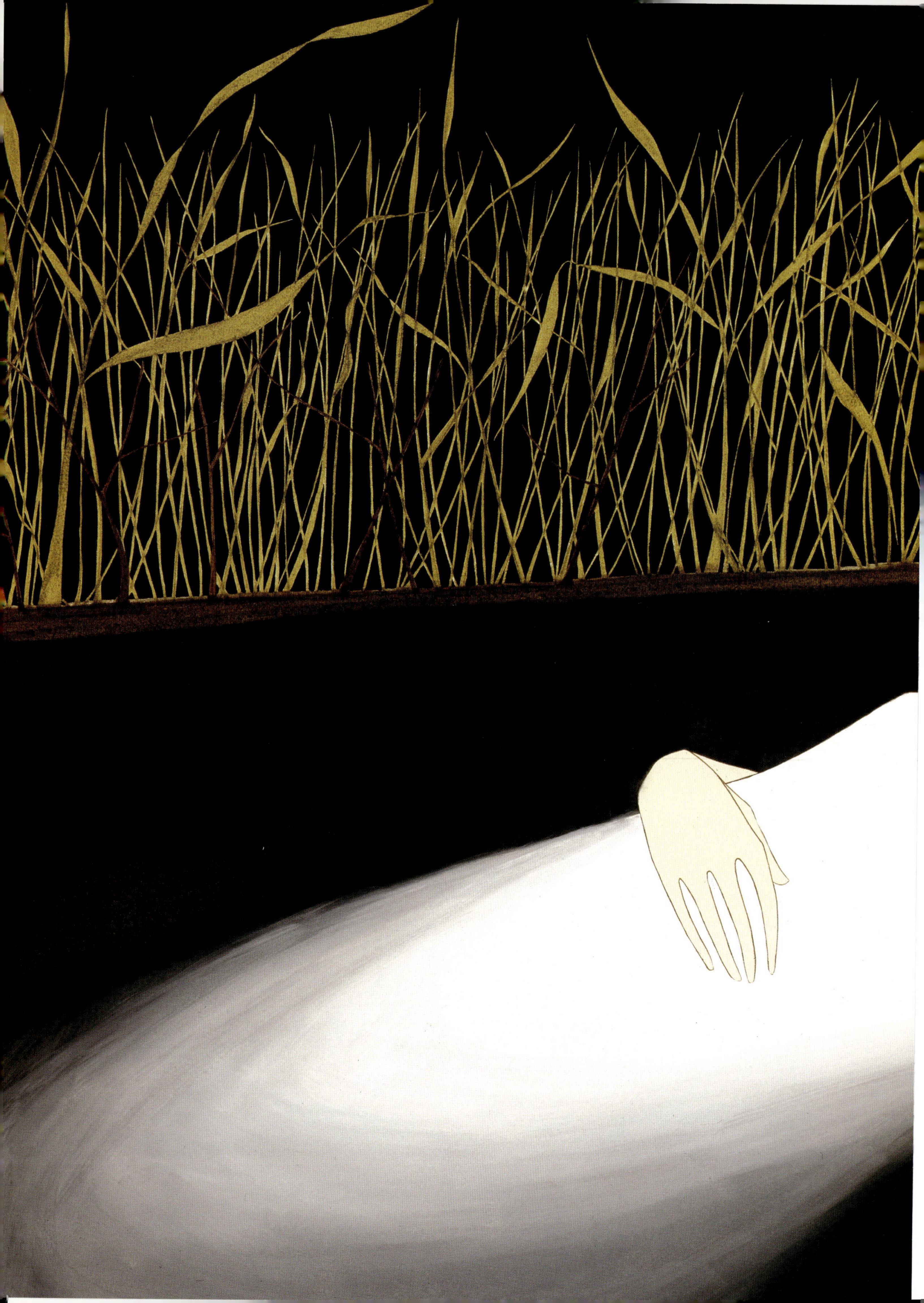

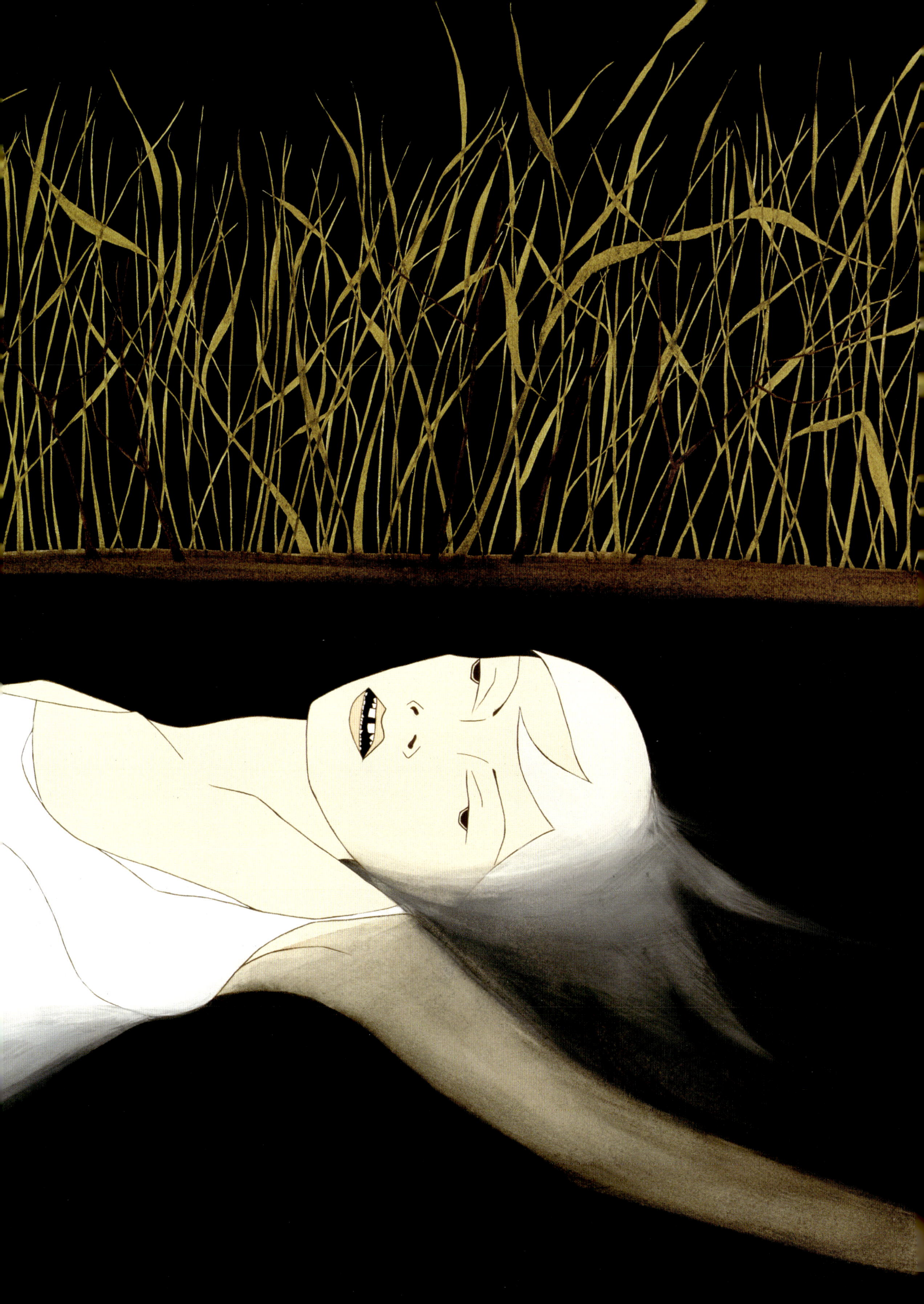

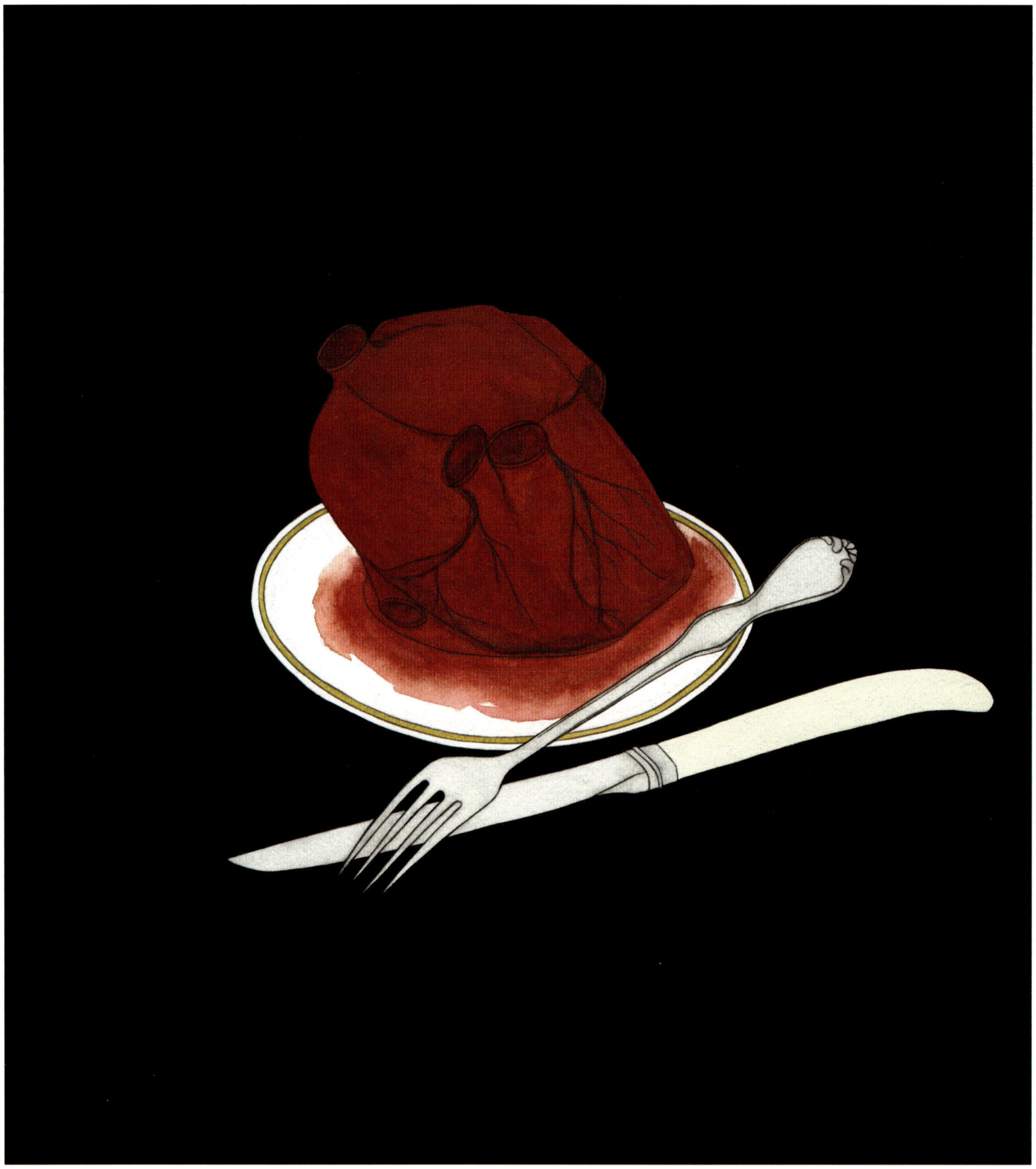

THE HEART
12 x 11″, 2010, Watercolor and Gouache on Paper

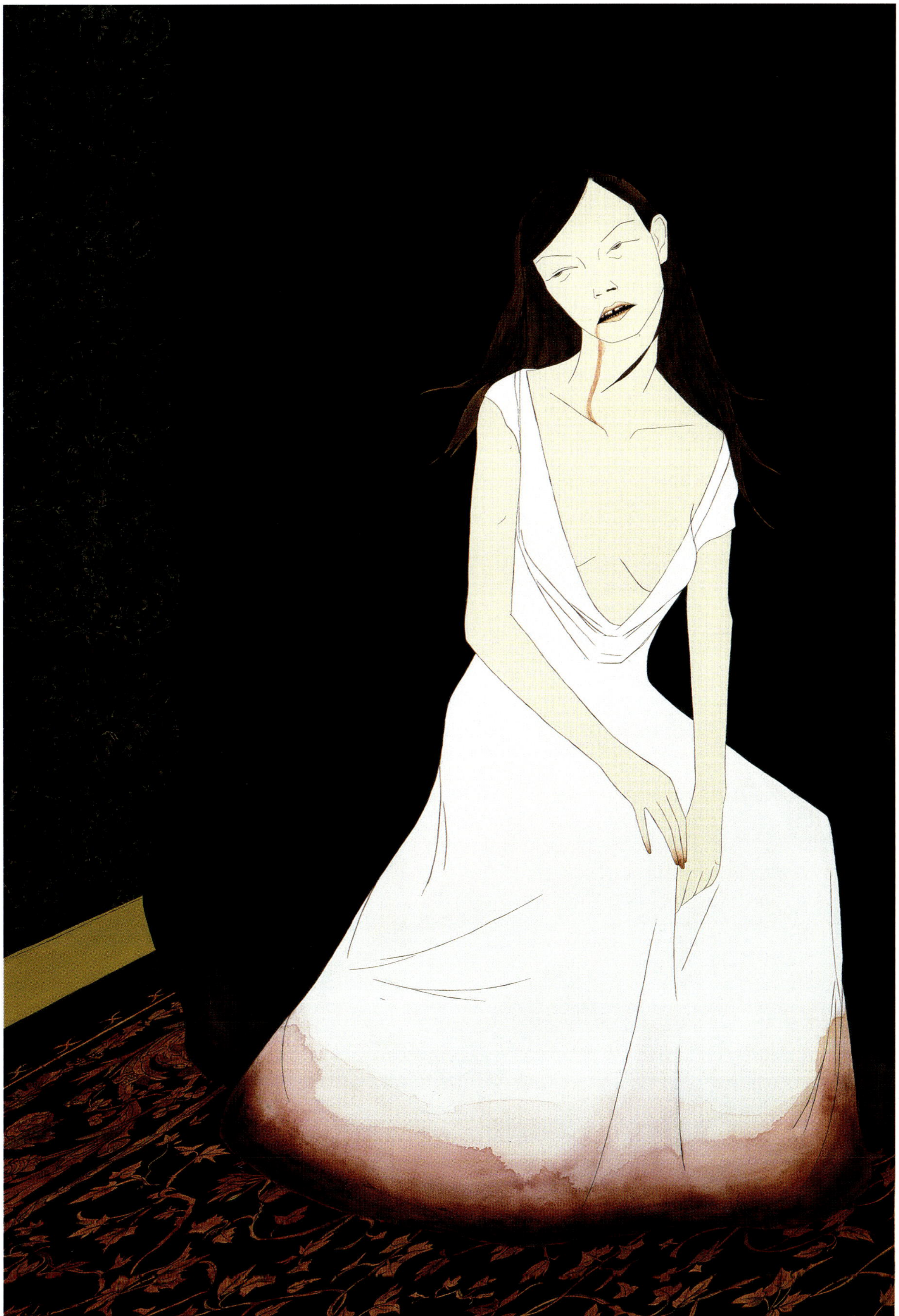

CURSED TO CHOKE ON THE SAME BLOOD
44 x 30″, 2008, Watercolor and Gouache on Paper

PREVIOUS SPREAD: **DROWNED**
24 x 32″, 2007, Watercolor and Gouache on Paper

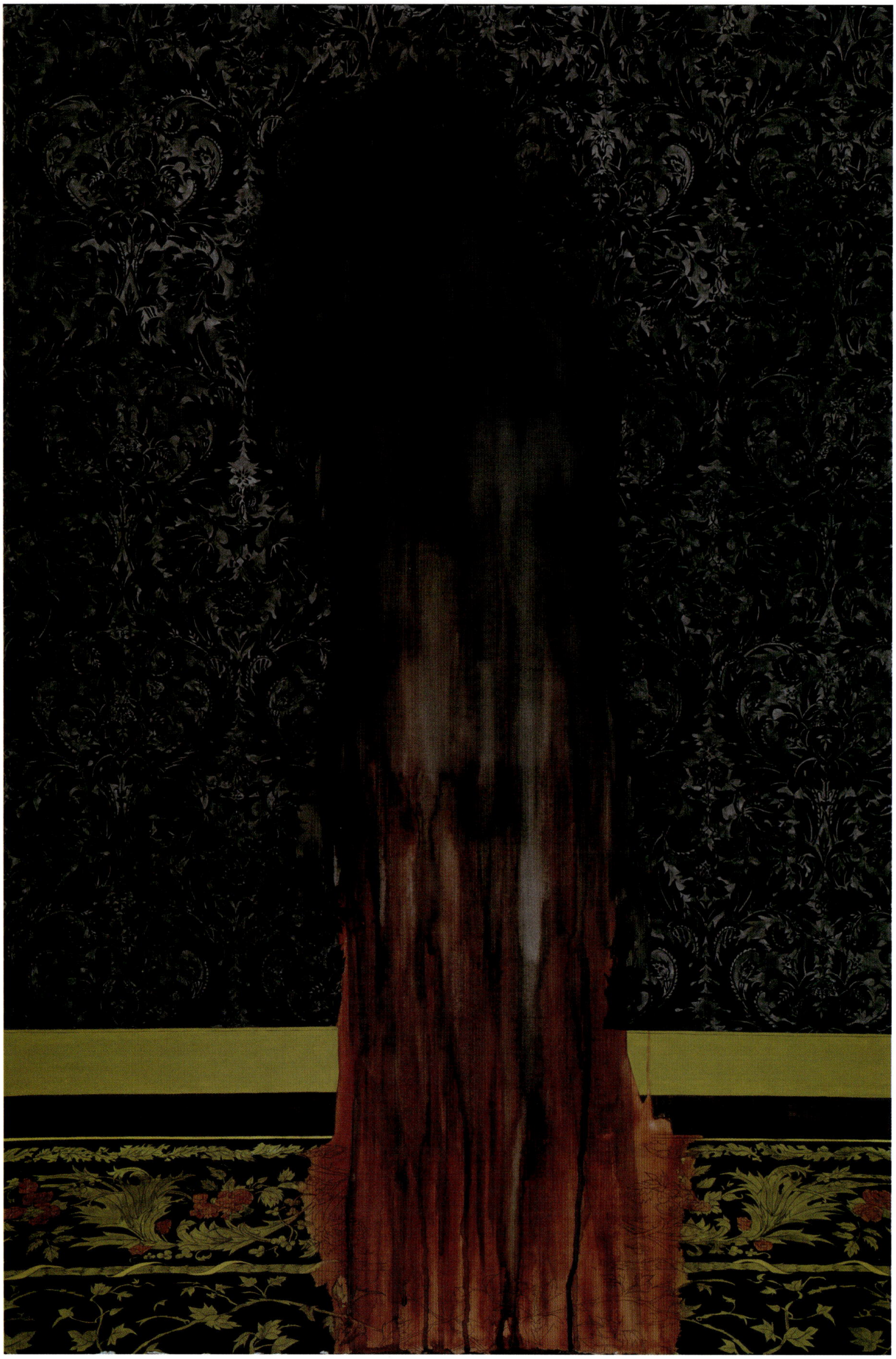

AND THE BLOOD WILL RISE TO MEET THE SHADOWS
44 x 30″, 2008, Watercolor and Gouache on Paper

OPPOSITE PAGE: **IN A DARK MIRROR**
36 x 25″, 2007, Watercolor and Gouache on Paper

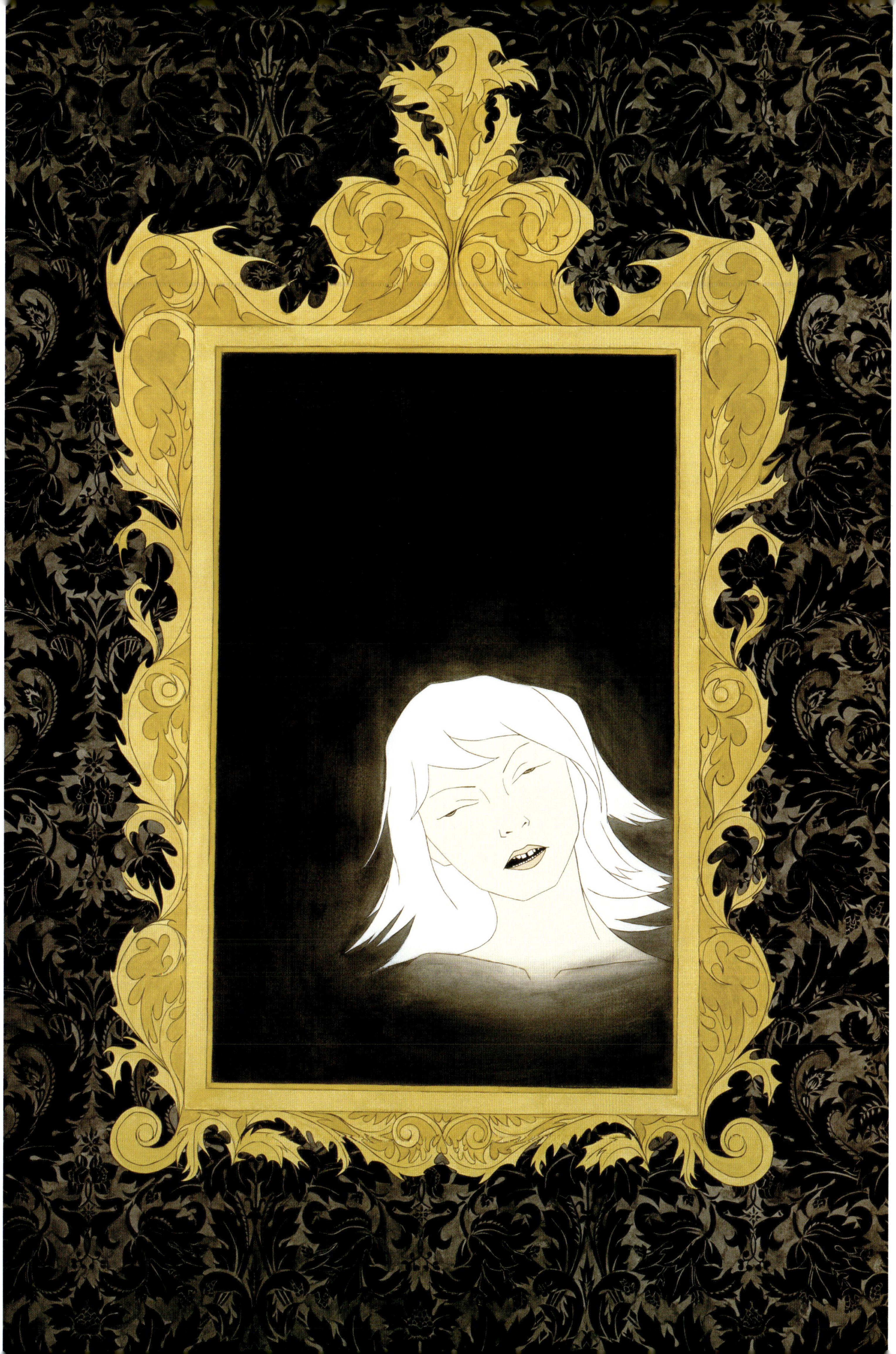

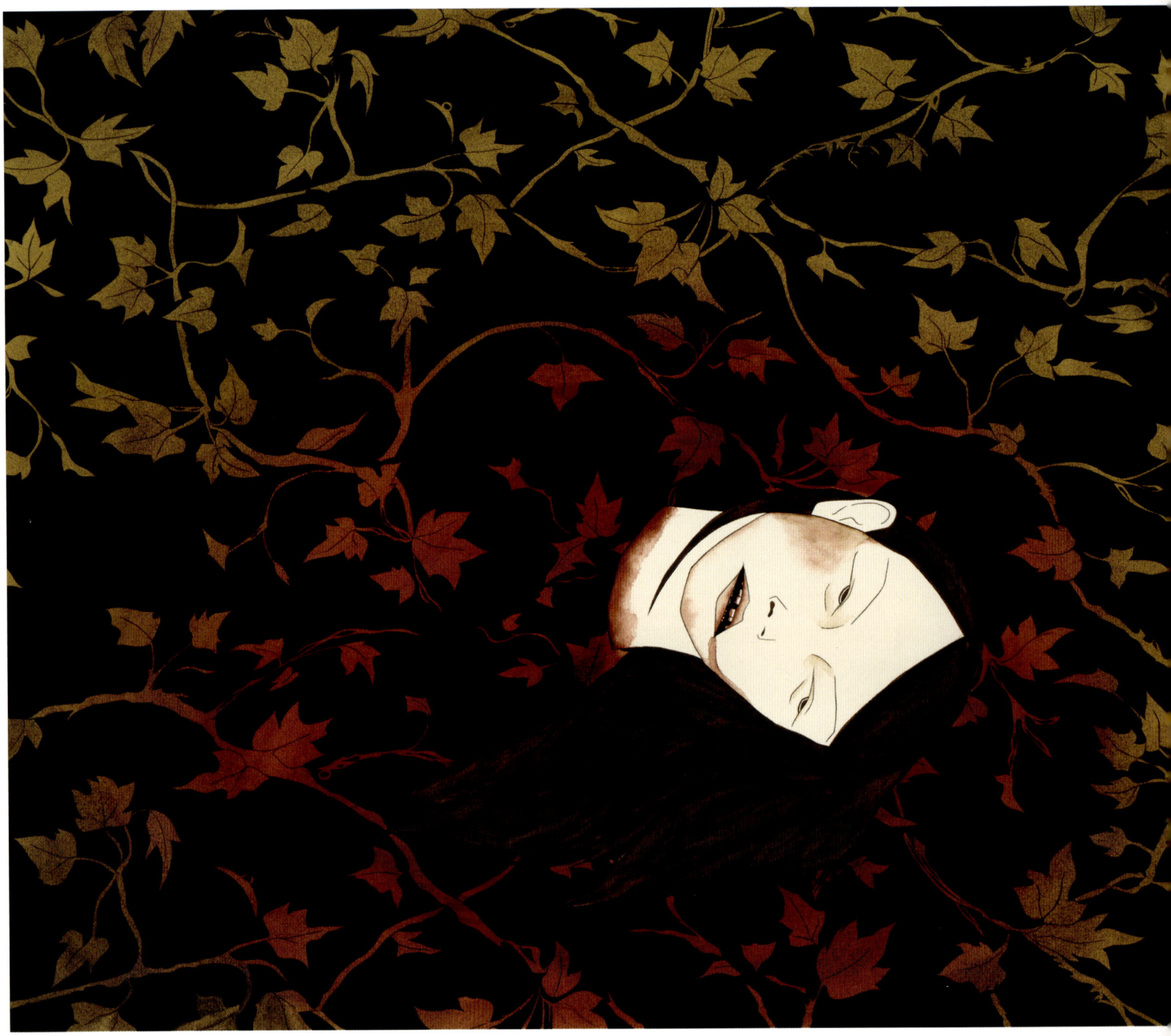

LOSING HER HEAD – ENTWINED
18 x 24″, 2008, Watercolor and Gouache on Paper

THE ARM
21 x 15″, 2007, Watercolor and Gouache on Paper

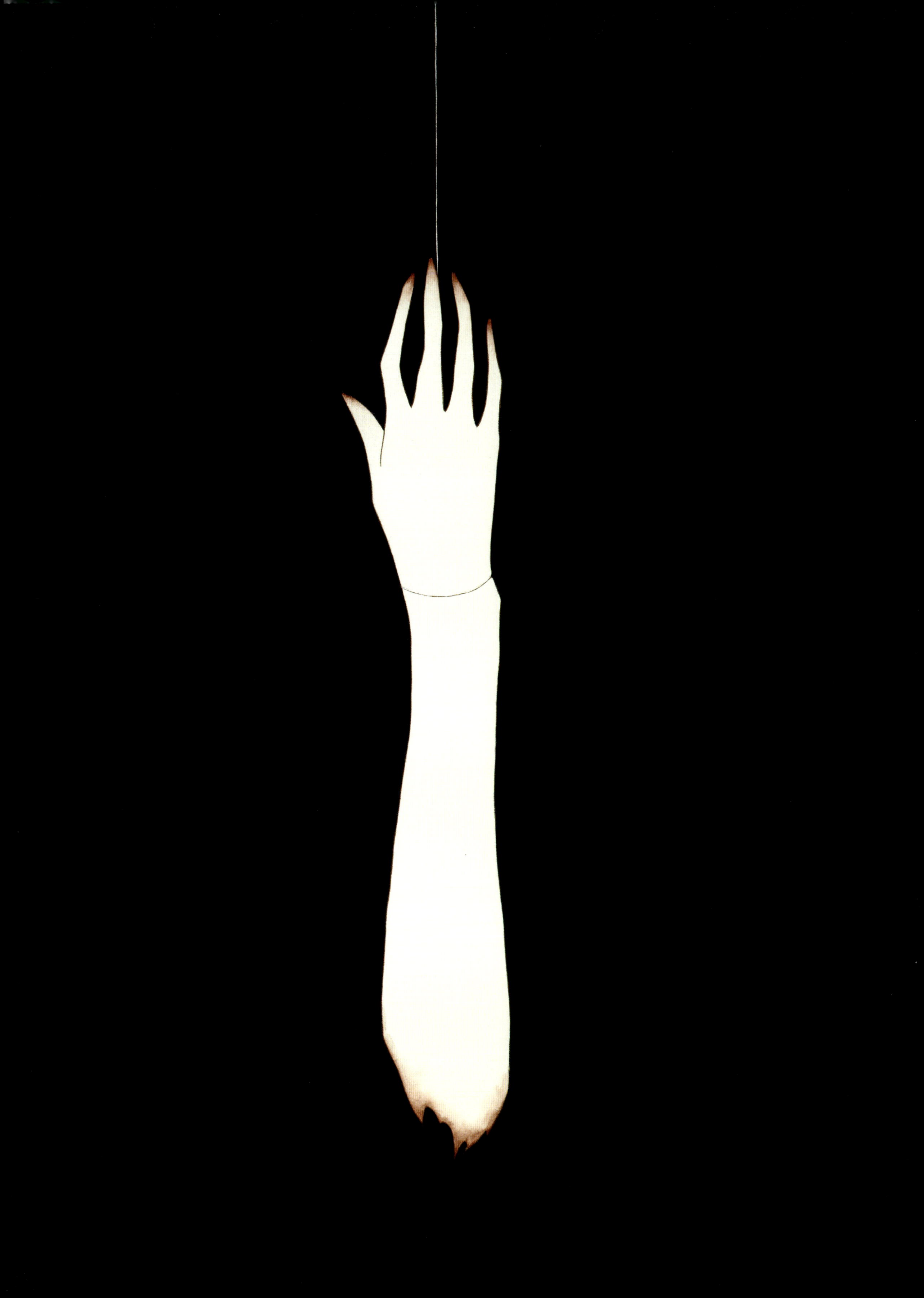

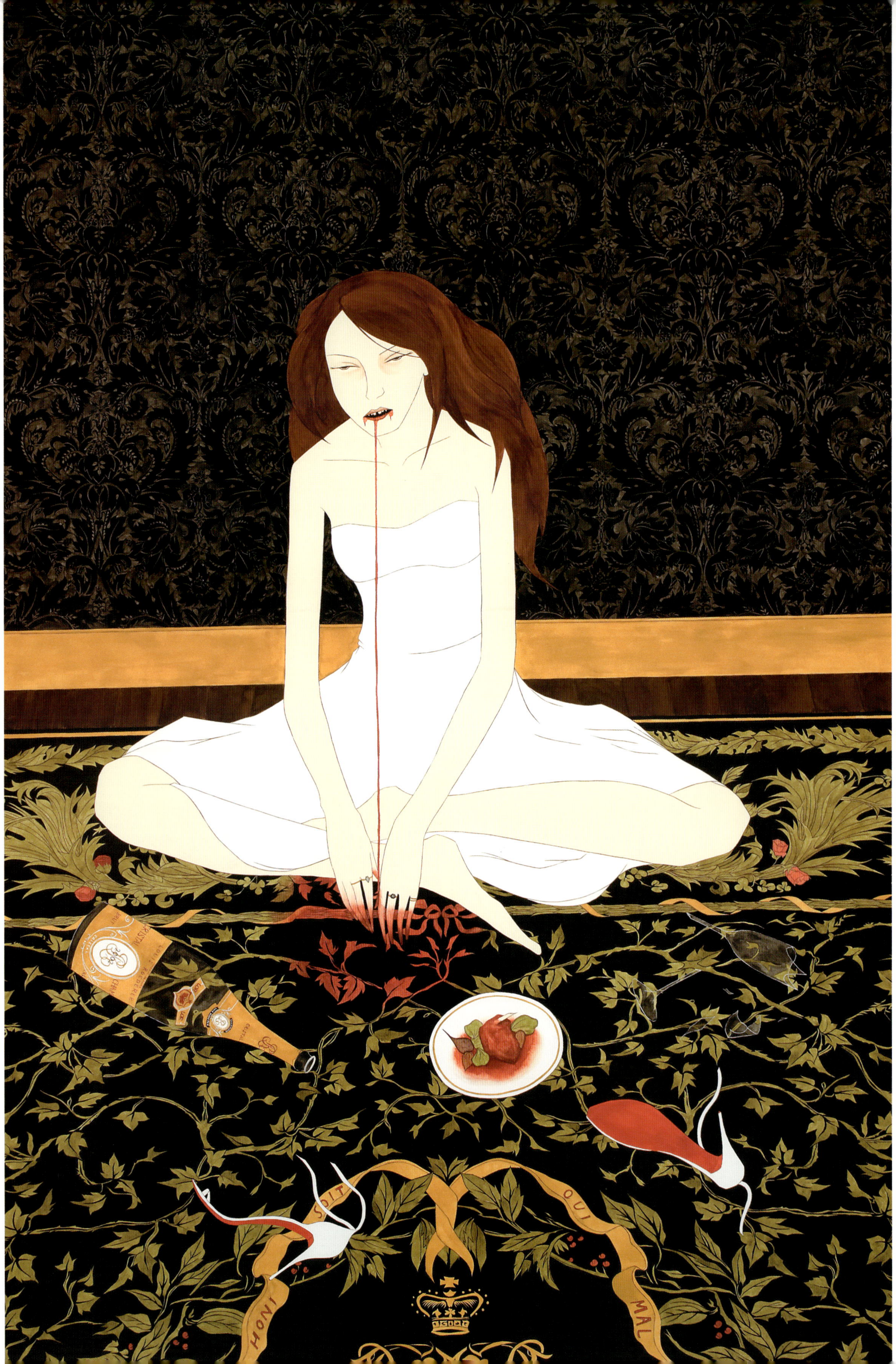
HONI
SOIT
QUI
MAL

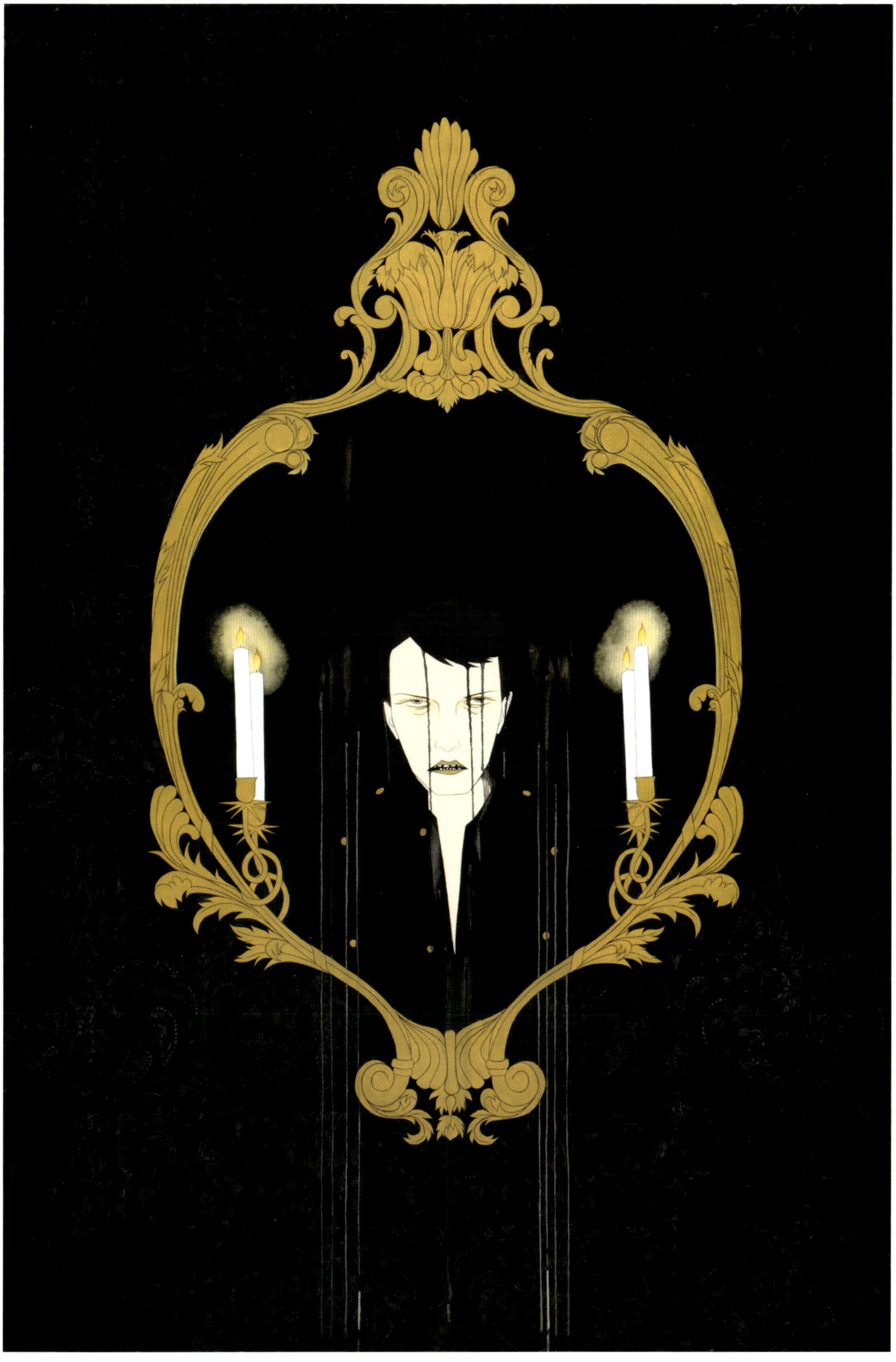

TO CONJURE THE NAMELESS
44 x 30″, 2010, Watercolor and Gouache on Paper

OPPOSITE PAGE: **AFTER THE DINNER PARTY**
54 x 36″, 2009, Watercolor and Gouache on Paper

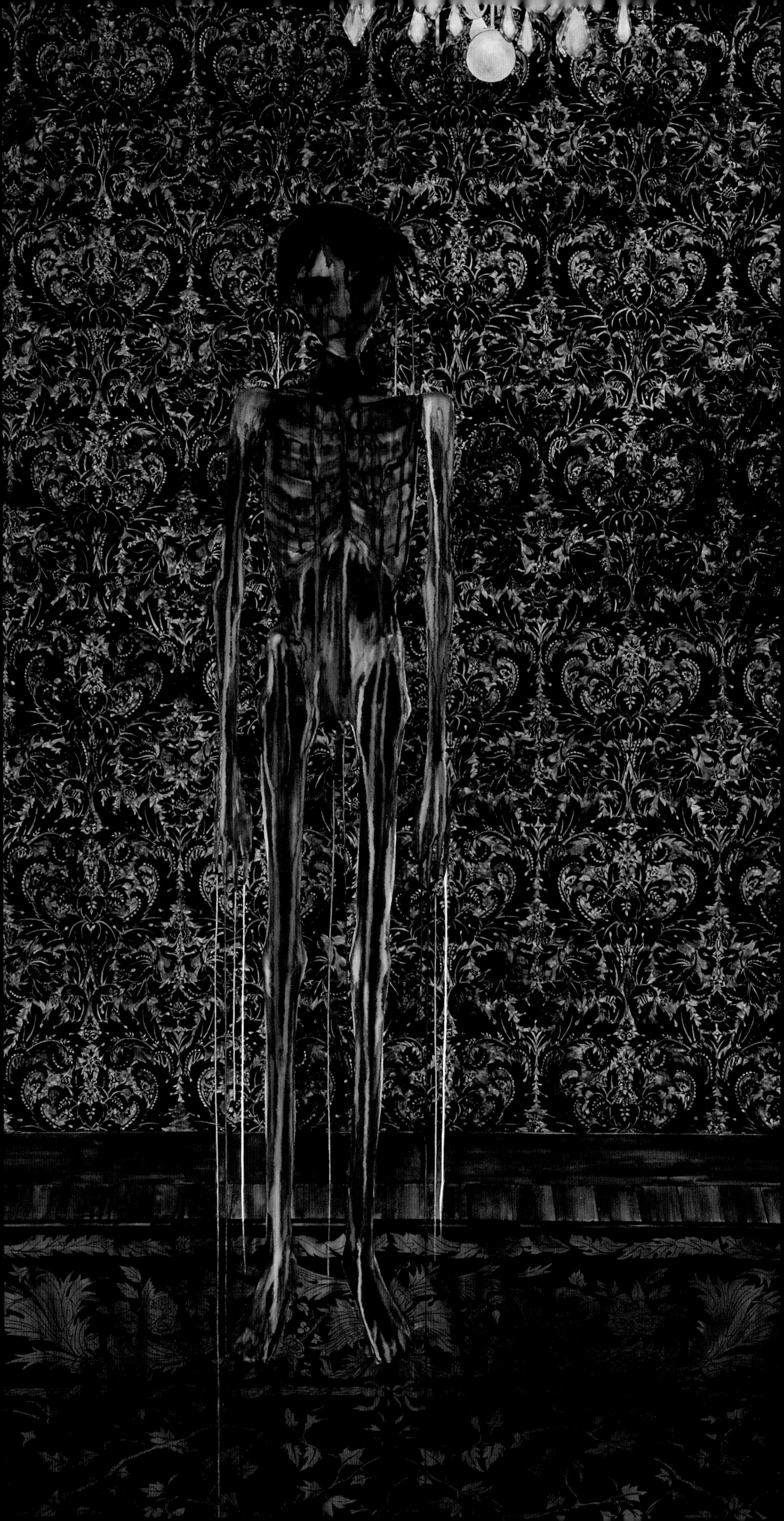

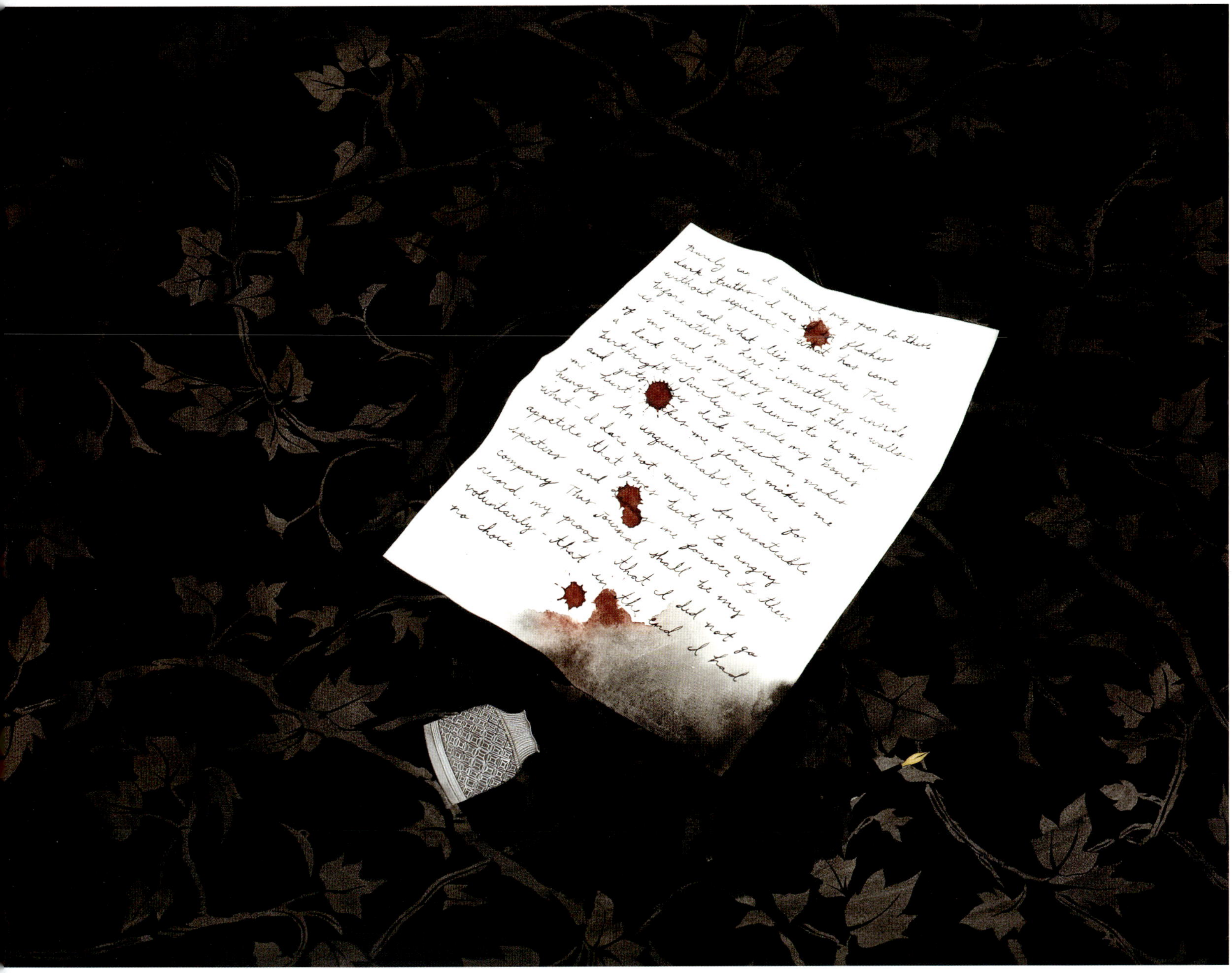

OPPOSITE PAGE: **TO WALK THESE HALLS–UNNAMED AND UNMOURNED**
72½ x 40″, 2009, Watercolor and Gouache on Paper

THE LETTER
22 x 28″, 2009, Watercolor and Gouache on Paper

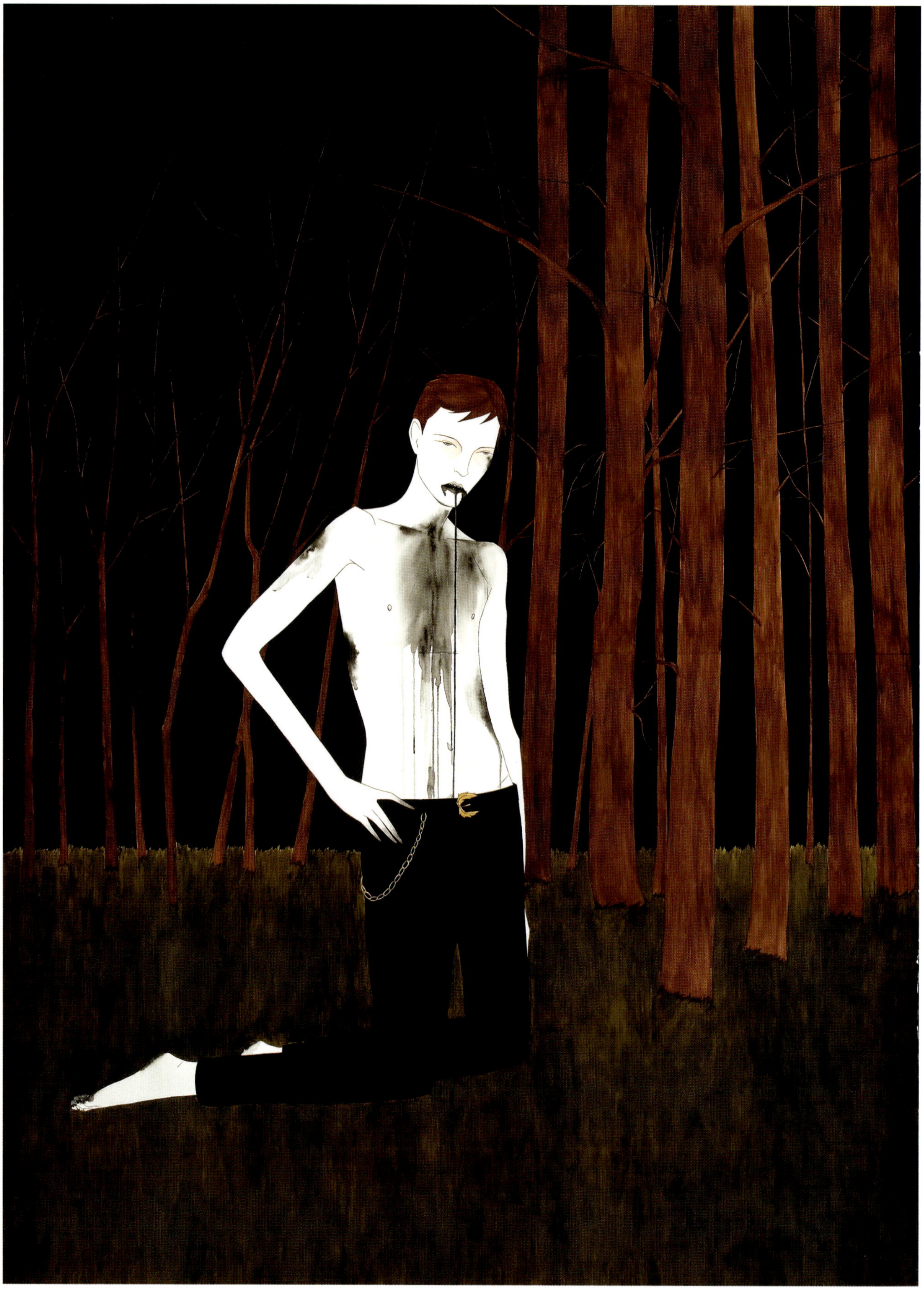

ESCAPE INTO THE WOODS–OVERCOME
64 x 48″, 2009, Watercolor and Gouache on Paper

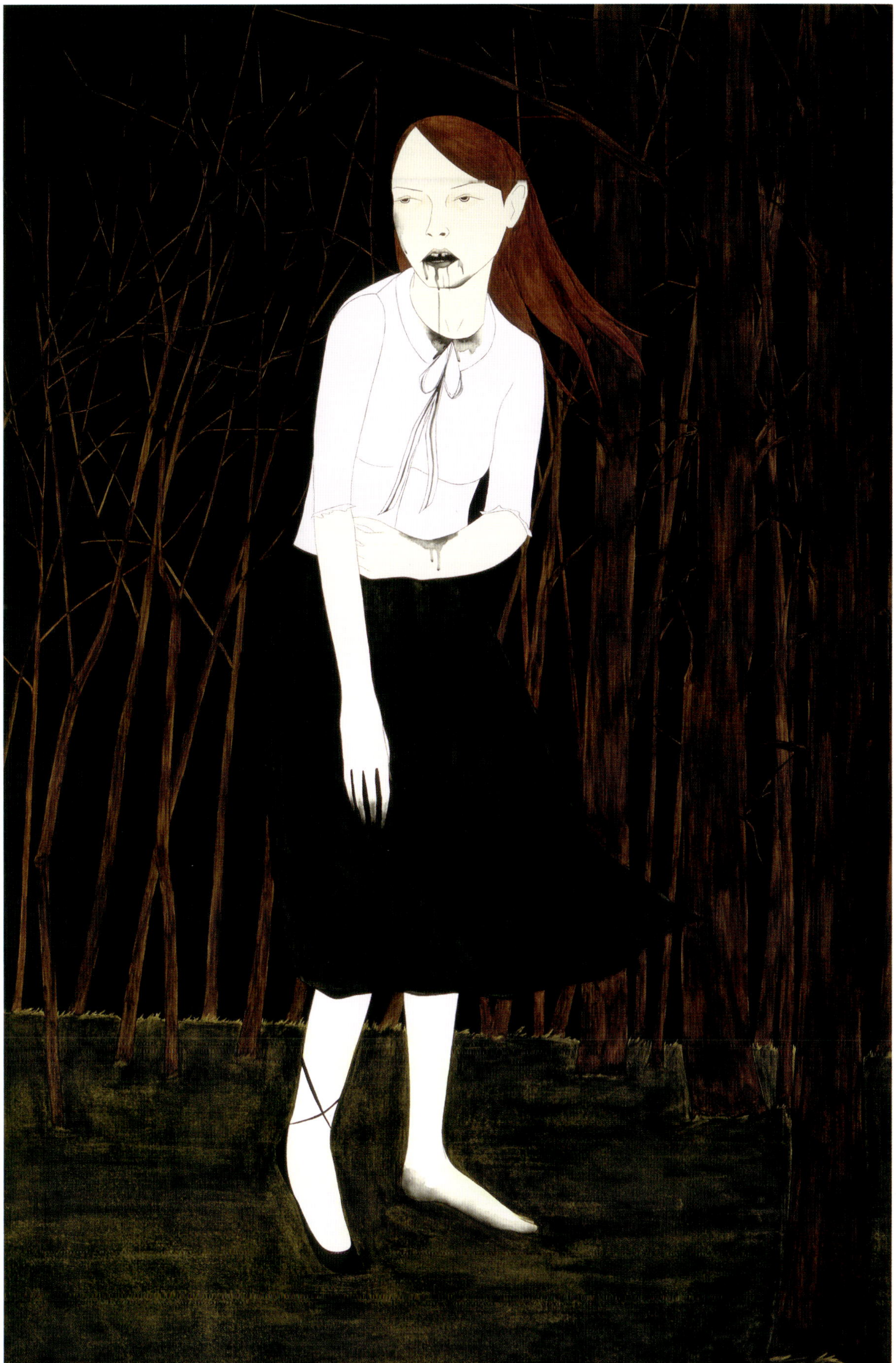

ESCAPE INTO THE WOODS–PURGING THE BLACK INFECTION
48 x 33″, 2008, Watercolor and Gouache on Paper

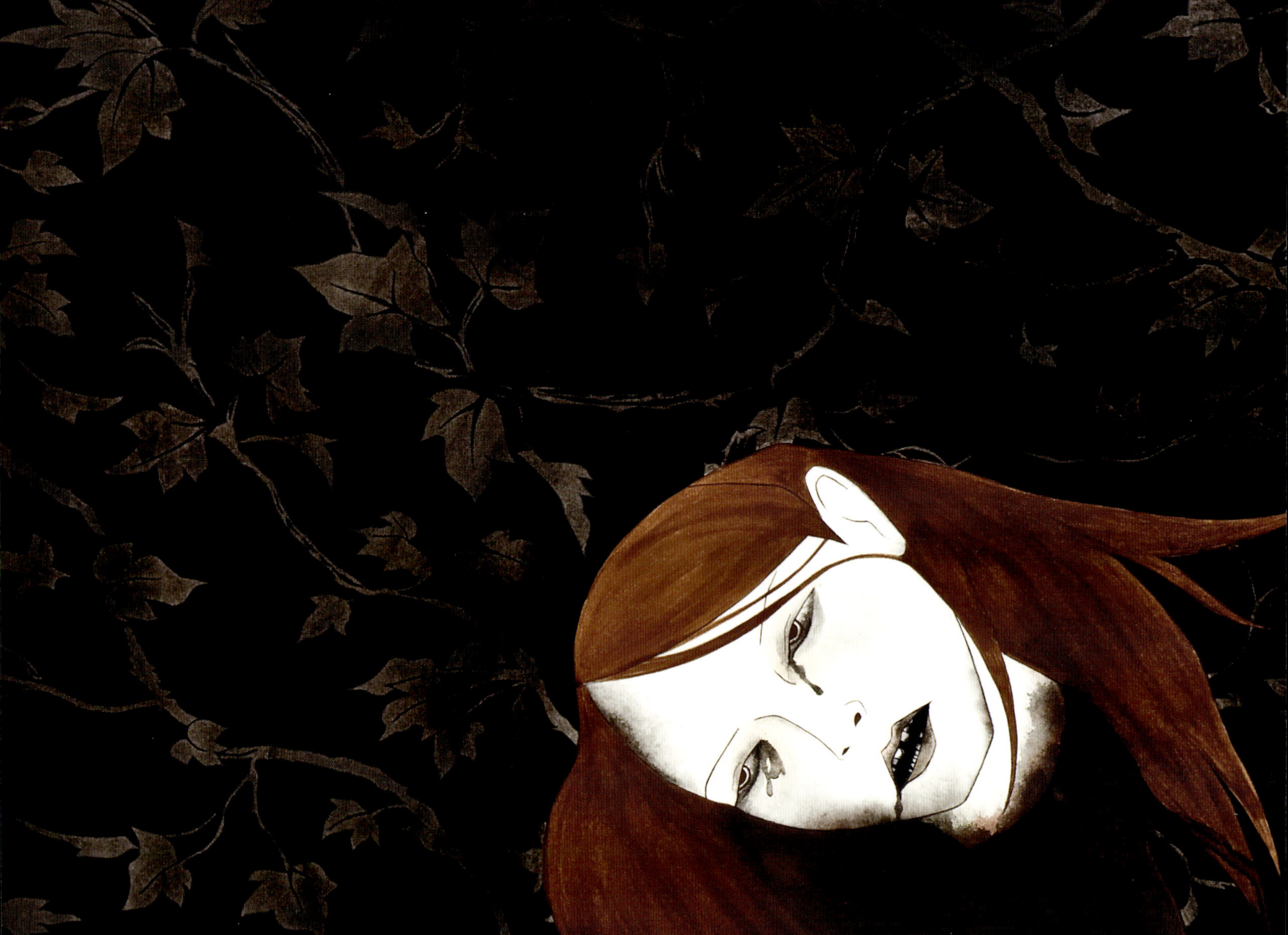

FROM WITHIN
22 x 26″, 2008, Watercolor and Gouache on Paper

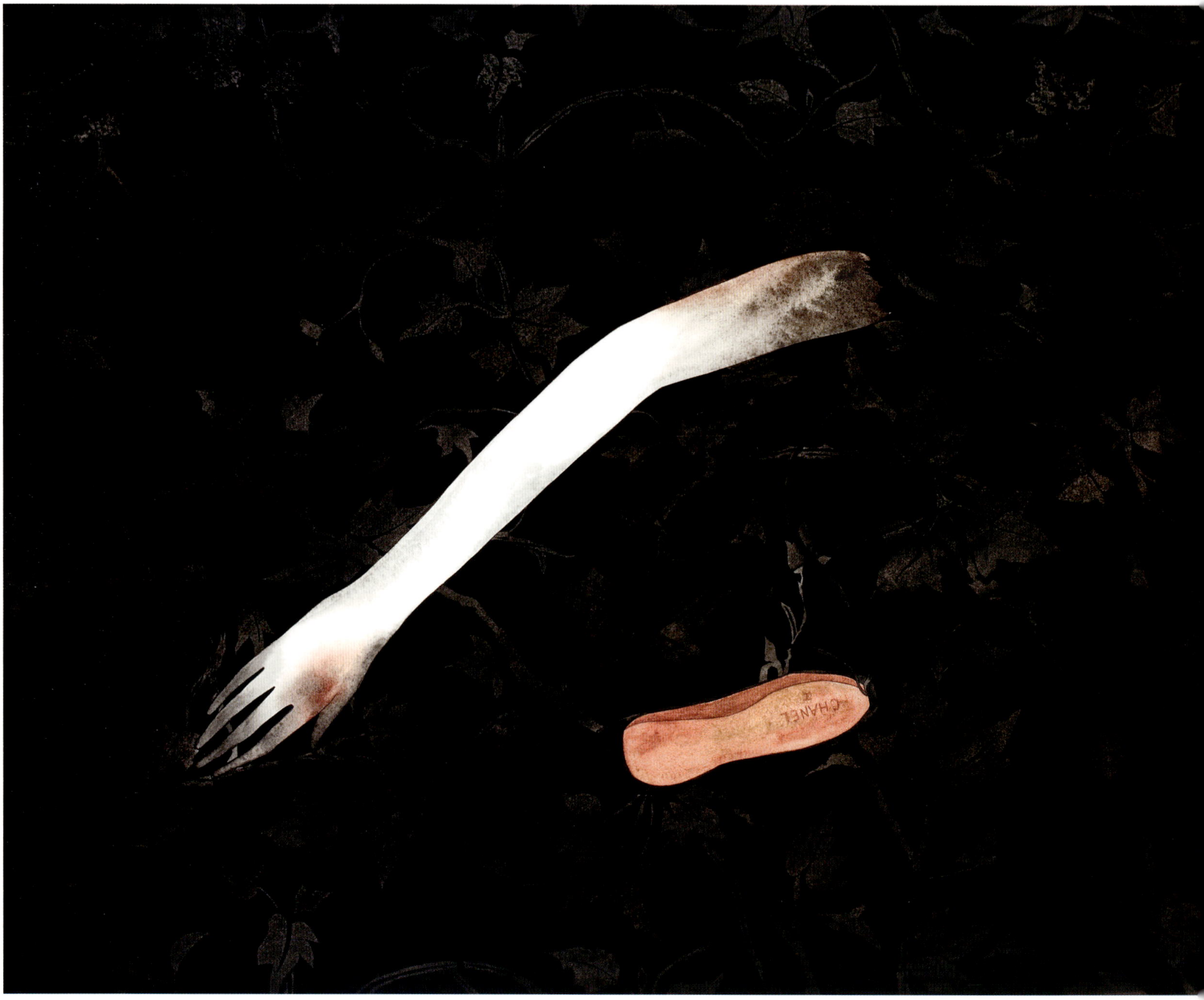

REMAINS
20 x 25", 2009, Watercolor and Gouache on Paper

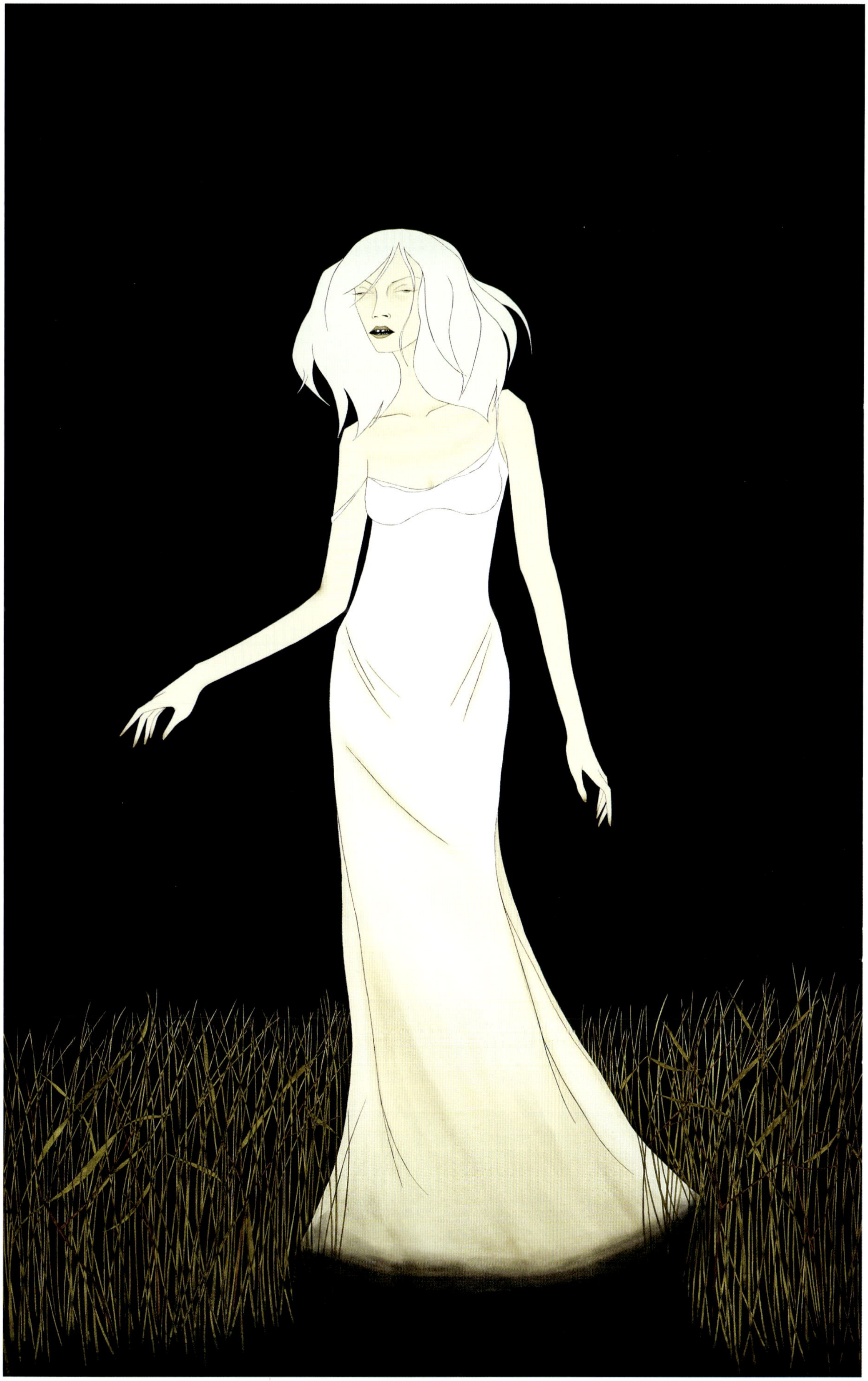

FROM THE DEPTHS
64 x 43″, 2009, Watercolor and Gouache on Paper

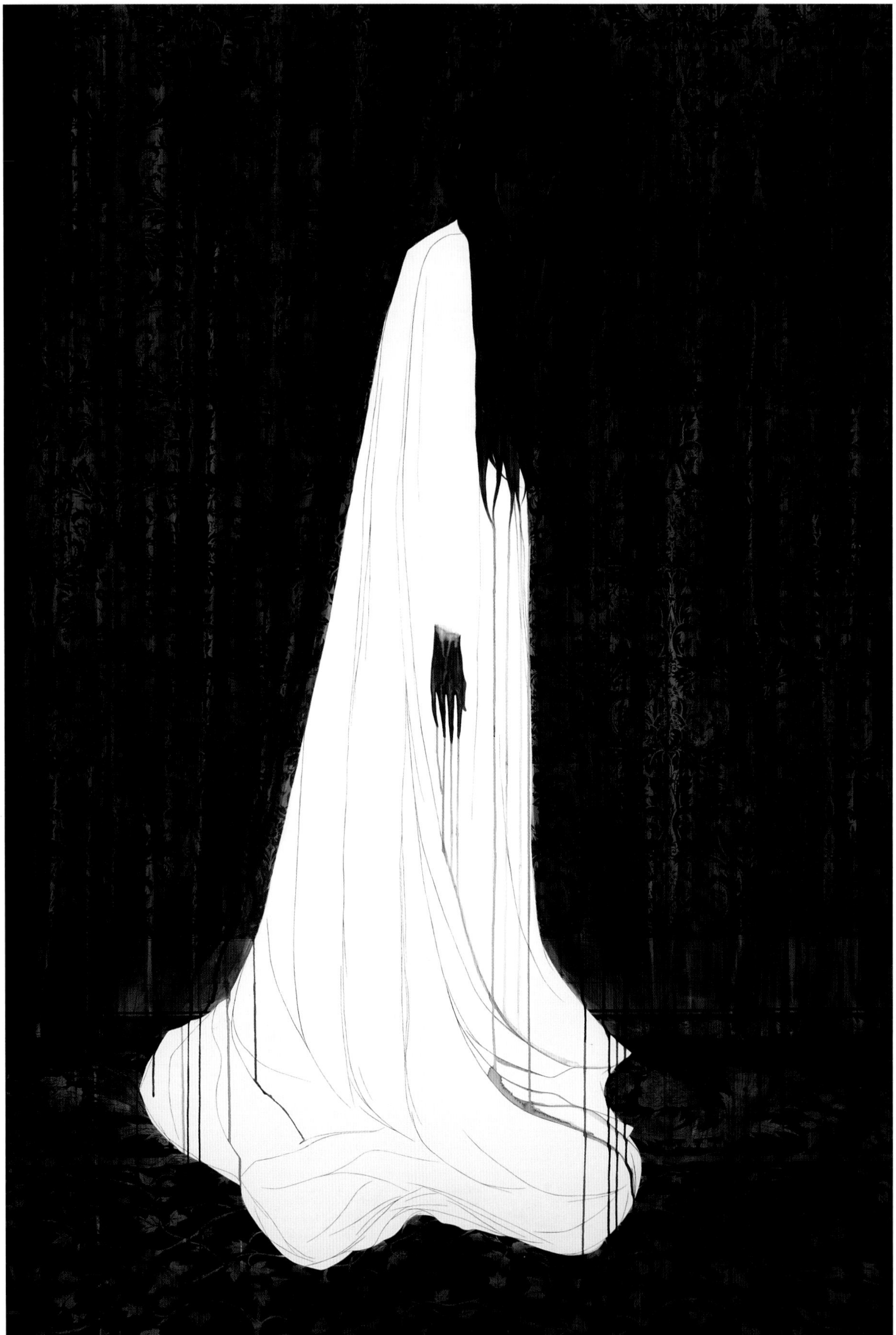

THROUGH THE THINNEST OF VEILS
71 x 48″, 2009, Watercolor and Gouache on Paper

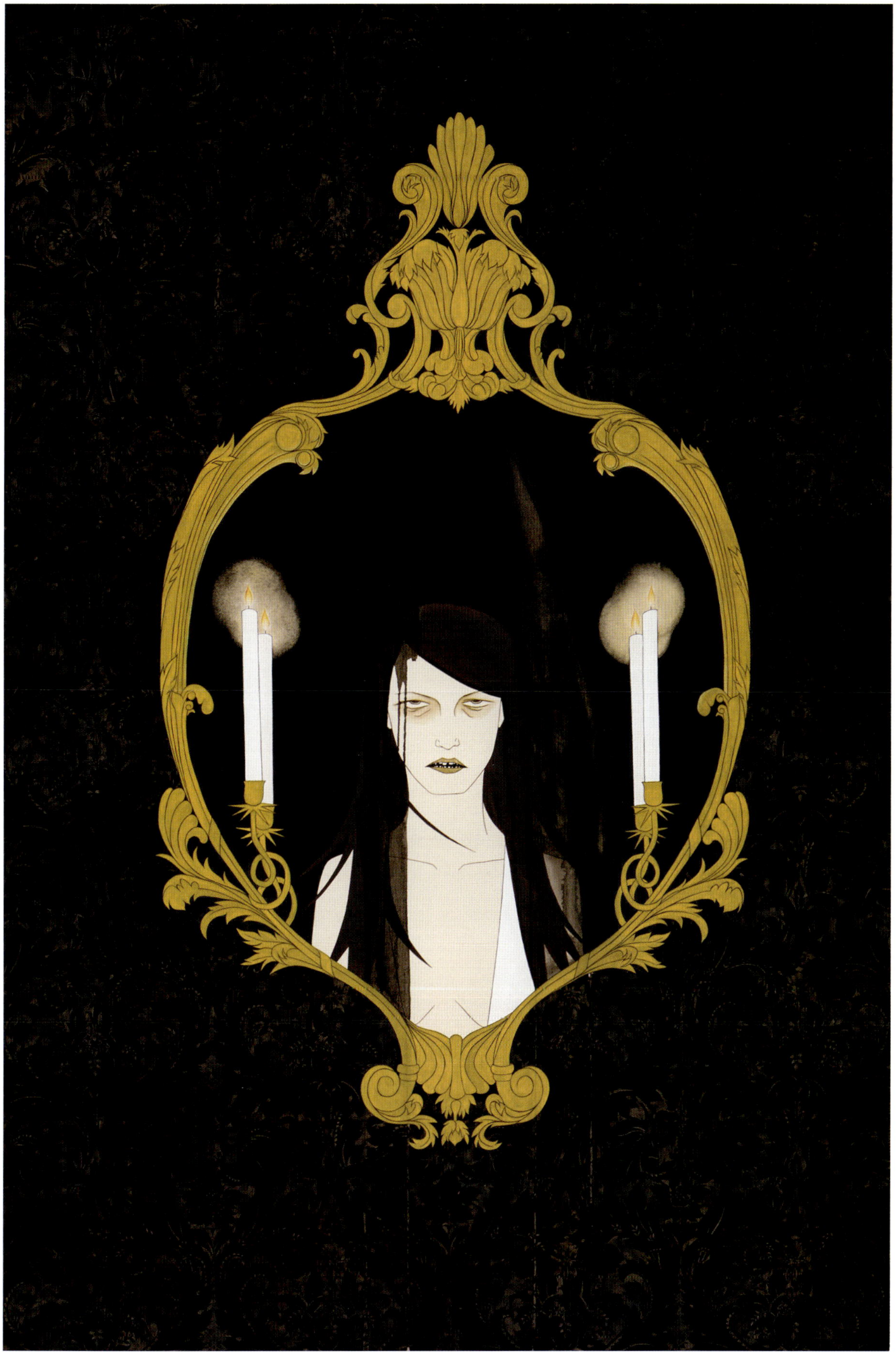

THE SUMMONING, A RECKONING
44 x 30″, 2010, Watercolor and Gouache on Paper

CHAPTER THREE

For Forever

I'll Be Here

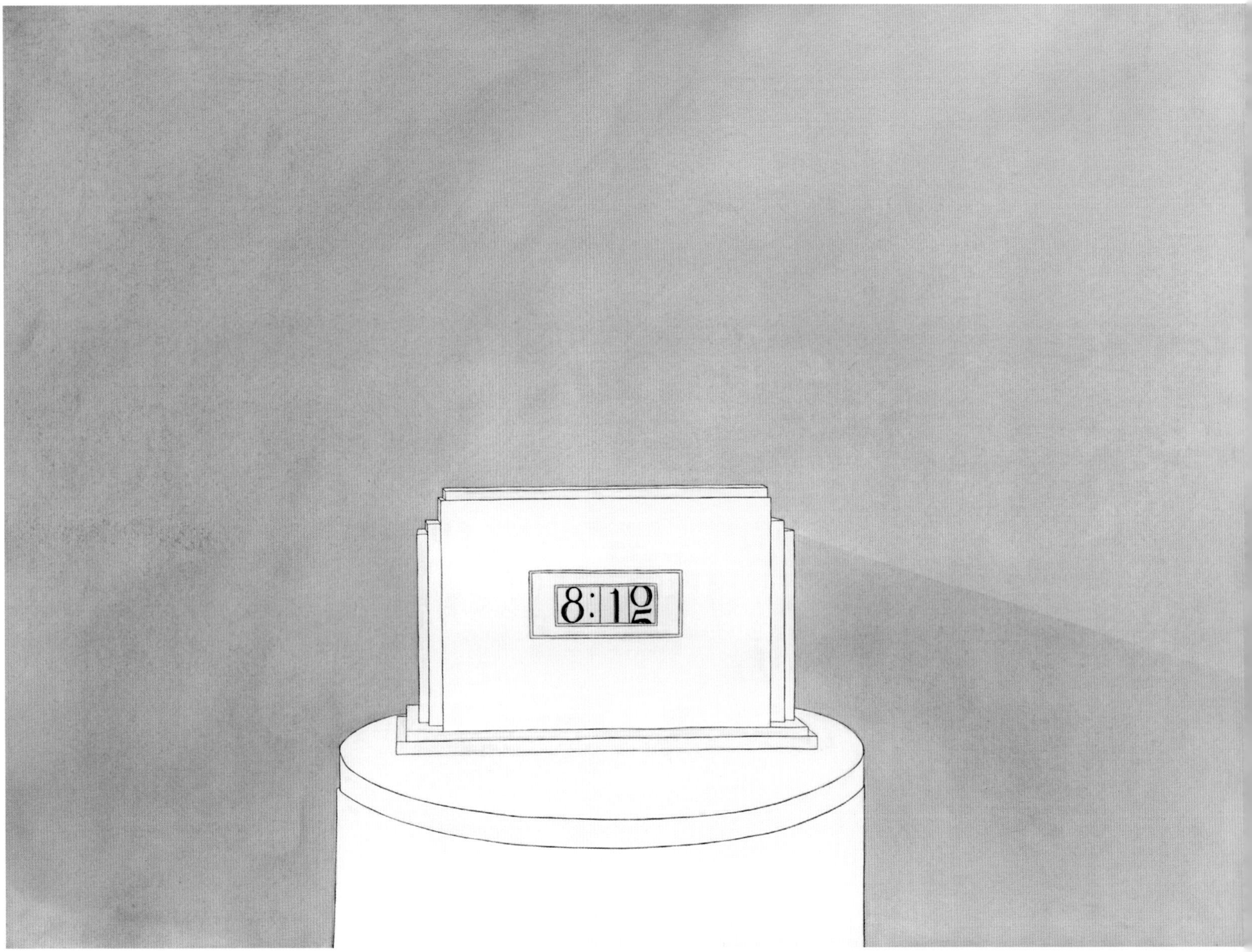

IN BETWEEN TIME
21 x 27″, 2010, Watercolor and Gouache on Paper

OPPOSITE PAGE: **NO PLACE**
48 x 34″, 2010, Watercolor and Gouache on Paper

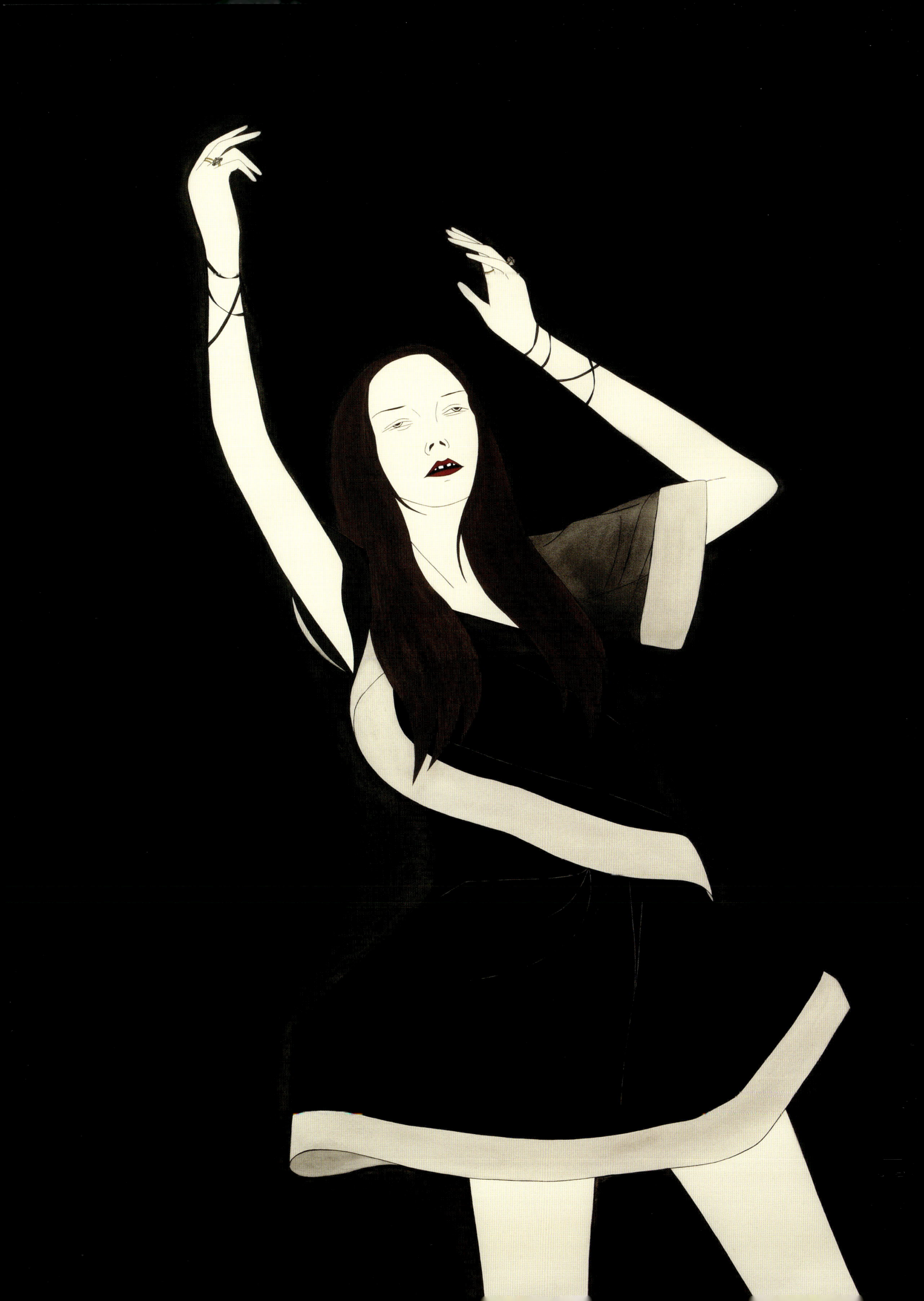

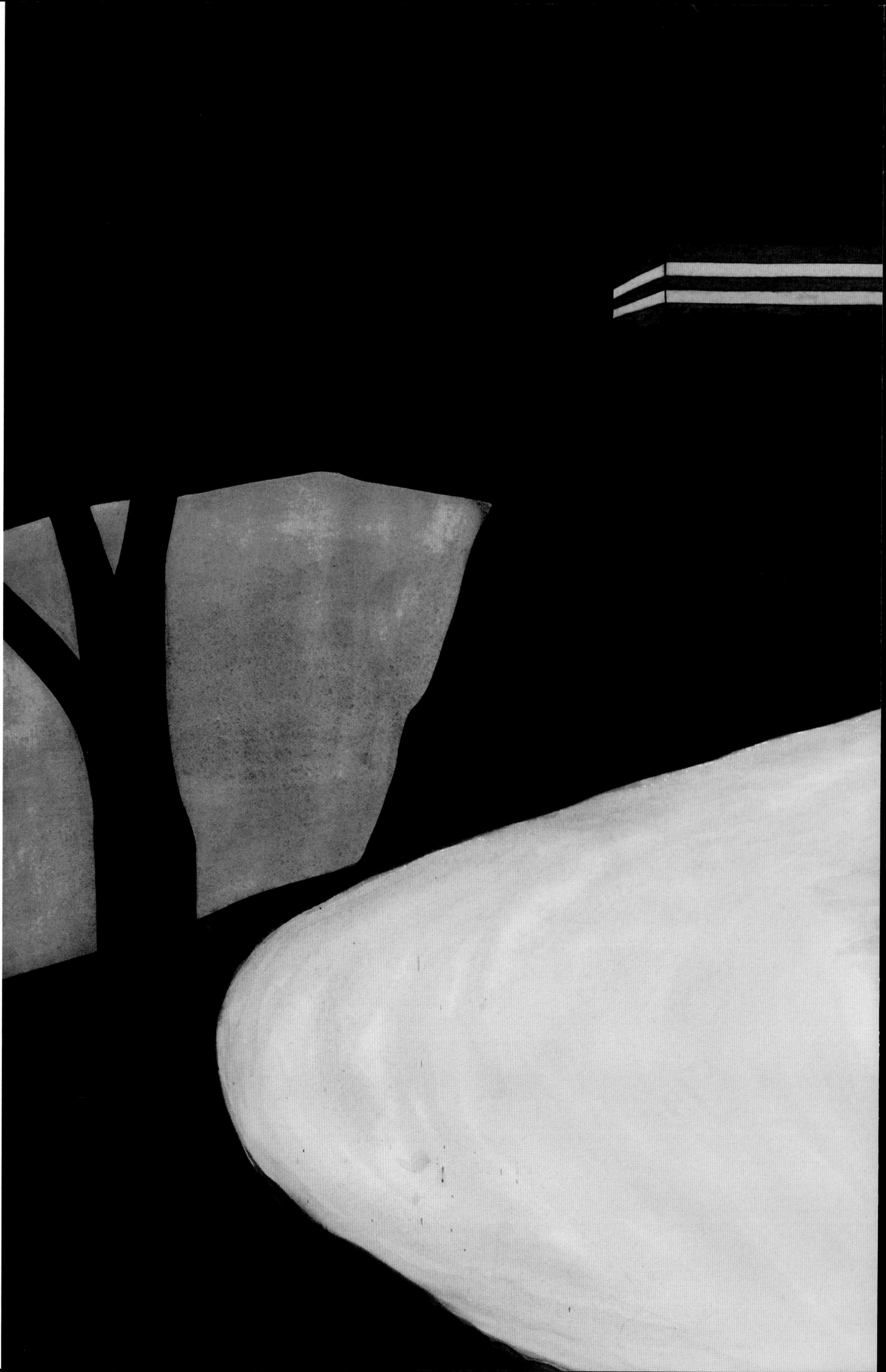

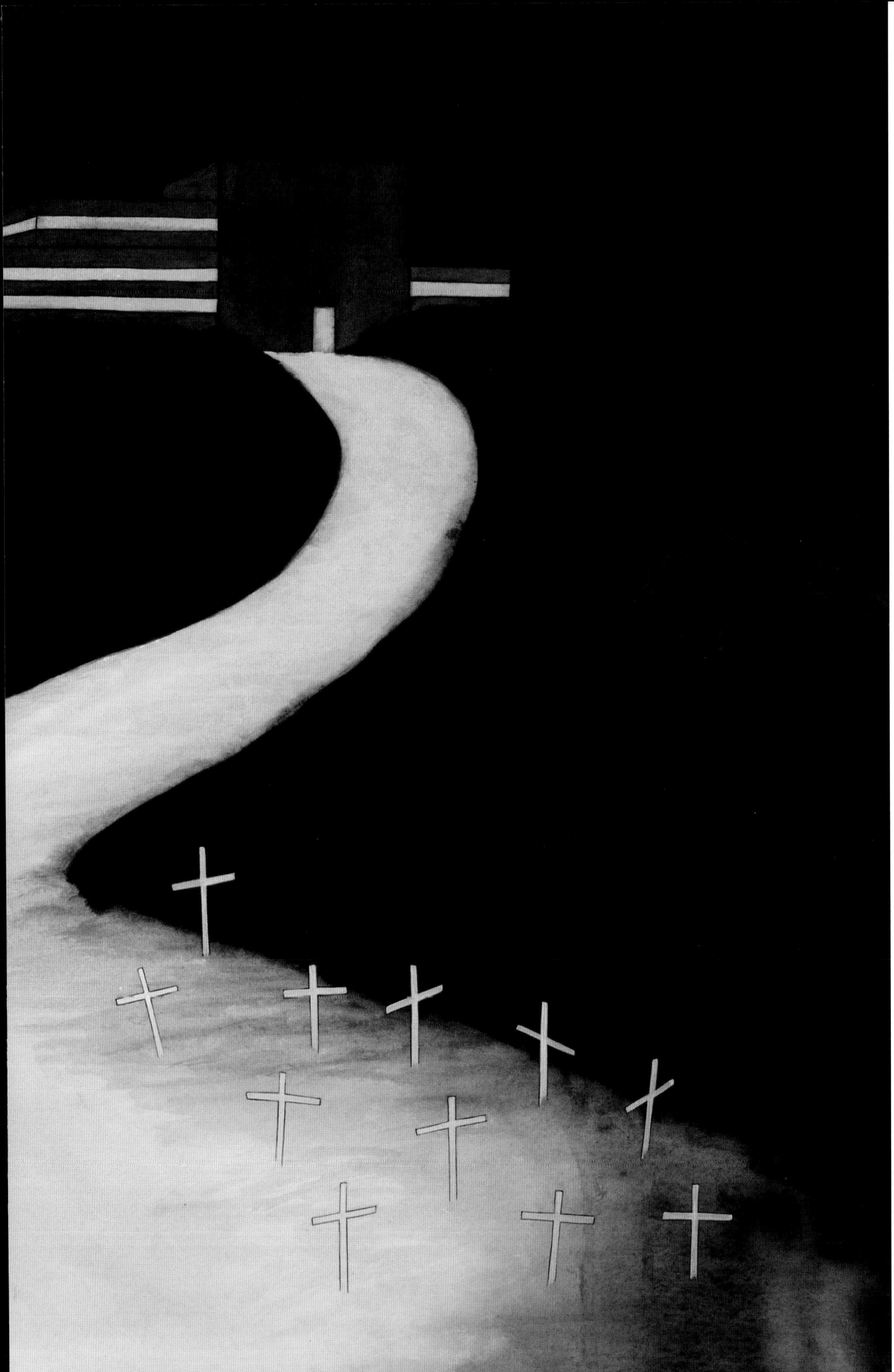

THE ARCHITECT'S HOUSE
21 x 27", 2010, Watercolor and Gouache on Paper

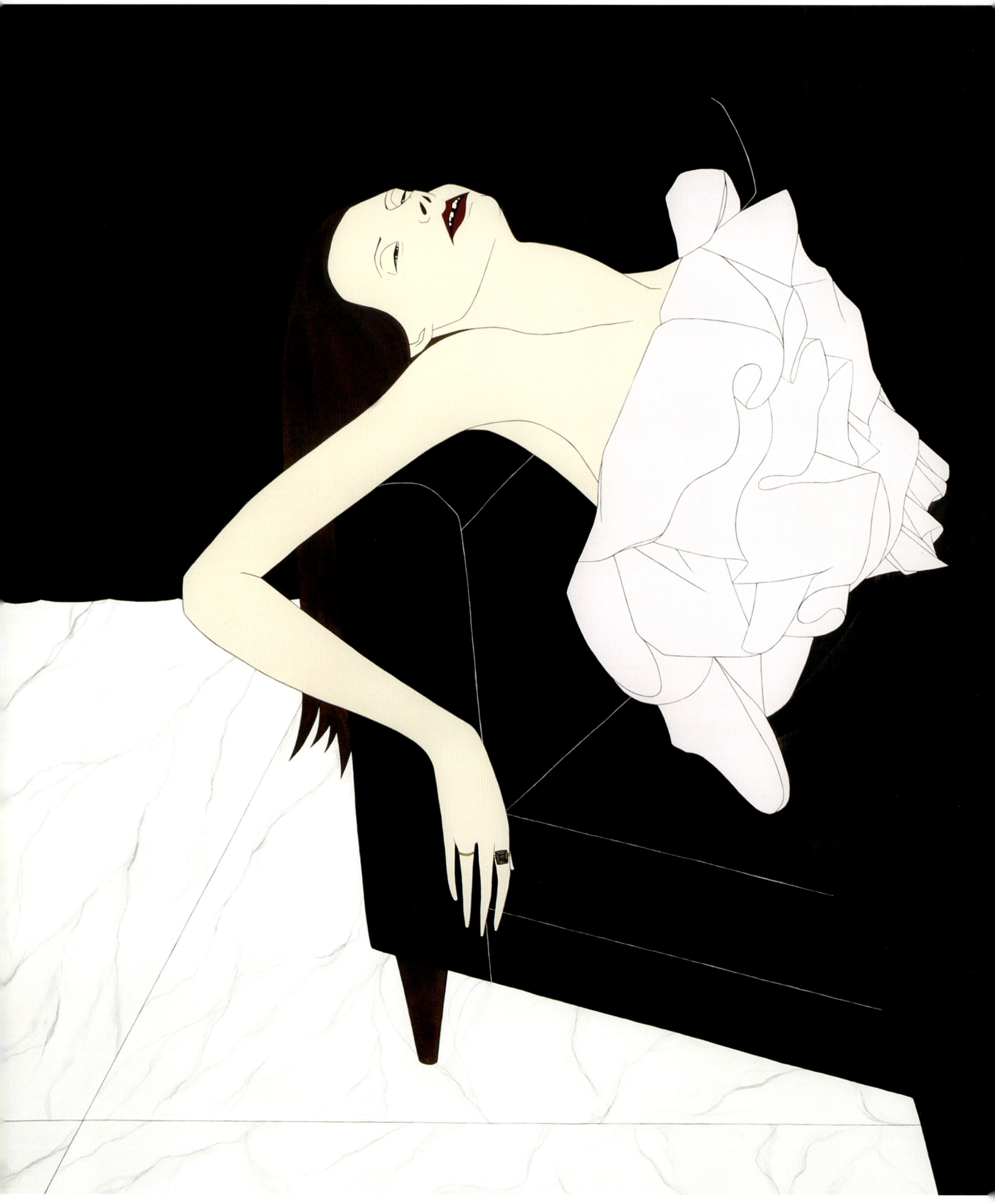

WITHOUT END
34 x 48", 2010, Watercolor and Gouache on Paper

OPPOSITE PAGE: **MONUMENT**
27 x 21", 2010, Watercolor and Gouache on Paper

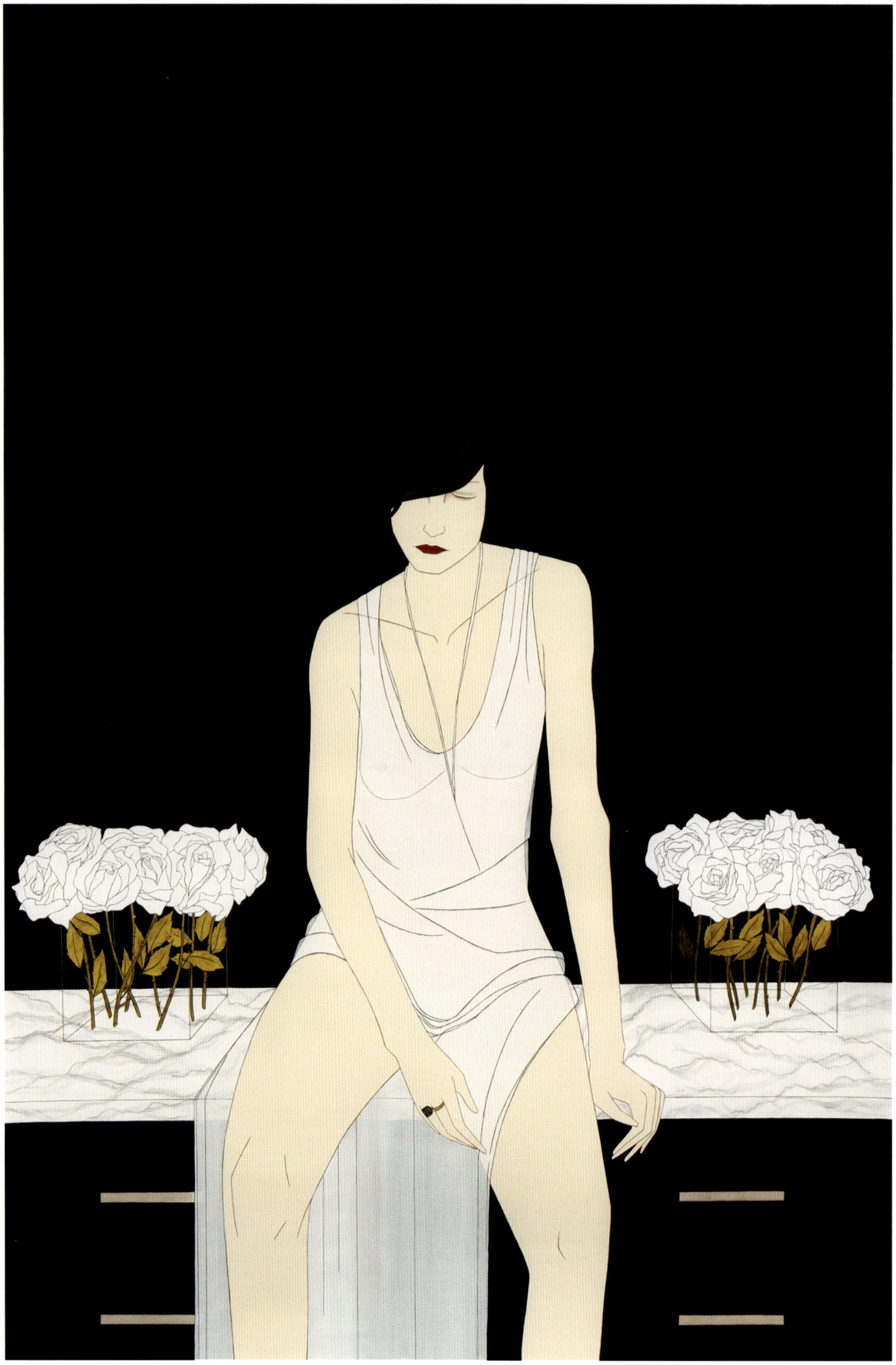

WHITE ROSES
48 x 34", 2010, Watercolor and Gouache on Paper

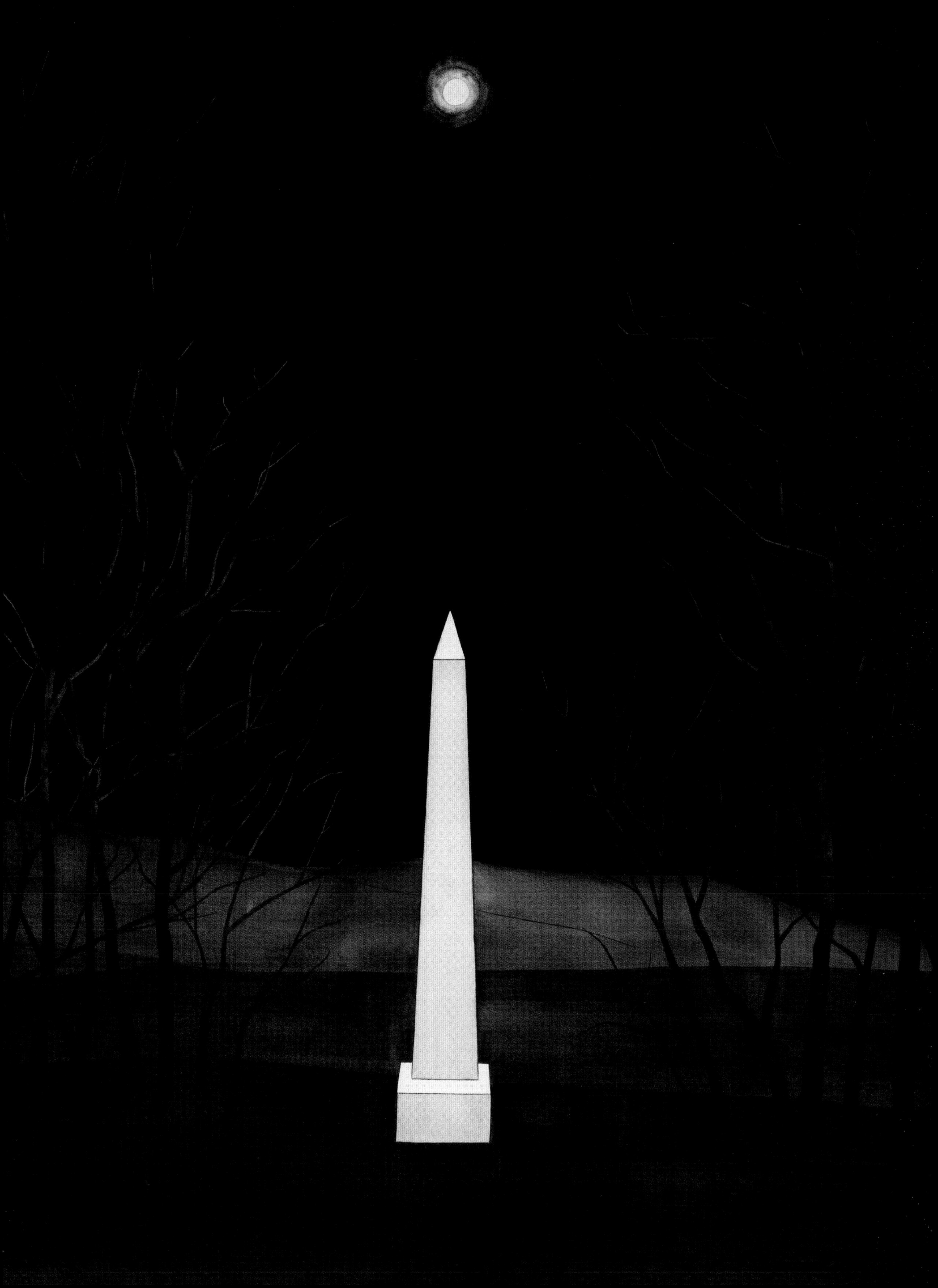

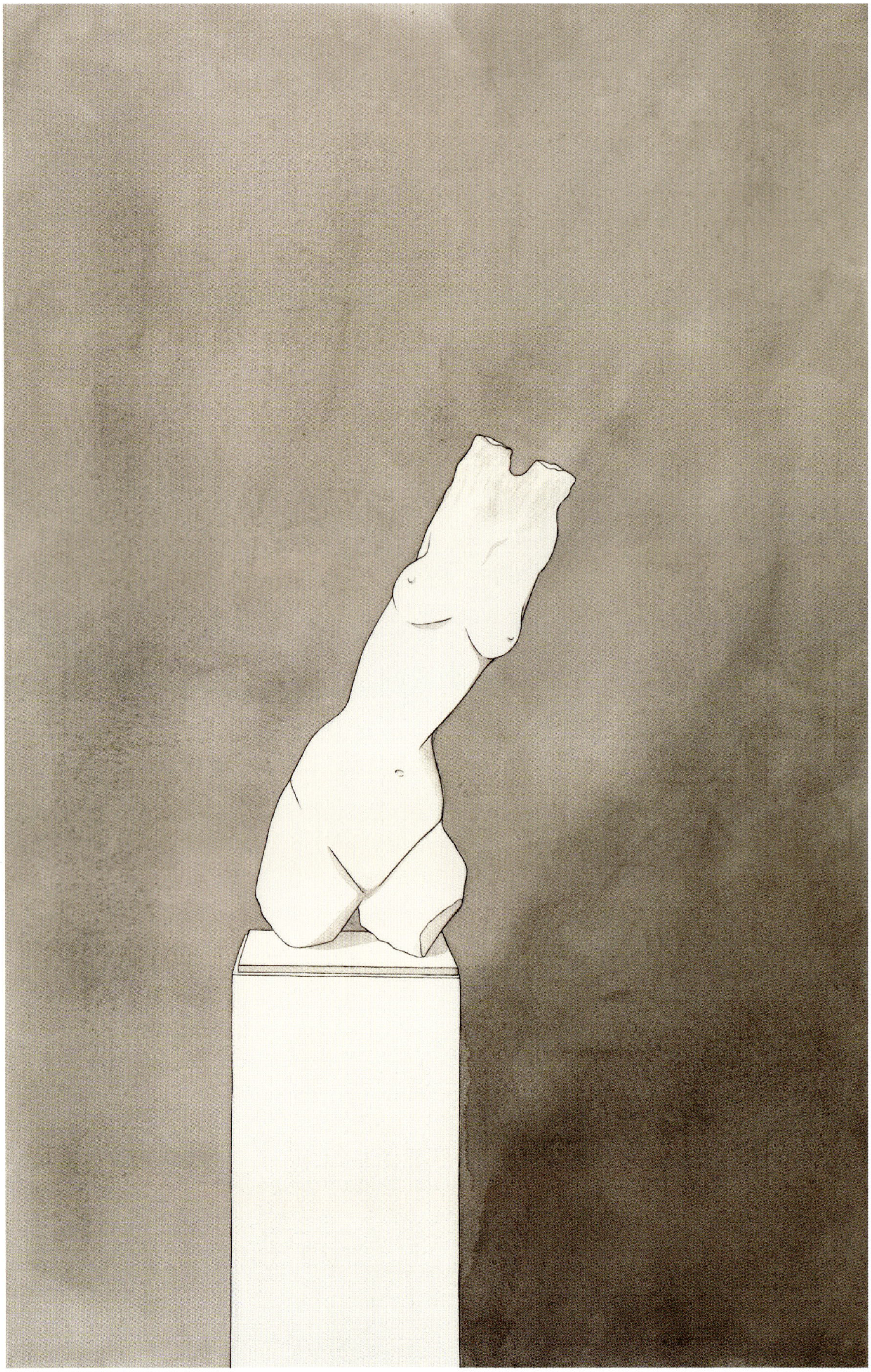

THE ARTIFACT (OUT OF TIME)
25 x 18″, 2011, Watercolor and Gouache on Paper

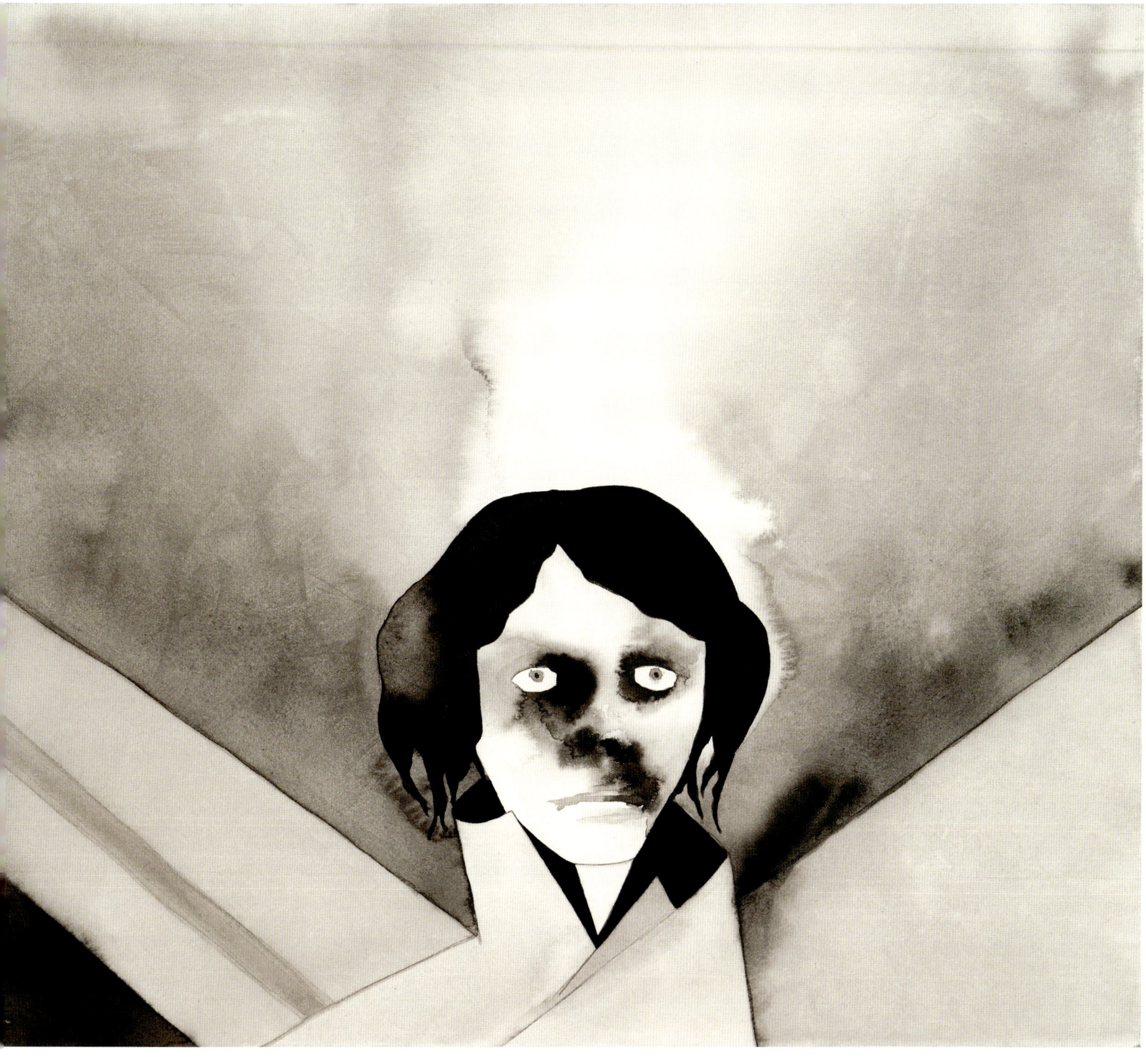

LIKE A FUCKED UP FACE
19 x 21", 2011, Watercolor and Gouache on Paper

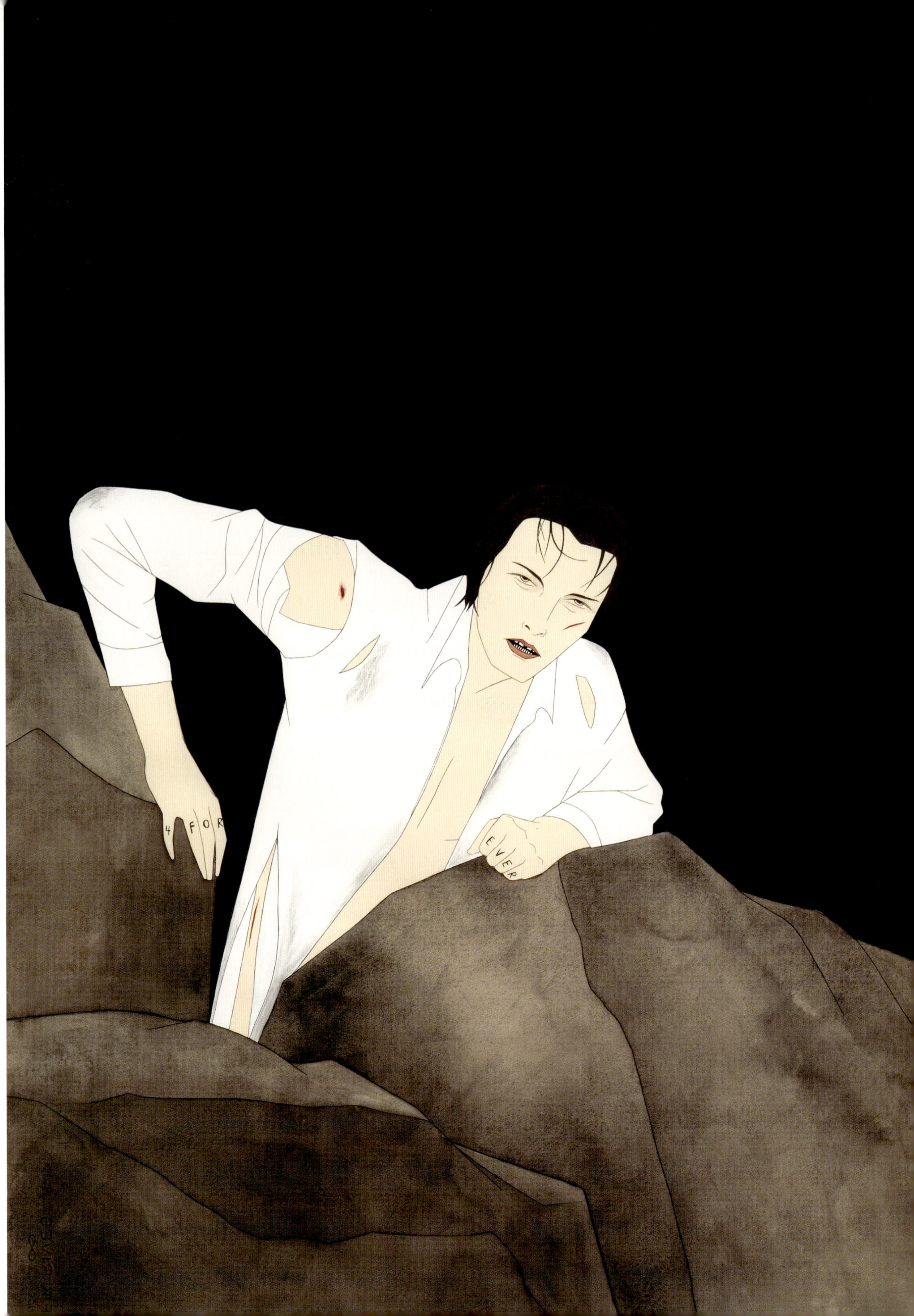
4 FOR
EVER

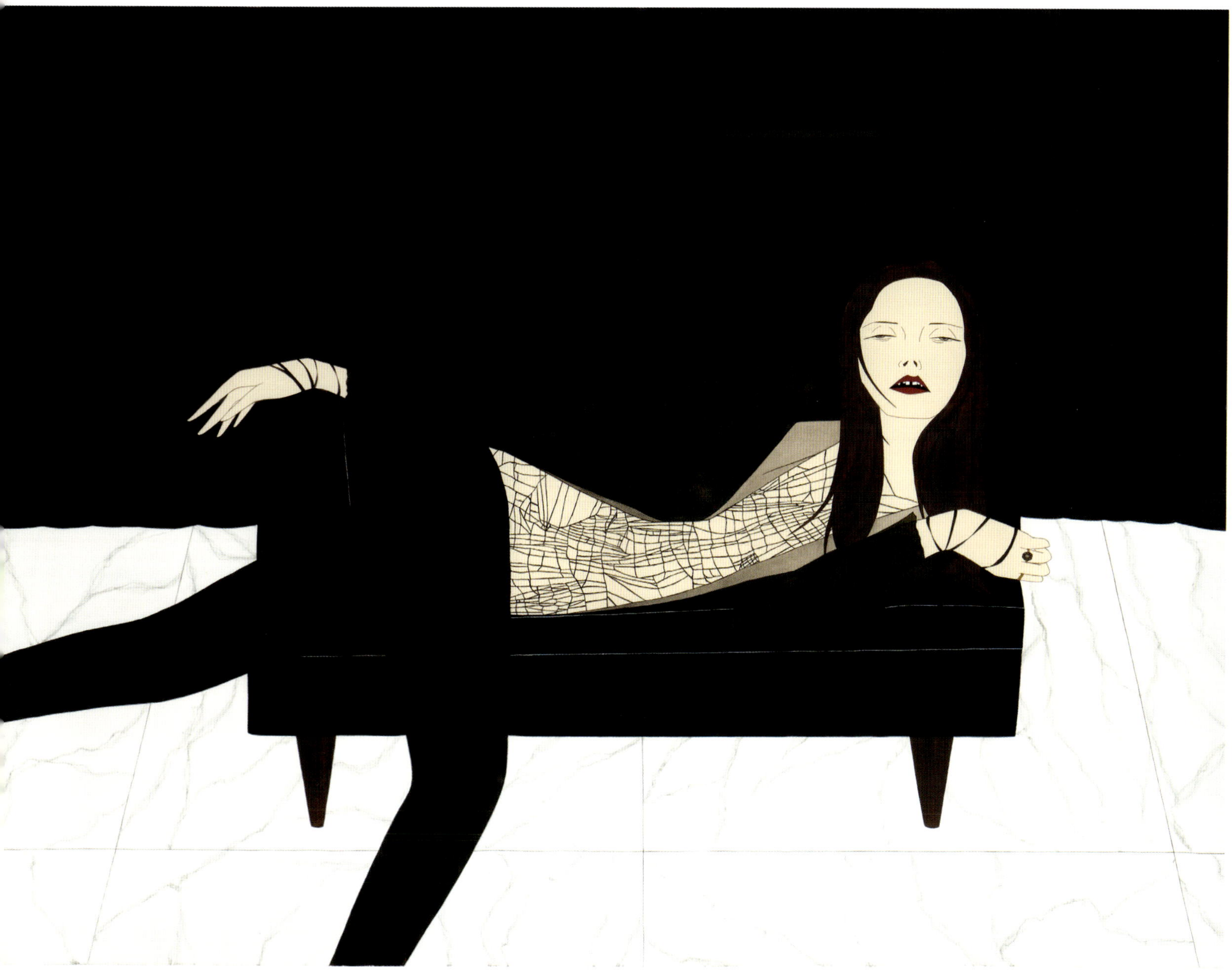

OPPOSITE PAGE: THE HUNTER
48 x 34″, 2011, Watercolor and Gouache on Paper

THIS WILL NEVER END CAUSE I WANT MORE
34 x 43″, 2011, Watercolor and Gouache on Paper

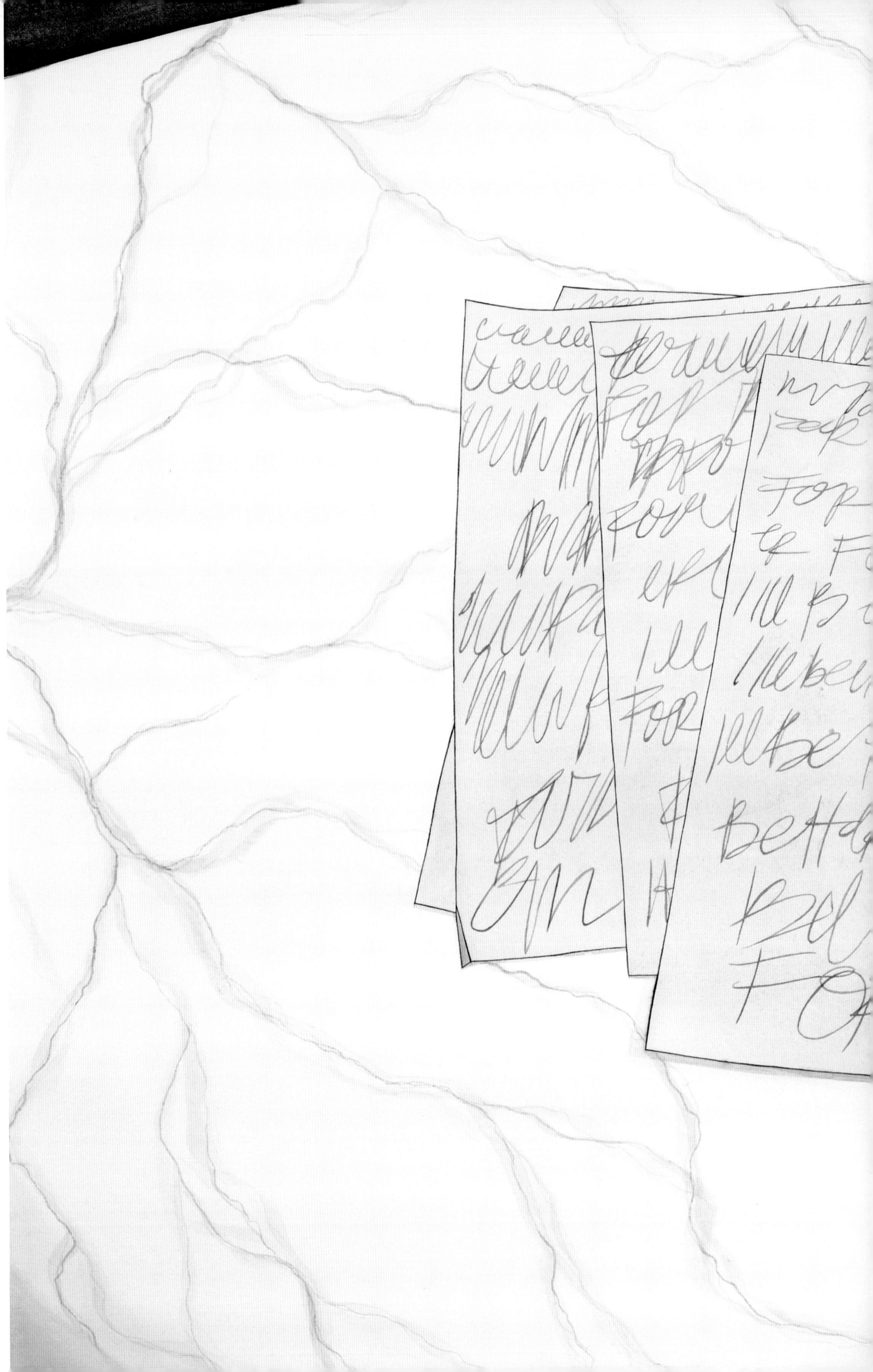

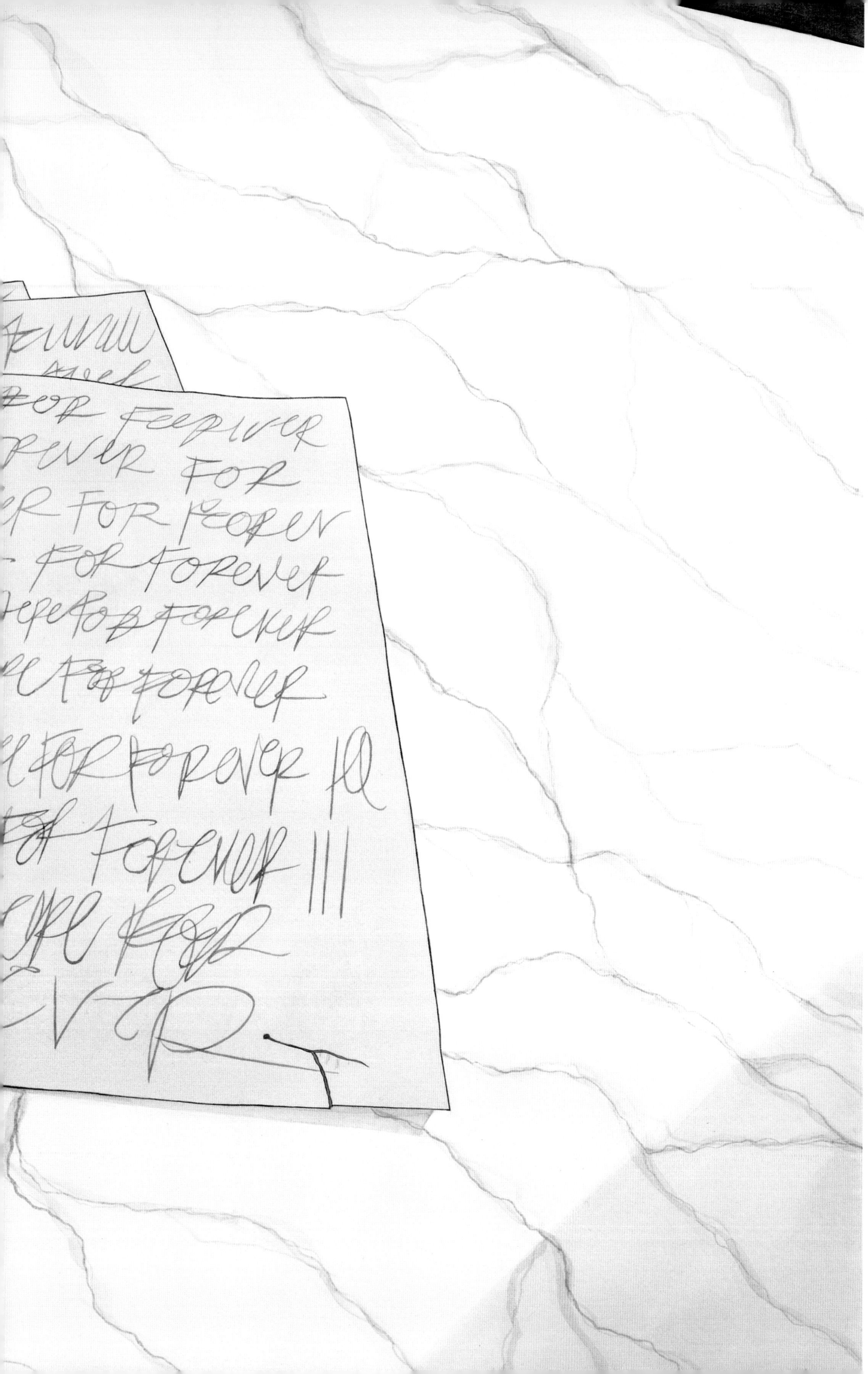

AUTOMATIC WRITING
21 x 27", 2011, Watercolor and Gouache on Paper

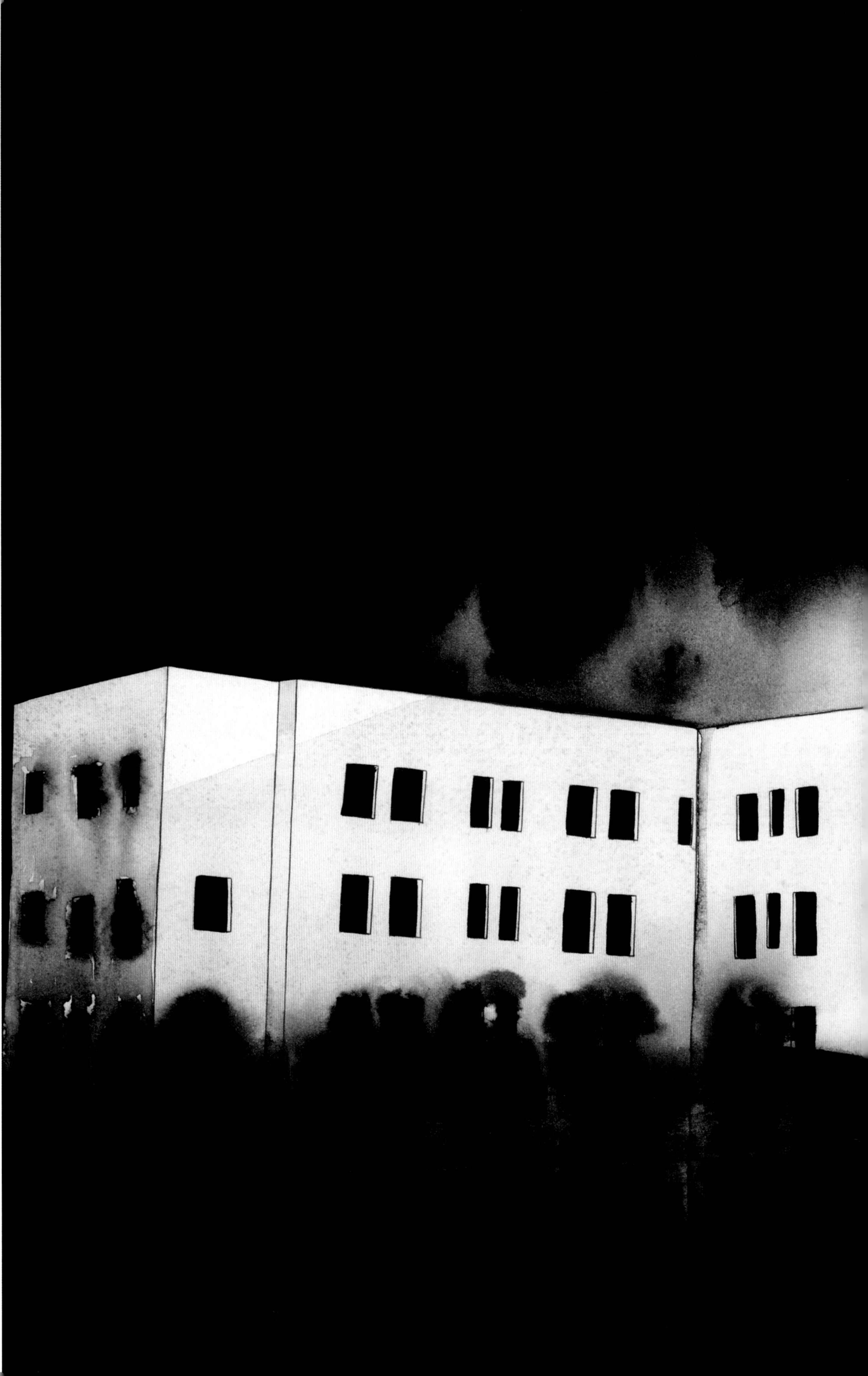

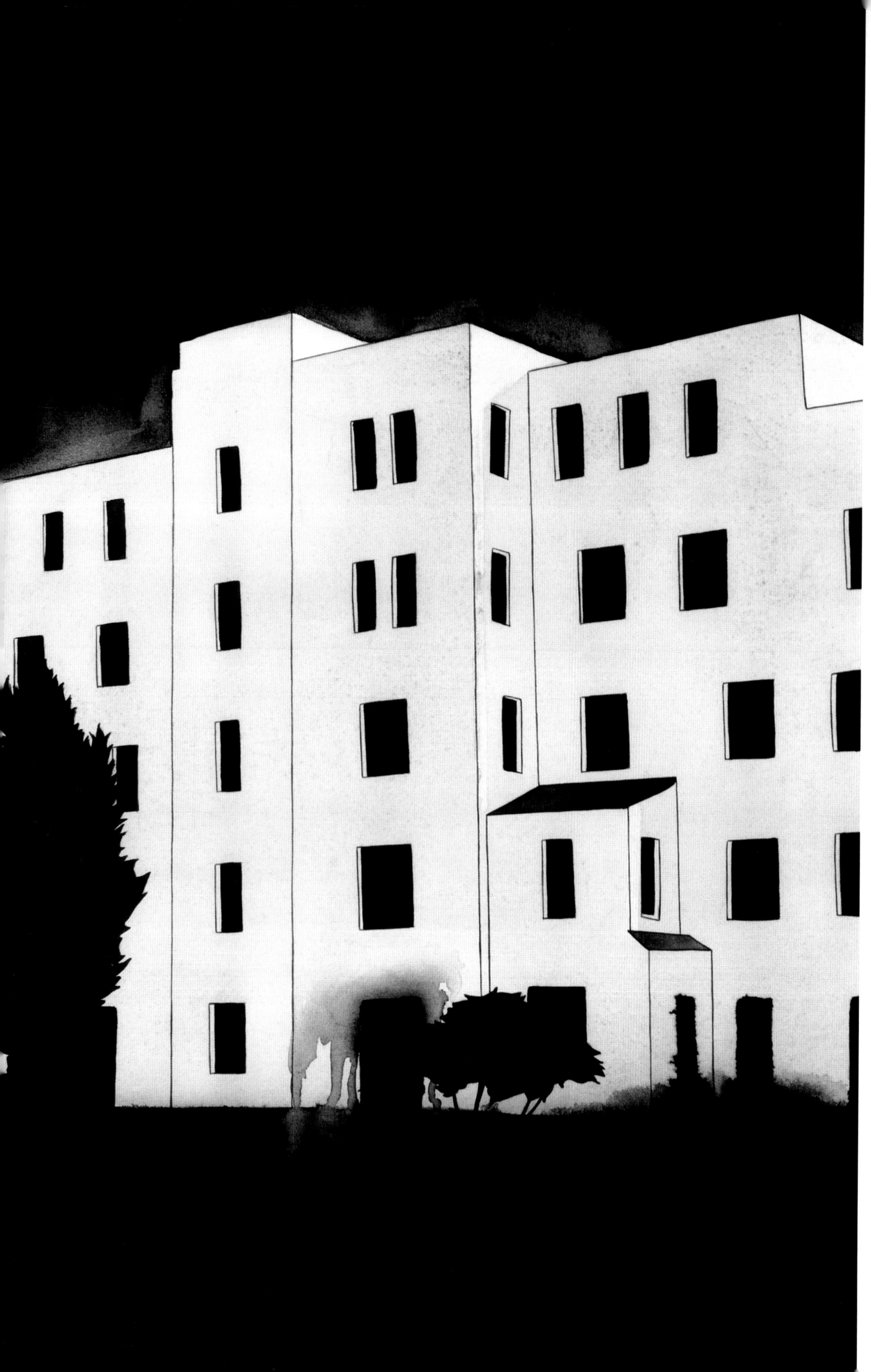

THE HOSPITAL
21 x 27", 2011, Watercolor and Gouache on Paper

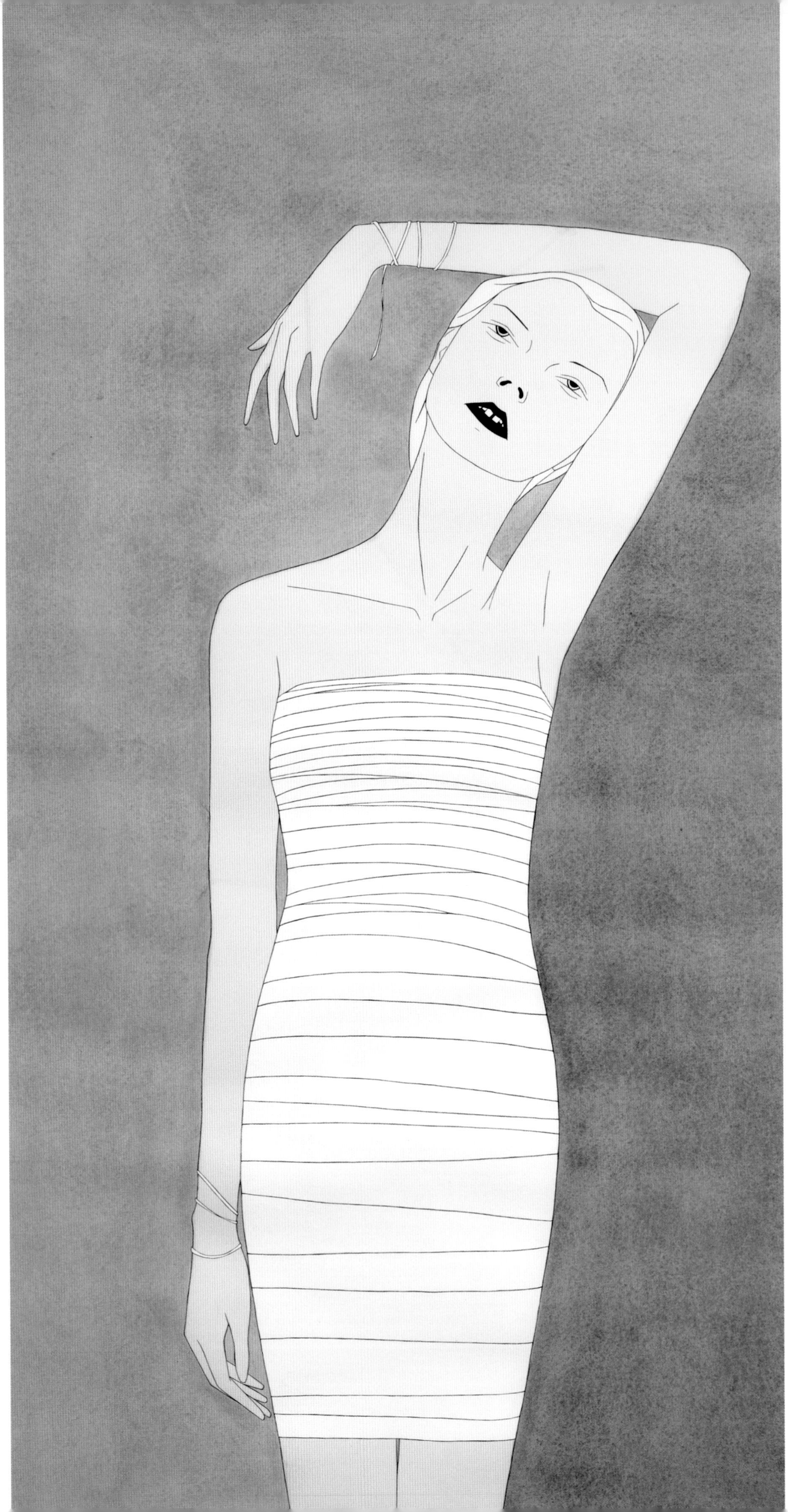

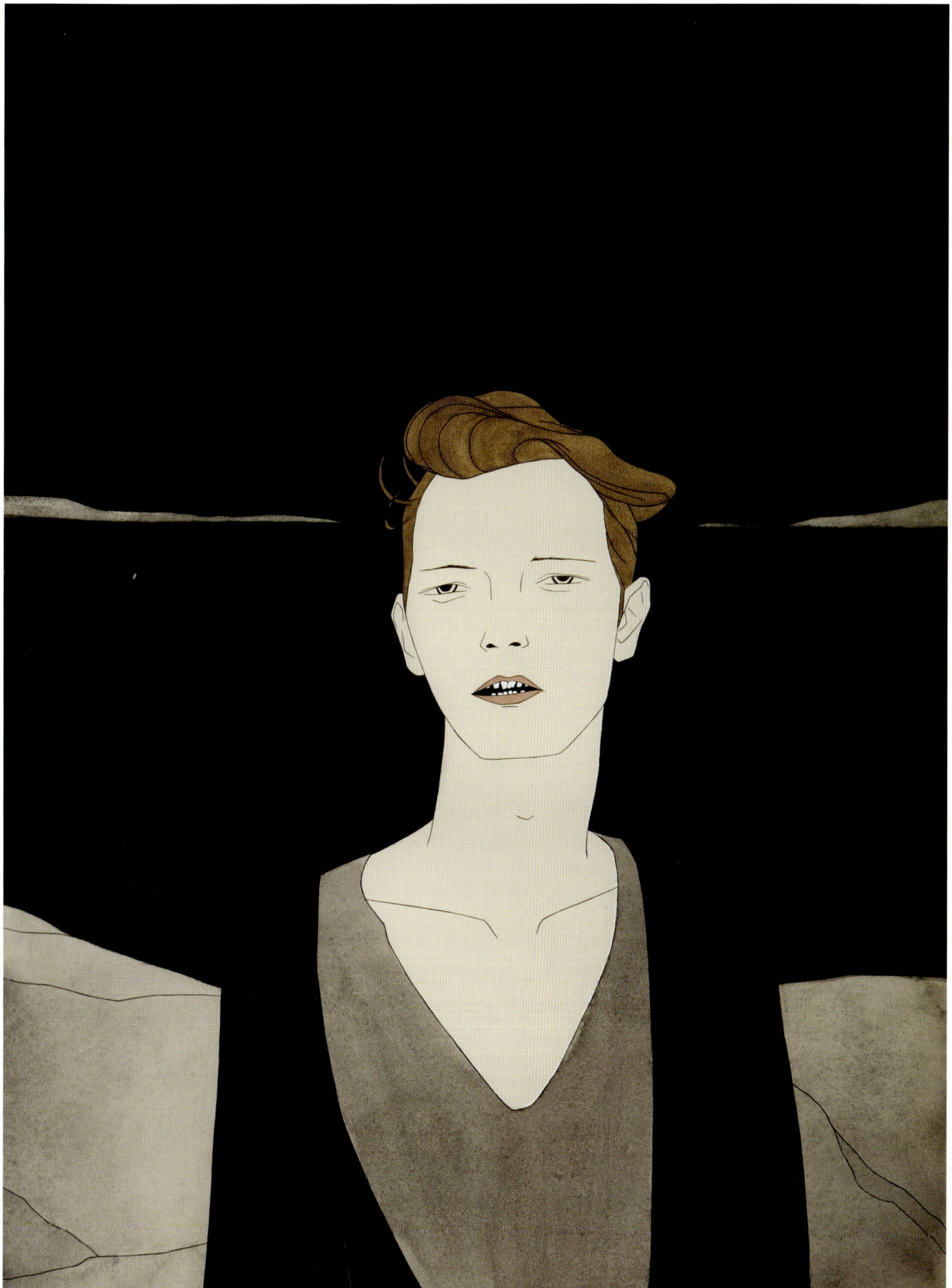

OPPOSITE PAGE: **CONCRETE WALLS**
39 x 21″, 2011, Watercolor and Gouache on Paper

IN BETWEEN
24 x 18″, 2011, Watercolor and Gouache on Paper

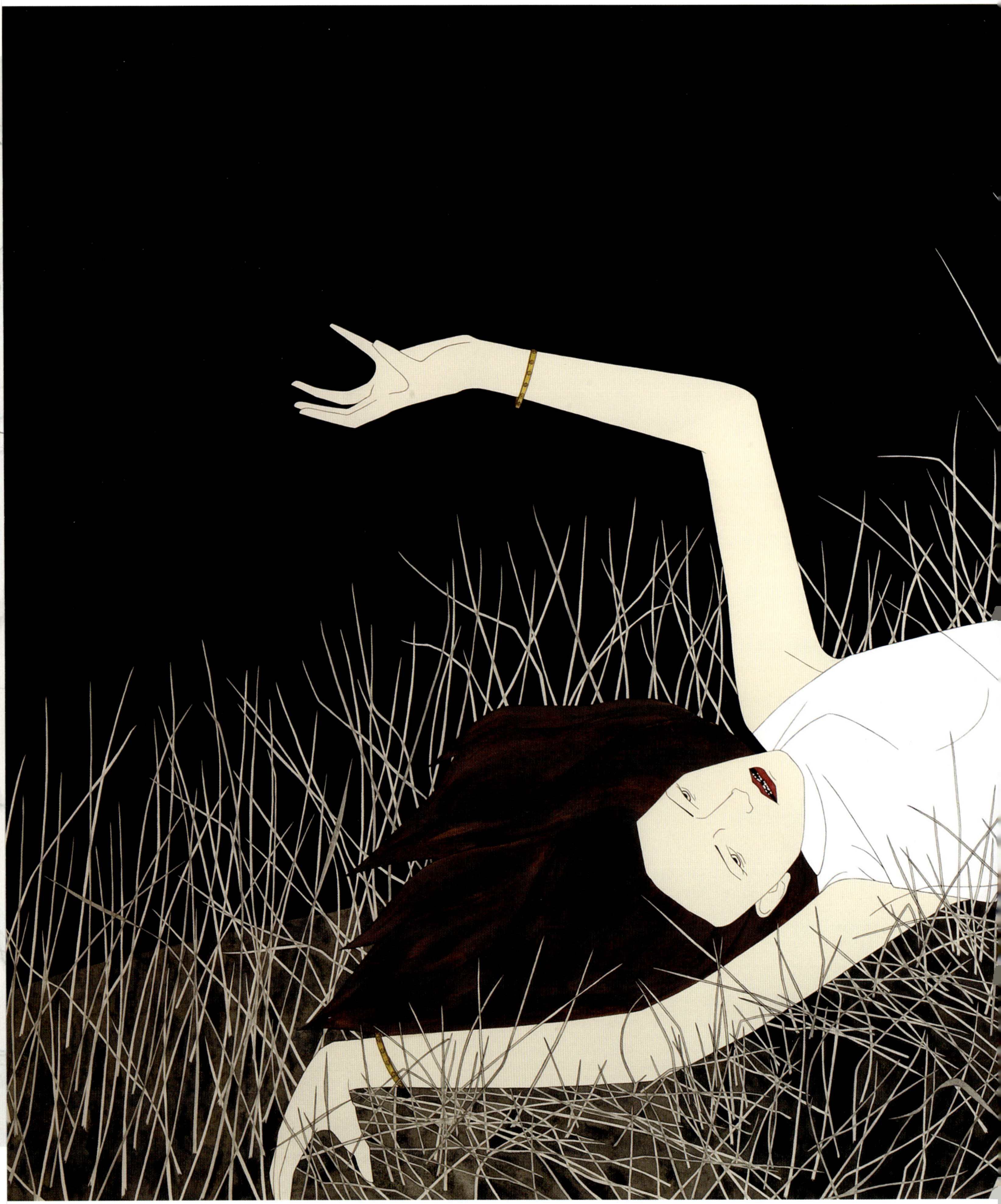

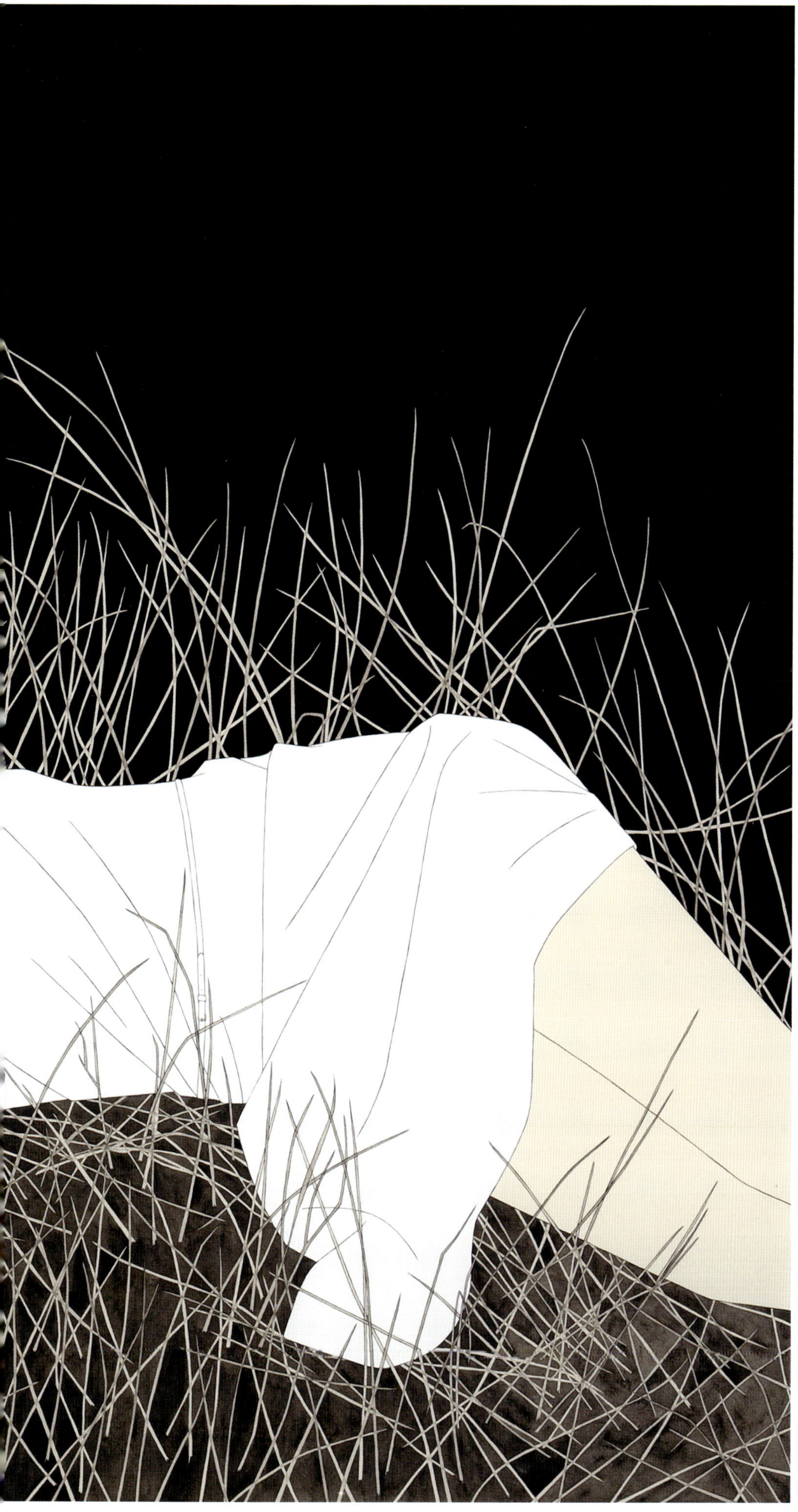

THE CAPTIVE
30 x 44", 2011, Watercolor and Gouache on Paper

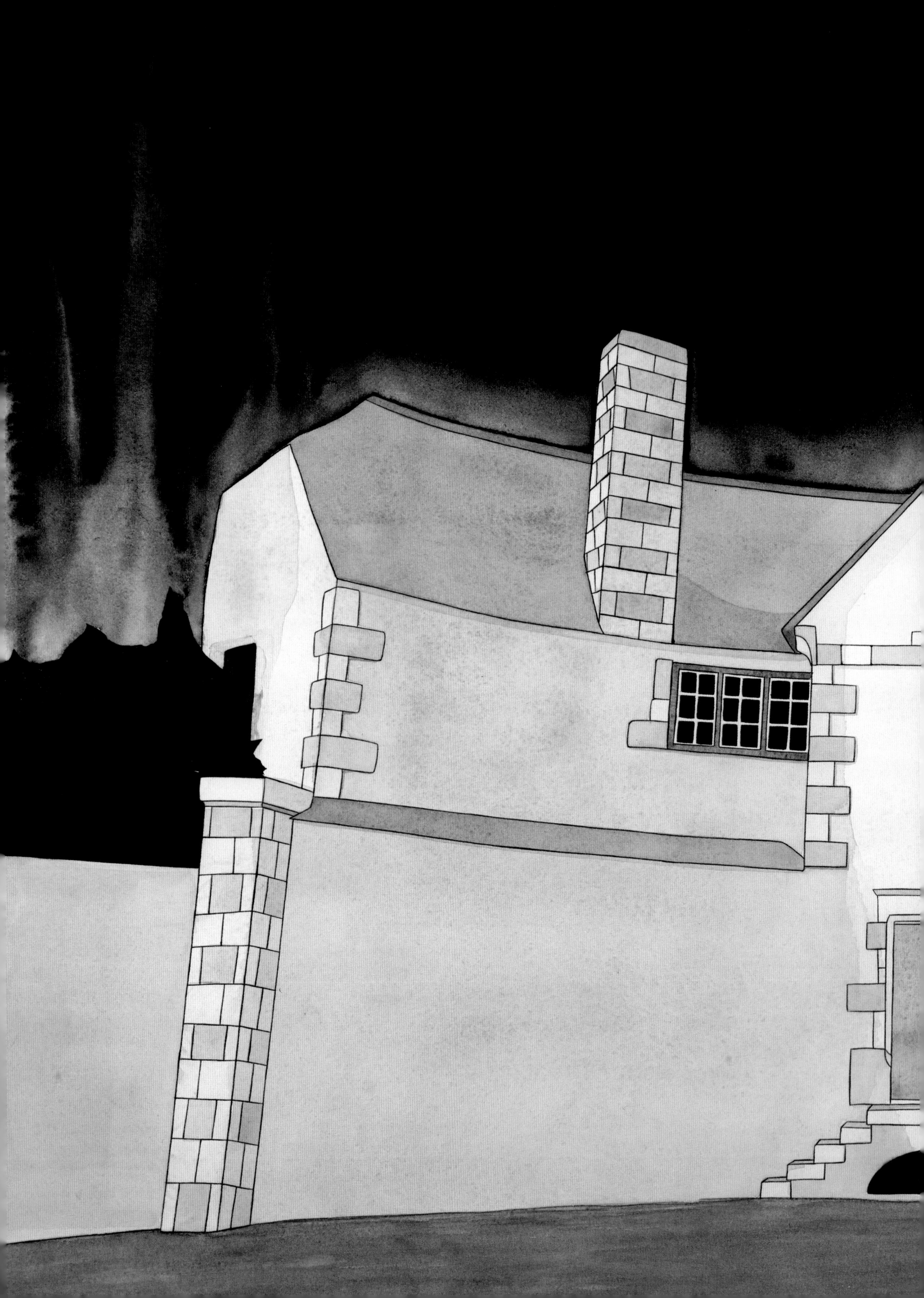

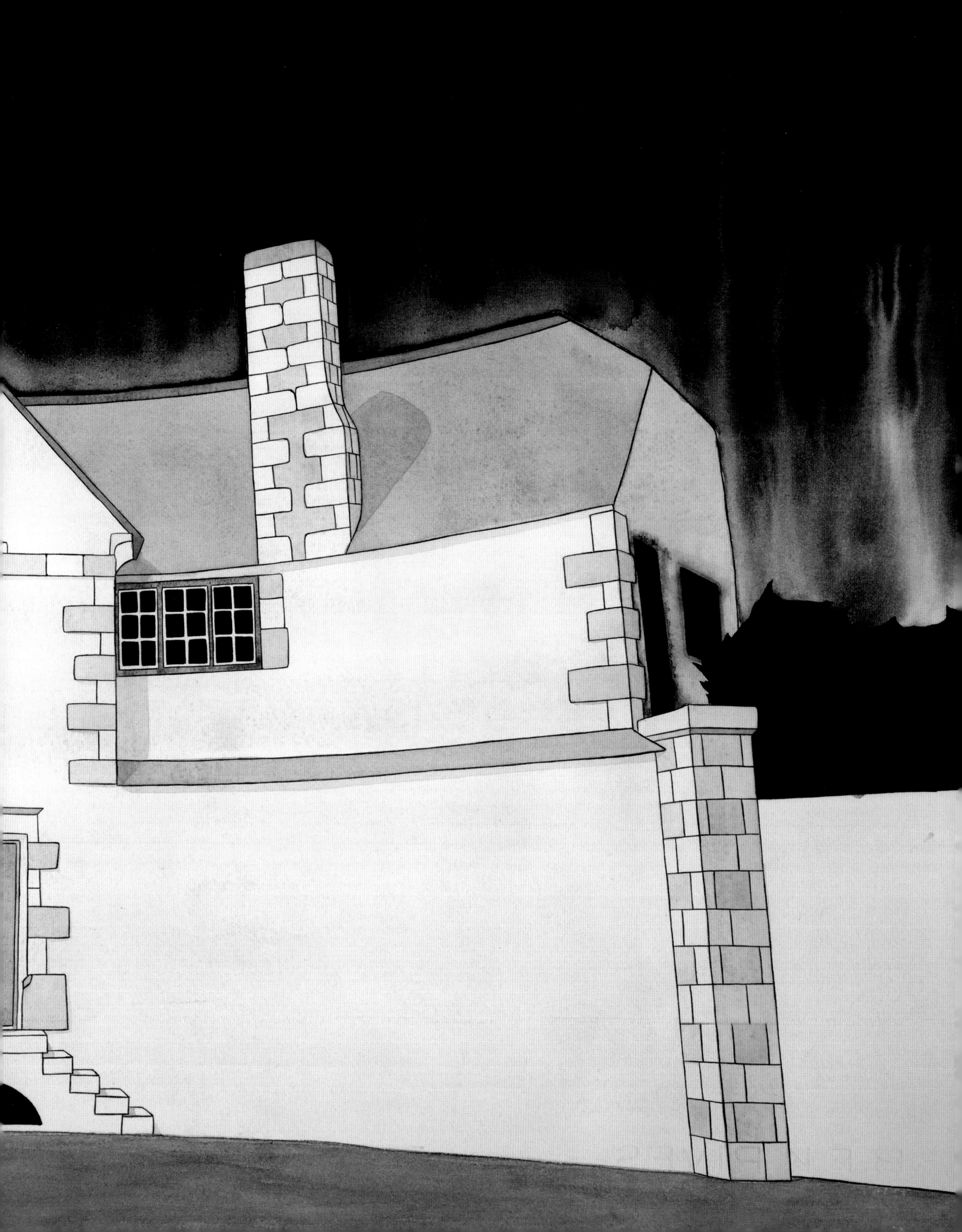

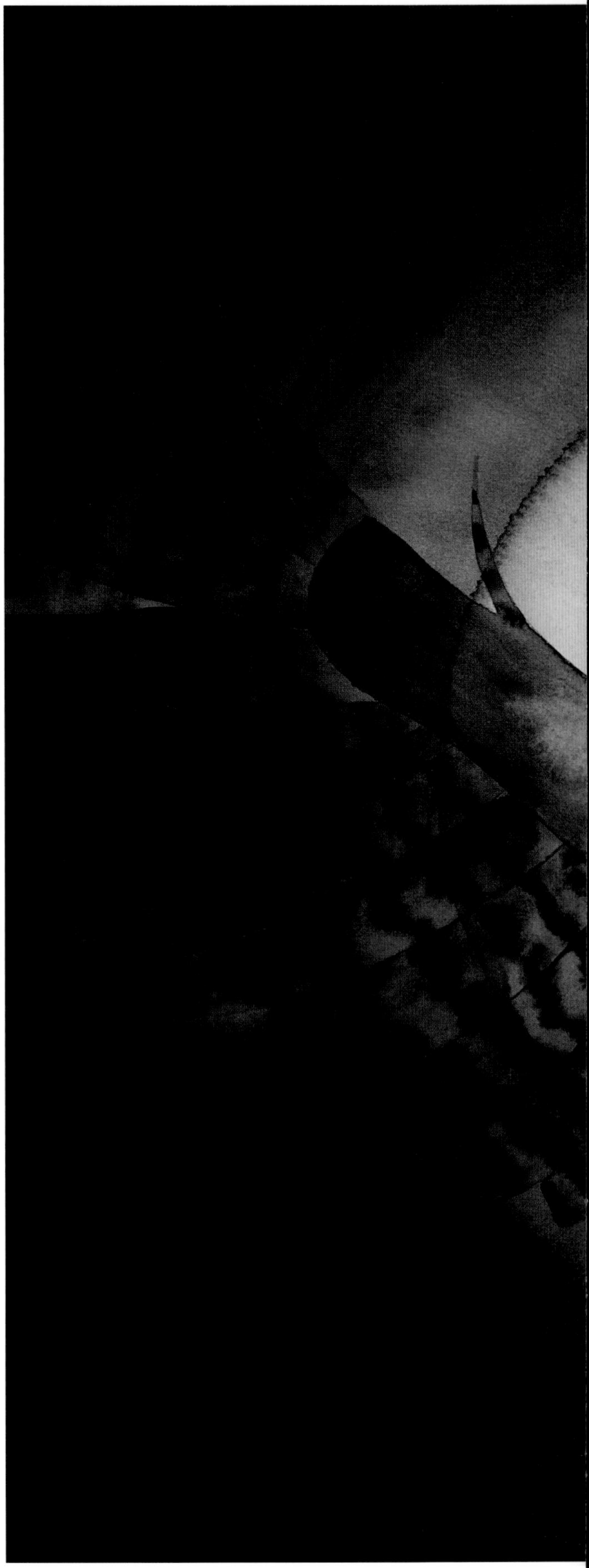

BOB
26 x 20", 2011, Watercolor and Gouache on Paper
PREVIOUS SPREAD: **THE GREY LODGE**
20 x 26", 2011, Watercolor and Gouache on Paper

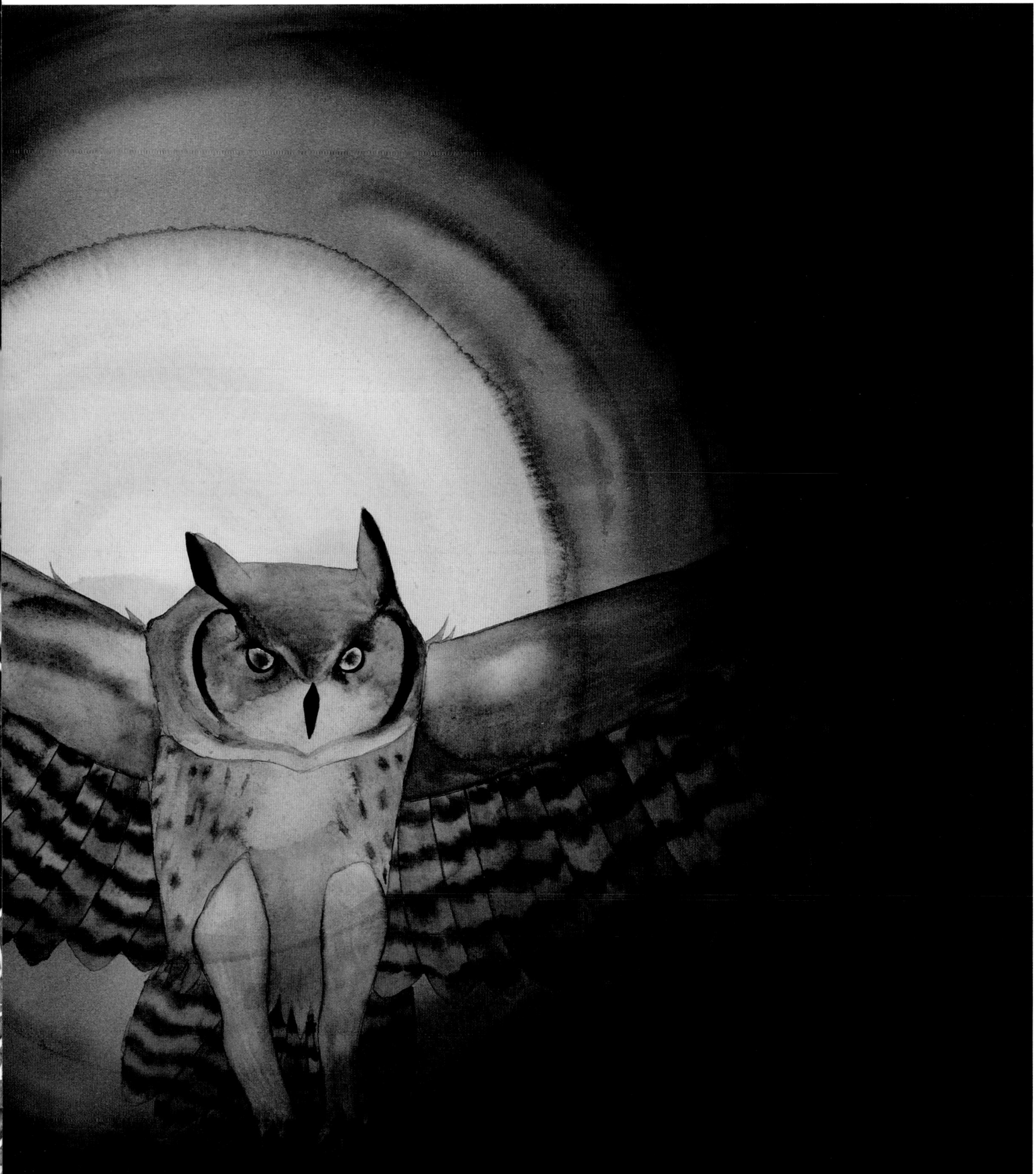

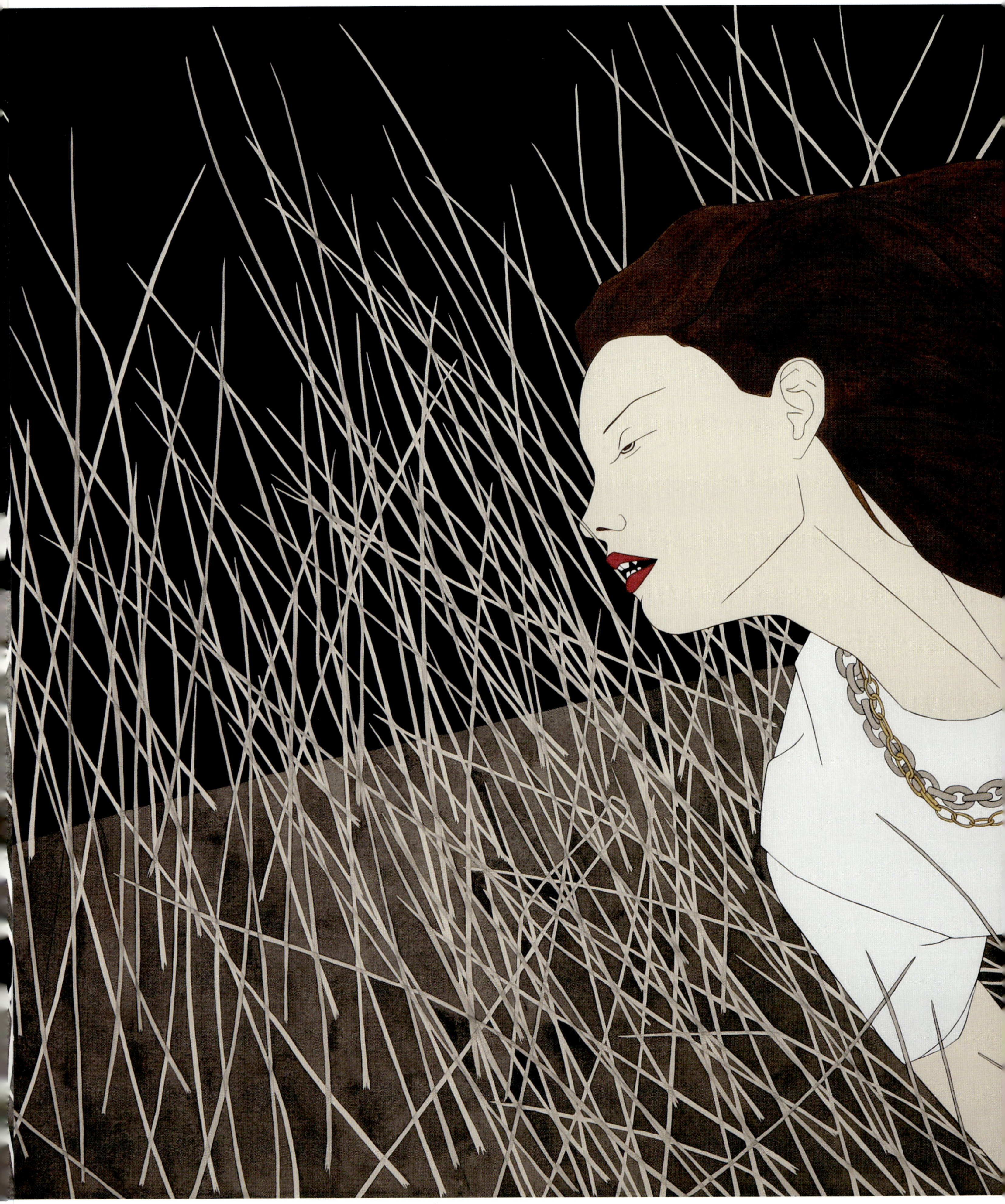

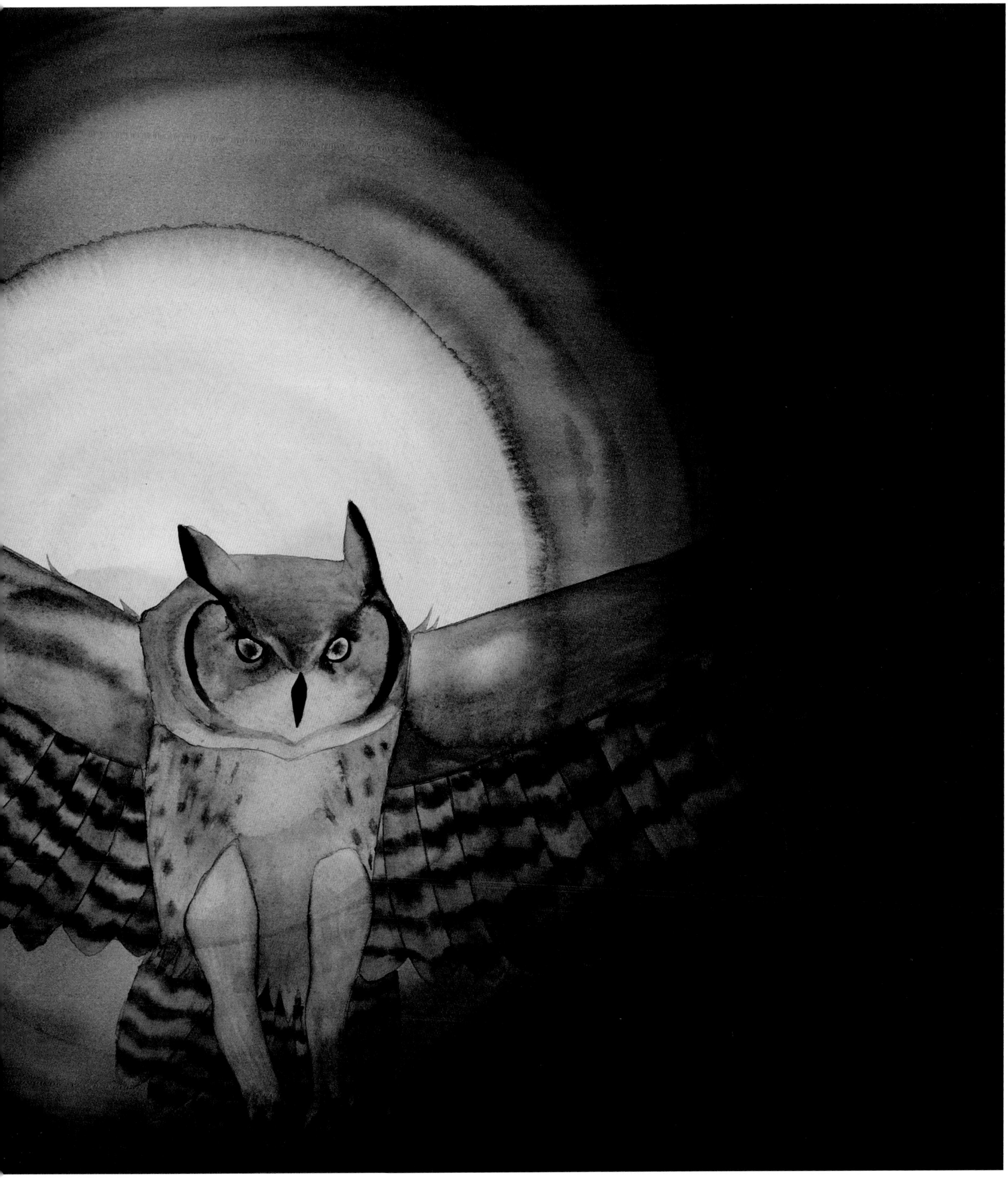

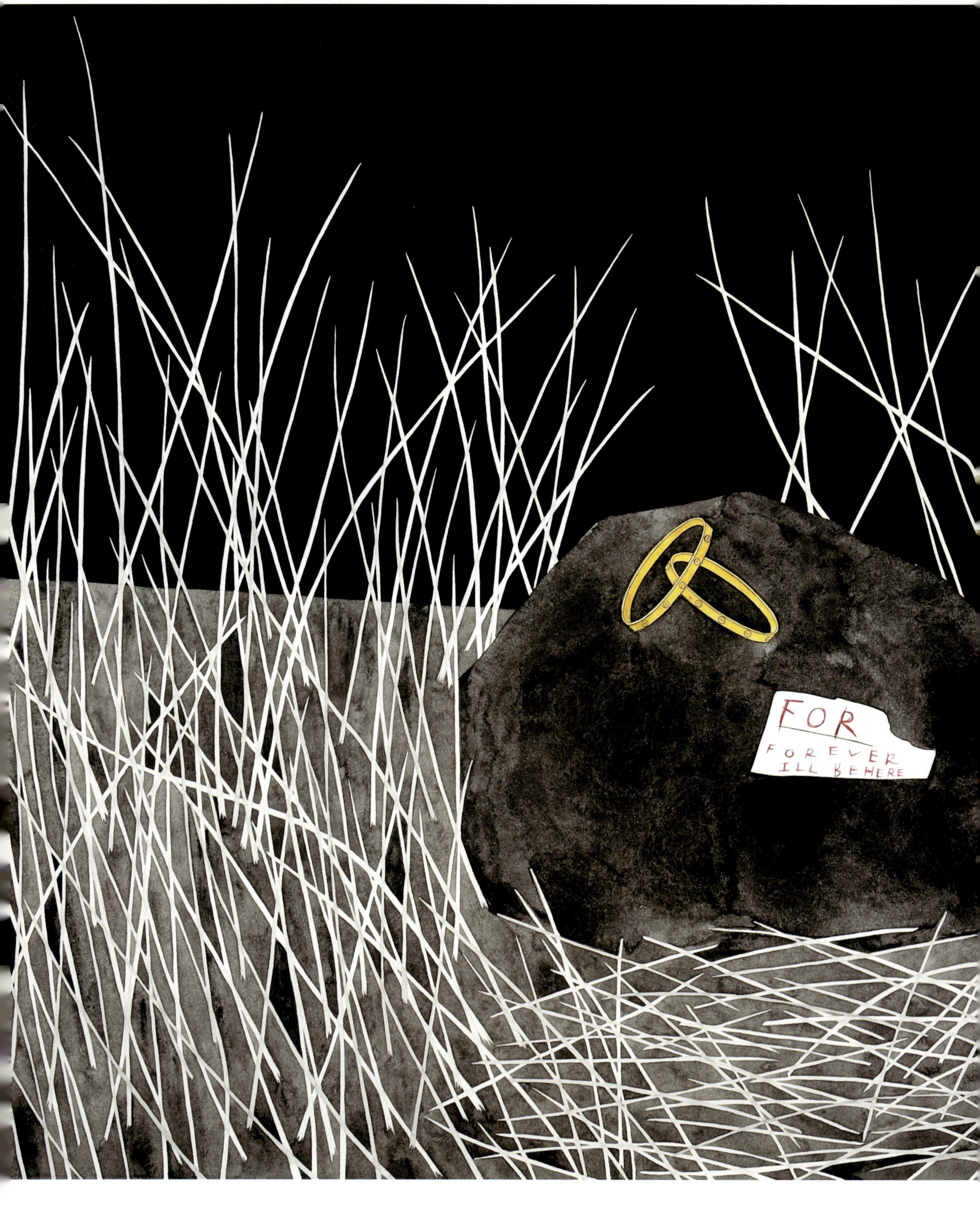
FOR
FOREVER
ILL BE HERE

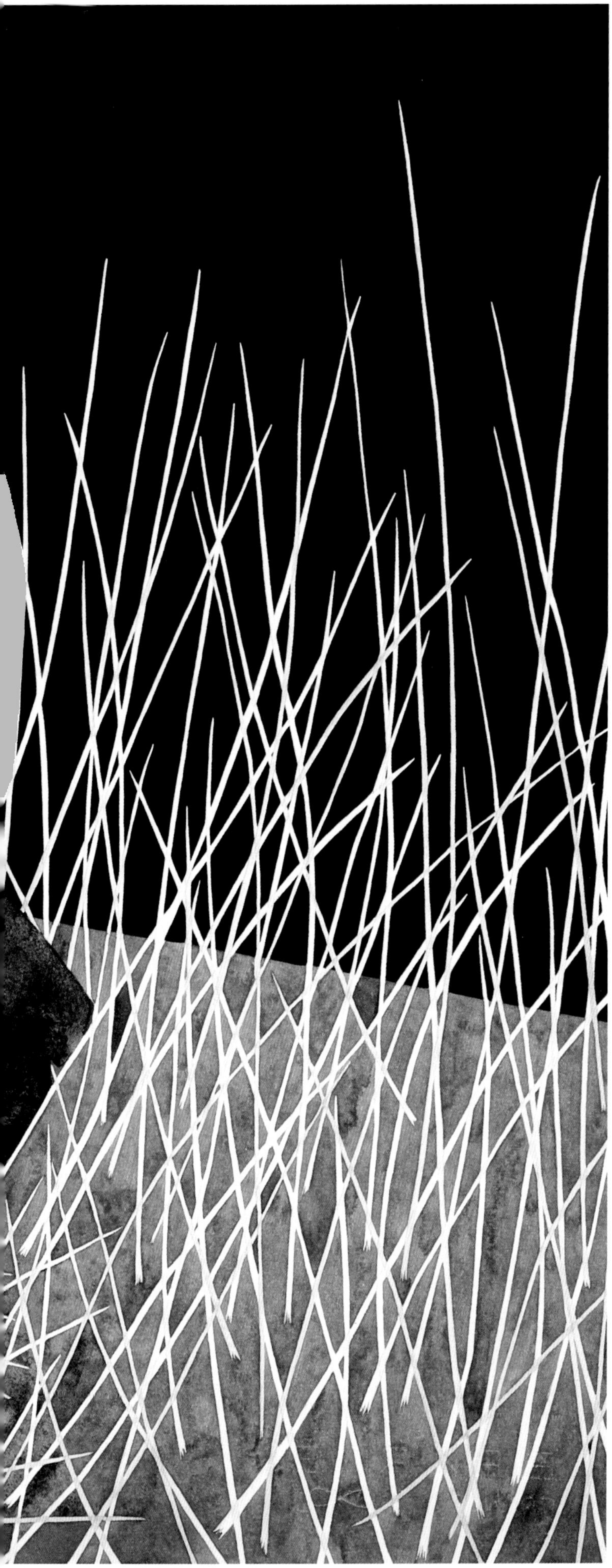

BRACELETS
20 x 26", 2011, Watercolor and Gouache on Paper

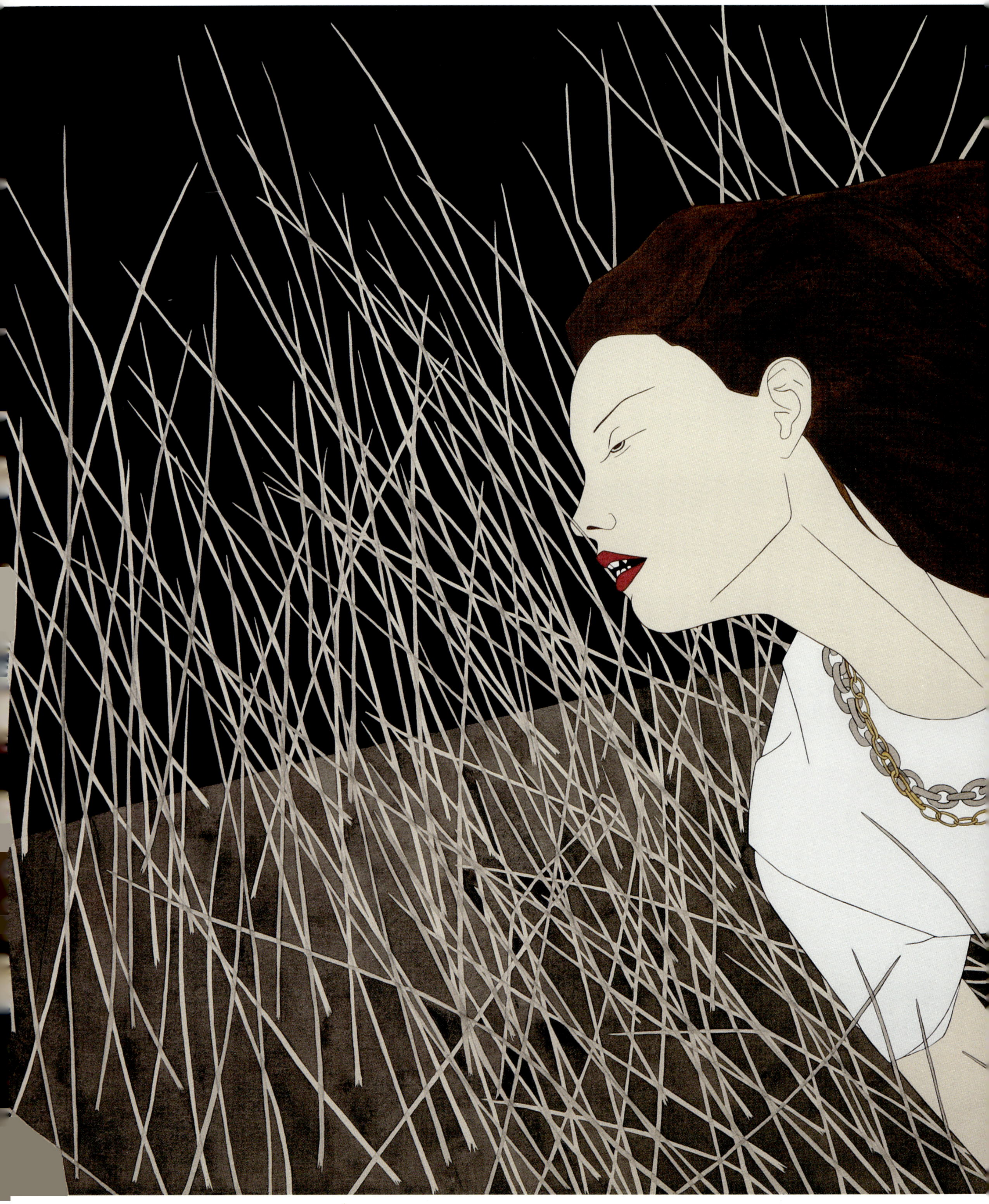

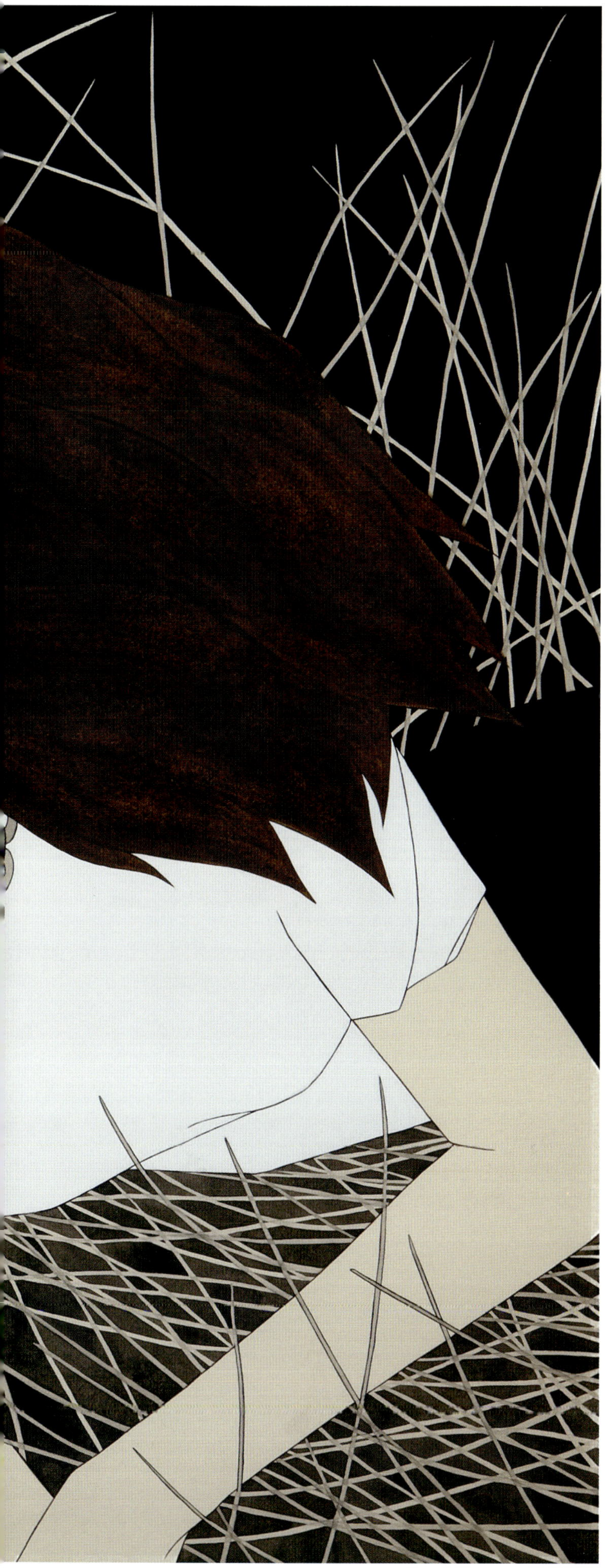

GOLD CHAINS
18 x 24", 2011, Watercolor and Gouache on Paper

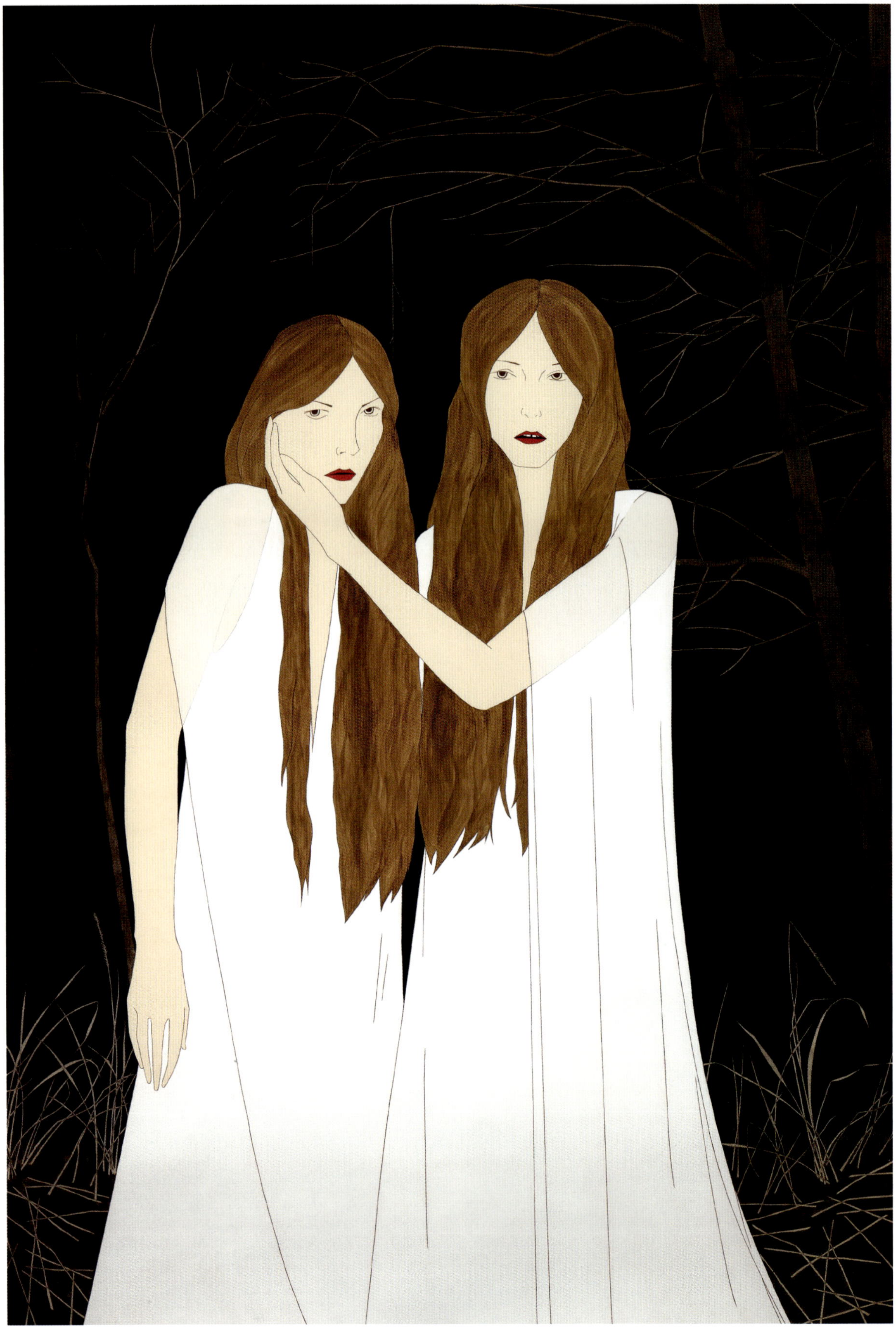

ESCAPE FROM THE TOMB
44 x 30", 2013, Watercolor and Gouache on Paper

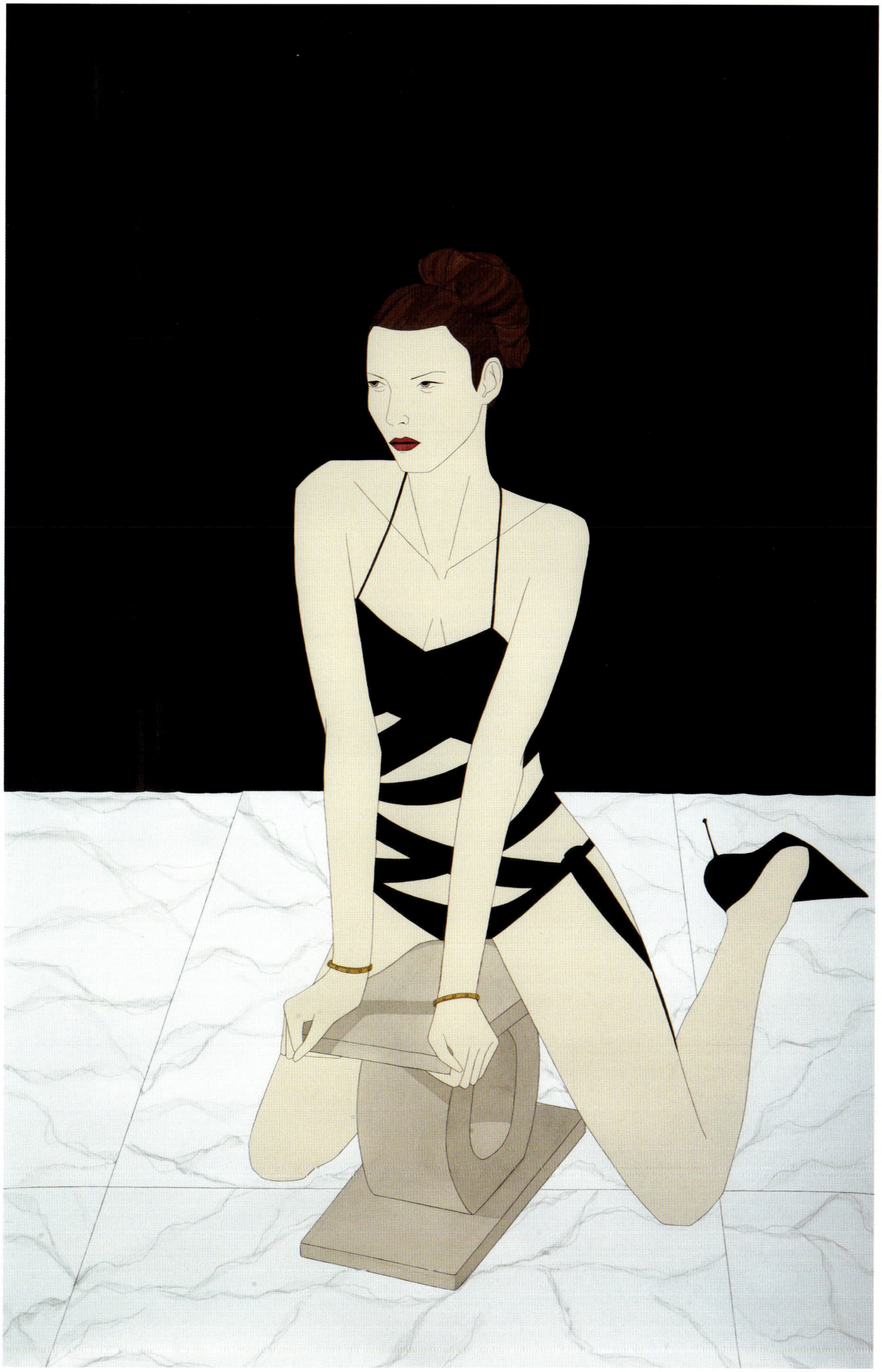

THE BIKINI
44 x 30", 2011, Watercolor and Gouache on Paper

THE SERVANT OF THE POWER
26 x 20", 2011, Watercolor and Gouache on Paper

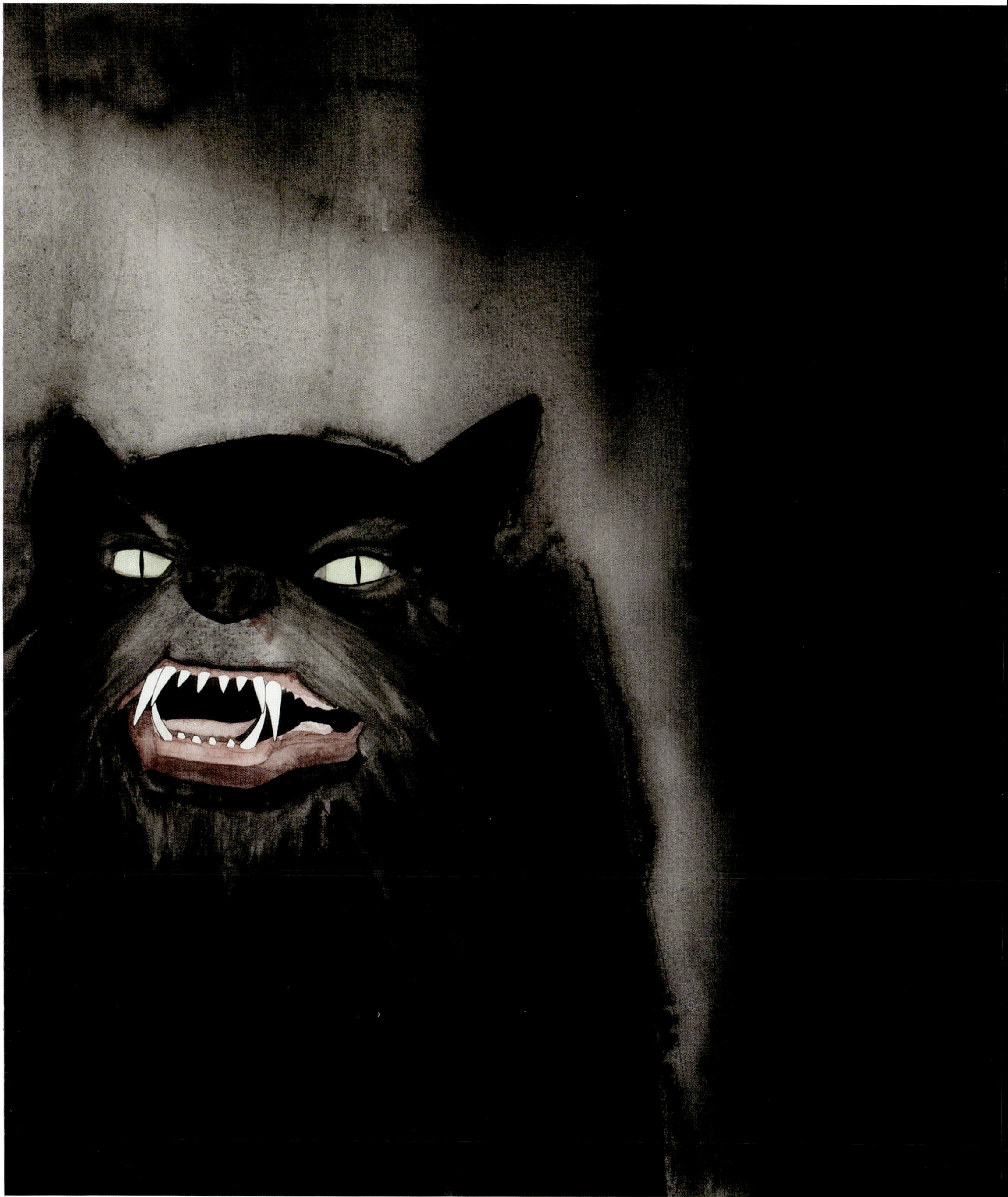

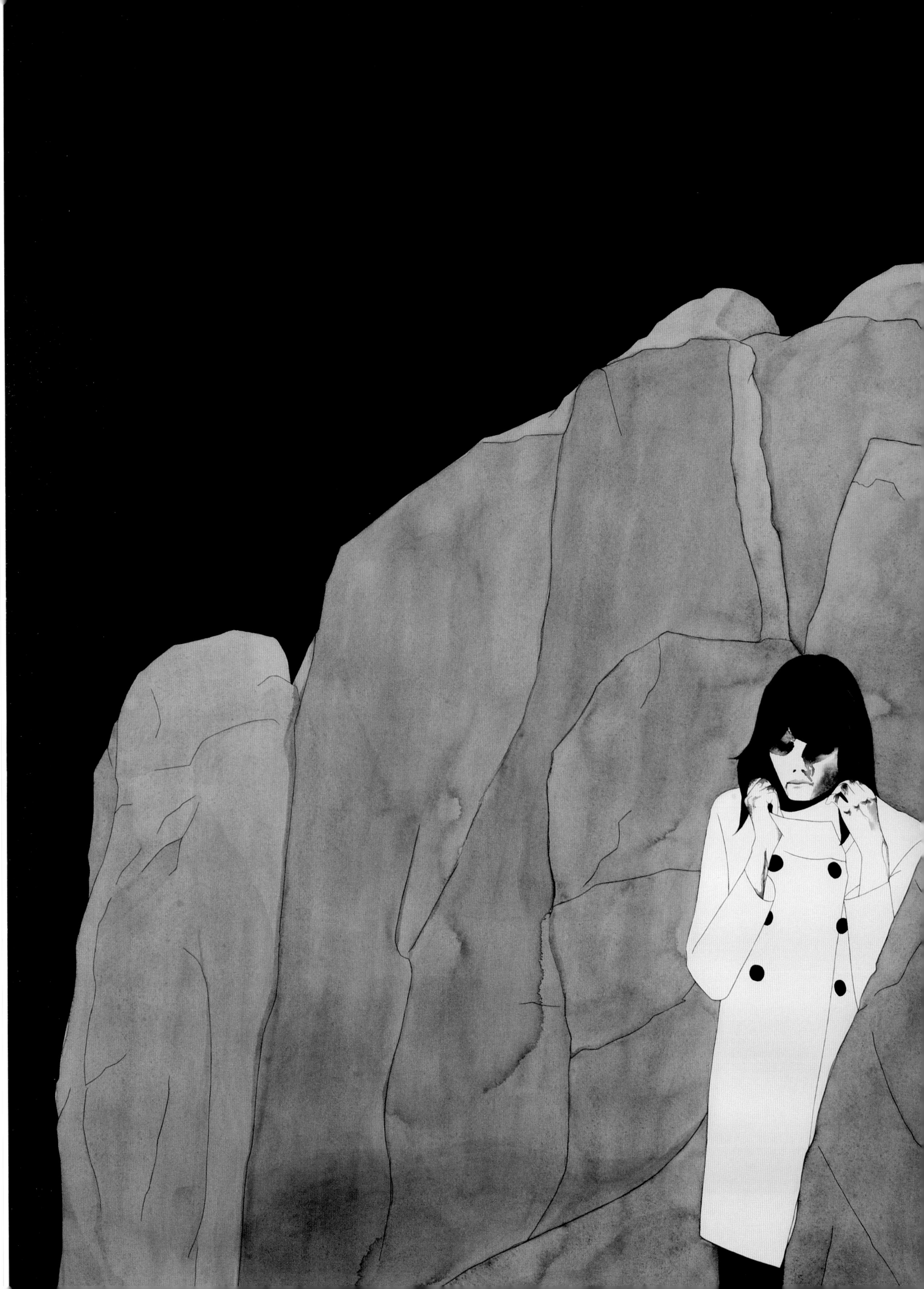

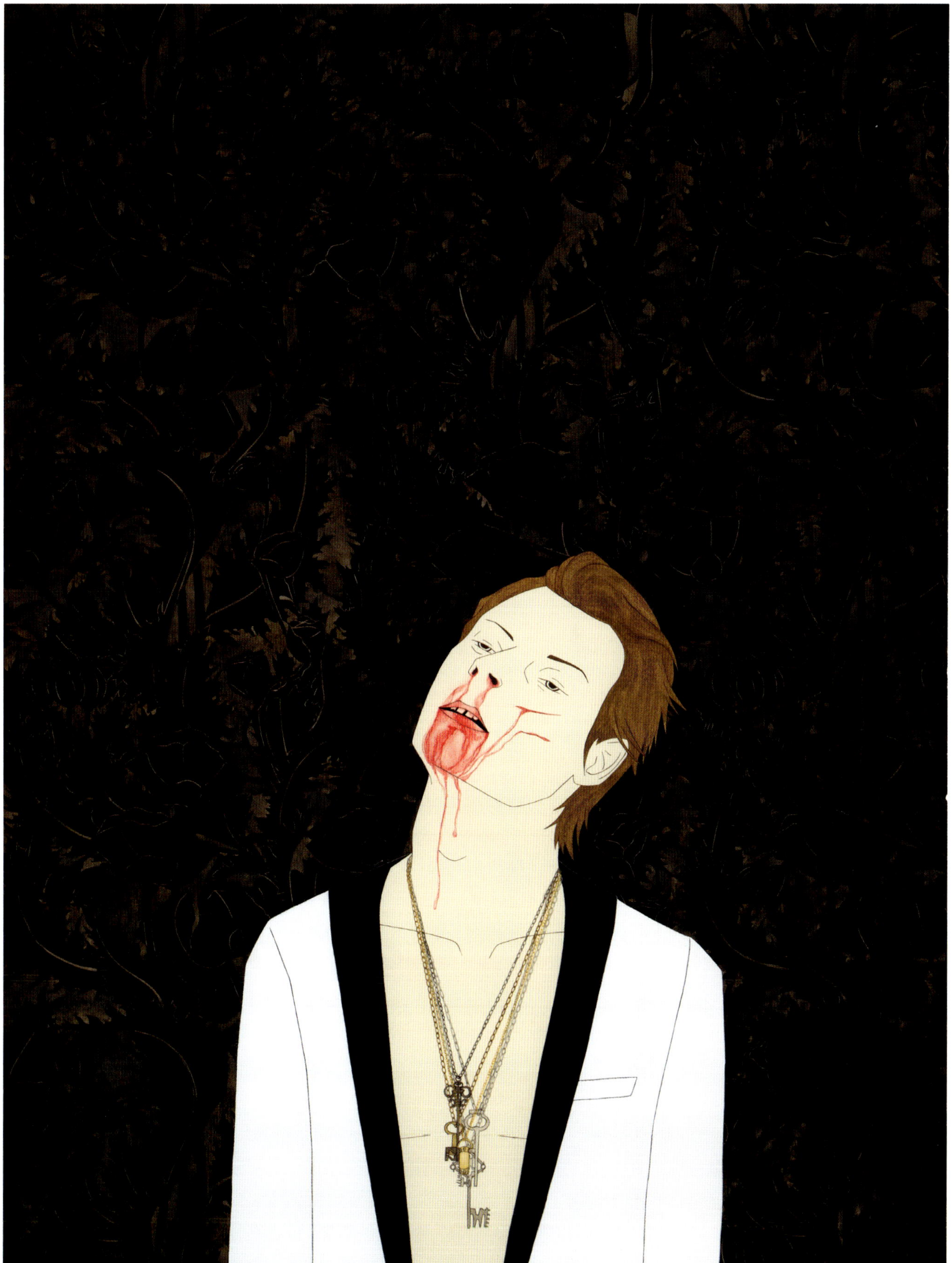

THIS MONSTER
30 x 22˝, 2013, Watercolor and Gouache on Paper

OPPOSITE PAGE: **WOMAN IN WHITE**
44 x 30˝, 2011, Watercolor and Gouache on Paper

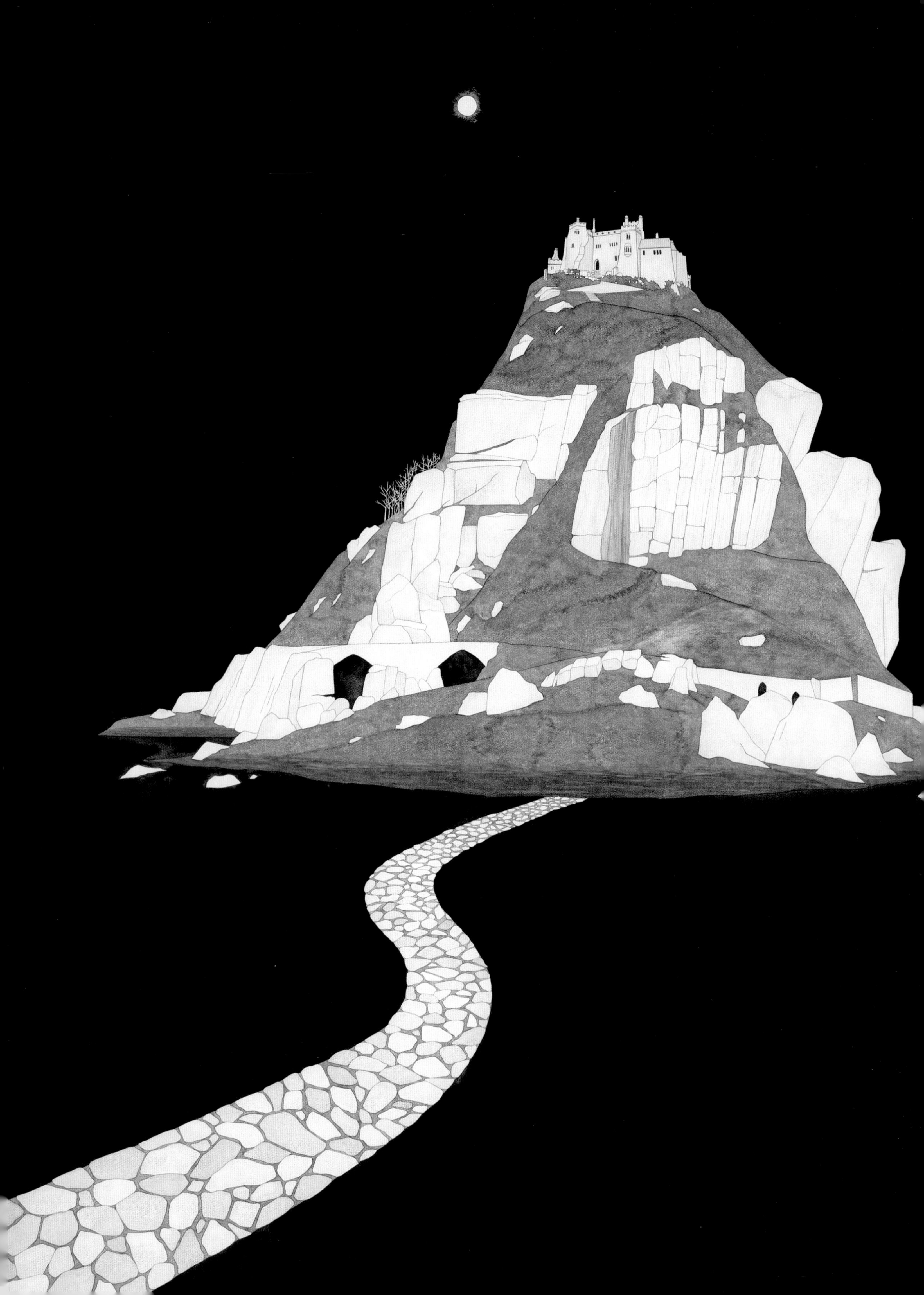

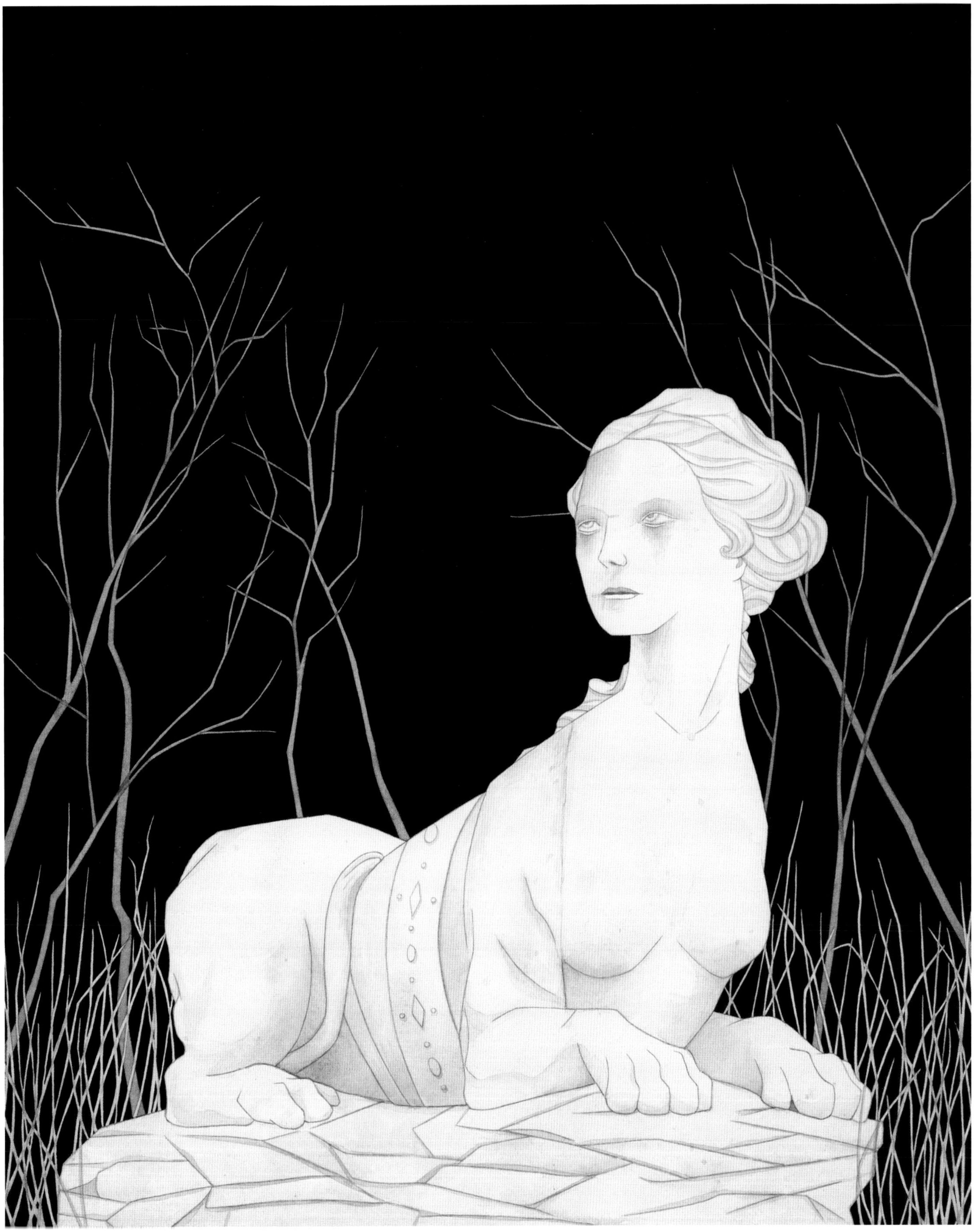

THE ENIGMATIC OBJECT
15 x 12″, 2013, Watercolor and Gouache on Paper

OPPOSITE PAGE: THE CASTLE
35 x 26″, 2013, Watercolor and Gouache on Paper

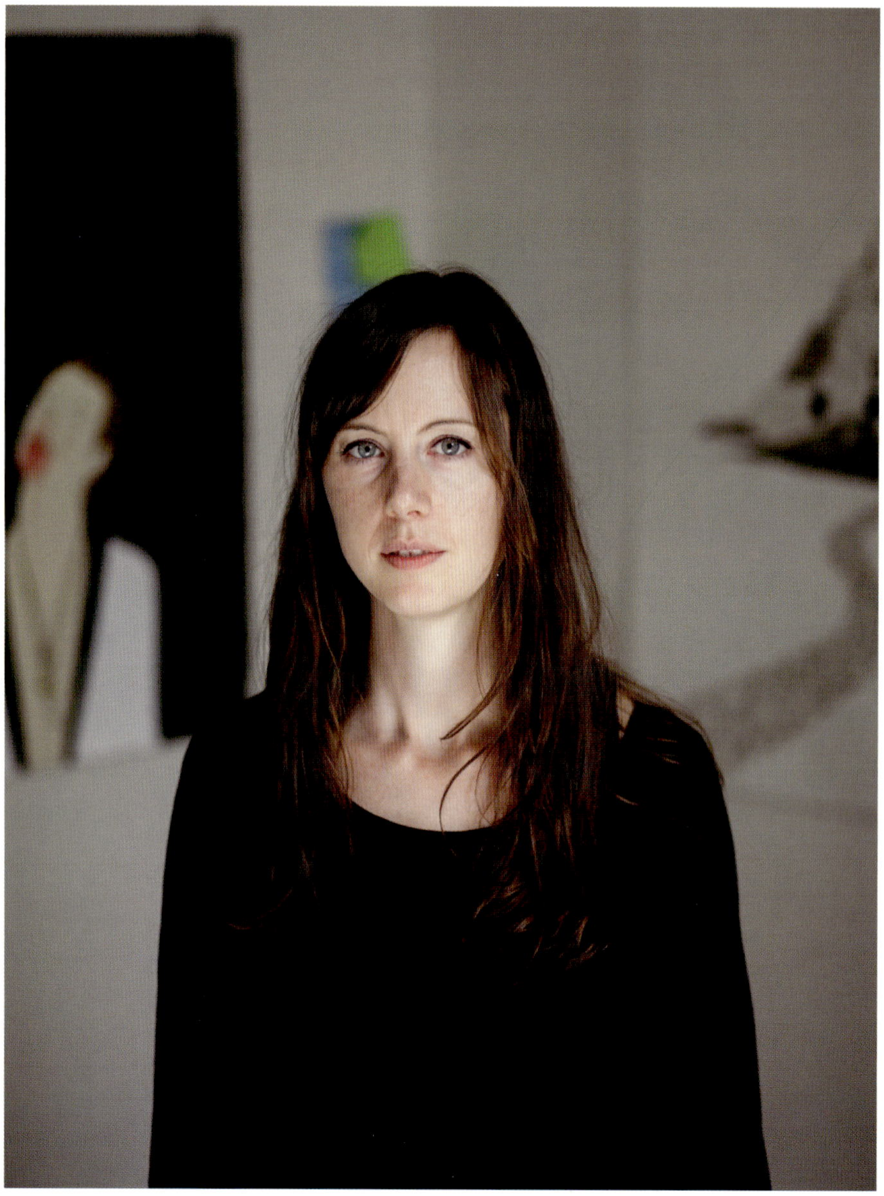

MARCI WASHINGTON IN HER STUDIO
Photographed by Myleen Hollero

Acknowledgements

I would like to thank Deth P. Sun, Amanda Washington, Shea'la Finch, Mark, Jennifer, Pat, and Dick Washington for their unending love and support. For help with this book, big thanks to Terence Jones and the Leeds College of Art, Jenny Baie and the lovely ladies of the Rena Bransten Gallery, and Jessica Skloven, Myleen Hollero, and Nathaniel Rich. Big love to all the friends that have kept me sane with home cooked meals, karaoke parties, river times, emergency ice cream / cheeseburgers, secret pond swimming, and movie nights — I love you guys and couldn't make these paintings without you.

